E.H. NORMAN: HIS LIFE AND SCHOLARSHIP

TO BARBARA

For sharing the conference experience and much, much more

E.H.Norman

His Life and Scholarship

EDITED BY ROGER W. BOWEN

UNIVERSITY OF TORONTO PRESS

Toronto Buffalo London

© University of Toronto Press 1984
Toronto Buffalo London
Printed in Canada

ISBN 0-8020-2505-6

Canadian Cataloguing in Publication Data

Main entry under title:
E.H. Norman : his life and scholarship
Bibliography: p.
Includes index.
ISBN 0-8020-2505-6
1. Norman, E. Herbert, 1909–1957 – Addresses, essays, lectures.
2. Diplomats – Canada – Addresses, essays, lectures.
3. Japan – Study and teaching (Higher) – Canada – Addresses,
essays, lectures.
I. Norman, E. Herbert, 1909–1957.
II. Bowen, Roger Wilson, 1947–
FC611.N67E4 1984   971.063'092'4   C83-099230-8
F10394.3.N67E4I1984

Contents

Preface / vii

Biographical Sketch / ix

PART ONE: LIFE

Edwin O. Reischauer   Herb Norman: The Perspective of a
                           Lifelong Friend / 3

Cyril Powles   E.H. Norman and Japan / 13

Victor Kiernan   Herbert Norman's Cambridge / 27

Roger Bowen   Cold War, McCarthyism,
                           and Murder by Slander:
                           E.H. Norman's Death in Perspective / 46

Arthur Kilgour   On Remembering Herbert Norman / 72

PART TWO: SCHOLARSHIP

Maruyama Masao   An Affection for the Lesser Names:
                           An Appreciation of E. Herbert Norman / 81

Richard Storry   Some Reflections on E.H. Norman:
                           A Historian in the English Tradition / 87

Kenneth B. Pyle   E.H. Norman and the New Stage in
                       Western Studies of Japan / 92

Gary D. Allinson   E.H. Norman on Modern Japan:
                       Towards a Constructive Assessment / 99

Toyama Shigeki   The Appreciation of
                       Norman's Historiography / 122

PART THREE: NORMAN ON FREEDOM

People under Feudalism / 143

Persuasion or Force:
The Problem of Free Speech in Modern Society / 155

On the Modesty of Clio / 170

The Place of East Asian Studies in a Modern University / 186

Roger W. Bowen   Irony or Tragedy? / 195

Selected Writings of E.H. Norman / 201

Contributors / 203

Index / 205

Preface

On 18–20 October 1979, over one hundred friends, one-time External Affairs colleagues, scholars of Japan, and Canadian, American, and Japanese admirers gathered at Saint Mary's University in Halifax, Nova Scotia, to pay tribute to the life and scholarship of E.H. Norman. As conferences go, ours was modest in terms of size of budget and audience, but it was none the less a most extraordinary event.

As the originator of the conference, and as its co-organizer along with Professor Paul Bowlby of SMU, I was in the enviable position of hearing almost everyone's thoughts on the idea and the actual workings of the conference. Incredibly, without exception each person remarked that this was the most open, stimulating, and *friendly* conference he/she had ever attended. No doubt to an immeasurable extent the overwhelmingly pleasant ambiance of the conference was due to the warmth and congeniality of our host, Saint Mary's University and its impressive staff of Asianists. But I would also like to think that our subject, E.H. Norman, and the daily presence of his most remarkable widow, Irene Norman, had much to do with the success of the conference. I most sincerely believe that Mrs Norman's presence helped the participants to revive (though not in any religious sense) the spirit of her late husband – his warmth, his gentleness, his civility, and above all his humanity. All these qualities somehow pervaded the proceedings.

There were of course many others who also contributed to creating the positive atmosphere at the conference. Here I would like to acknowledge and thank them. Besides those individuals who gave papers, a number of others shared the podium as discussants: Professor Donald Burton, then visiting Asianist at SMU; Professor John

Howes of the University of British Columbia; William 'Bill' Holland, former editor of *Pacific Affairs*; Dr Eleanor Hadley of George Washington University and the General Accounting Office; Professor John Brownlee of the University of Toronto; Richard 'Dick' Finn, now retired from the Department of State; and Michiko Tanaka of the El Colegio De Mexico. Also in attendance and contributing from the audience was Gordon Robertson, recently retired from the Privy Council Office; Professor James Eayrs of Dalhousie University; Professor Frank C. Langdon of the University of British Columbia; Dallas Finn; Professor Jack MacCormack of Saint Mary's; and Judge Sandra Oxner of Halifax, who also, most graciously, hosted a dinner reception following the conference.

The conference was funded by a variety of sources, the most important of which was the Japan Foundation. In addition, significant financial assistance was given by the Social Sciences and Humanities Research Council (Canada), the Tanaka Fund administered by the Association of Universities and Colleges of Canada; the A.B.C. Trading Company of Tokyo; Saint Mary's University; and private donations from friends and colleagues of E.H. Norman.

A special note of thanks must also go to Shirley Buckler, who helped both with the day-to-day organizing problems of the conference and later with the job of transcribing the conference proceedings. Also assisting with the preparation of the manuscript for publication were Deborah Clark and Vincent Isles. Final typing of the manuscript was done by Karen Bourassa. Mark Harmon served as a very able assistant in checking the copy-edited version of the manuscript, and Colby College generously provided the grant funds to employ Mark. In this regard as well, I am pleased to acknowledge the impressive editing talents of John St James, working for the University of Toronto Press. Minor stylistic modifications have been made to the conference papers and reprinted articles that will, it is hoped, improve their readability.

To all these individuals and organizations, I would personally like to express my gratitude in this twenty-seventh anniversary year of Norman's death.

ROGER W. BOWEN
Colby College
Waterville, Maine
8 August 1983

Biographical Sketch

Egerton Herbert Norman was born on 1 September 1909 in Karuizawa, Japan. He was the third child and second son of the Reverend
Daniel Norman (1864–1941) and Katherine Heal Norman (1870–
1952). Herbert's mother and father were both from the farmlands of
Ontario and educated at Victoria College, Toronto; they were married
in Mitchell, Ontario, on 22 May 1901. The summer of that year they
left together for missionary work in Japan, where all three children –
Grace (b. 1903), Howard (b. 1905), and Herbert – were born.

Herbert was educated at home by his mother until his eighth year,
when he followed his older brother and sister to the Canadian Academy at Kobe. Except for one year in Toronto (1923–24) when the
family was on furlough, Herbert's formative years were spent in
Japan. His studies were interrupted in 1925 when he contracted
tuberculosis. Following several months of unsuccessful treatment, in
late 1926 he left Japan, accompanied by his mother, for a sanitorium
in Alberta. Recovered by 1928, he finished matriculation at Albert
College in Belleville, Ontario, and the following autumn entered his
parents' alma mater, Victoria College, University of Toronto. There he
majored in classics. In his last year he was awarded a Kylie Scholarship in history, permitting him to take a second B.A. at Trinity College,
Cambridge University, which he finished in the spring of 1935.

On 31 August 1935, Herbert married Laura Irene Clark in Hamil-
ton, Ontario. Immediately thereafter, Herbert taught classics part-time
at Upper Canada College while taking post-graduate courses in history at the University of Toronto. In the fall of 1936, having been
awarded a Rockefeller Foundation Fellowship in Far Eastern studies,
Herbert left with Irene for Harvard University. He completed his M.A.

in one year and by late 1938 had completed his doctoral dissertation while serving as a research associate with the Institute of Pacific Relations (IPR) in New York. He successfully defended his dissertation at Harvard in early May 1940.

Two weeks later, on 18 May 1940, Norman sailed for Japan on the *Empress of Russia*, having been appointed, through an Order in Council, to serve as language officer in the embassy. Though tempted to leave the foreign service in mid-1941 when he was offered a teaching post by the University of Washington, Norman chose to remain in Japan following a promotion to third secretary, only to be interned with fellow embassy staff following the outbreak of the Pacific war in December 1941. In mid-1942 Norman and the others were returned to Canada as part of a prisoner exchange with the Japanese government. For the remainder of the war, he served in the Examination Unit of External Affairs where he organized a Japanese intelligence section.

Towards the close of the war another promotion (to second secretary) helped him to decide to remain with External rather than accept a teaching position at Yale University. Yet another promotion coincided with his post-surrender assignments, first to assist in the repatriation of Canadians from the Philippines and then to serve in Allied intelligence in the occupation of Japan; for the latter assignment, lasting from September 1945 to January 1946, he held rank equivalent to major in the American counter-intelligence service.

From March to July 1946 Norman acted as Lester Pearson's surrogate on the Far Eastern Commission in Washington, DC. During this time he was promoted to first secretary, and on 1 August 1946 he was appointed head of the Canadian Liaison Mission, accredited to the Supreme Commander of the Allied Powers (SCAP). He took up his new post in Tokyo on 14 August and held it until mid-October 1950.

Besides heading the Canadian mission those four years, Norman remained academically active. He delivered several papers (in Japanese) before scholarly conferences; attended an IPR conference in England in 1947 and helped to reorganize the Japan branch of the IPR; was elected president of the Asiatic Society of Japan; and in 1949 published his still highly regarded *Andō Shōeki*.

Norman was recalled from Japan in October 1950 and subjected to a security investigation that had been prompted by American intelligence branches which suspected Norman of being a communist. Cleared by the RCMP, Norman was appointed to head the American and Far Eastern Division of External Affairs in early December. In mid-1951 he briefly left that position to become acting permanent representative to the United Nations. In September he participated in the San Francisco Conference on the Japan Peace Treaty. It was around this time that his name figured prominently in the news after allegations were made by Professor Karl Wittfogel before the McCarran Committee identifying Norman as a communist in 1938. Following the unwanted publicity External Affairs moved Norman in July 1952 from the sensitive post heading the American desk to administer the Information Division.

In May 1953 Norman was assigned a foreign posting, this time as high commissioner to New Zealand, which he held for three years. During this time Norman enjoyed heightened productivity as a scholar, writing a series of philosophical and historical essays, most of which were published in Japanese. Once again he was offered an academic post, this time by the University of British Columbia, but again Lester Pearson intervened to assure Norman that more exciting work abroad was imminent.

Pearson delivered on his promise in early 1956, gaining cabinet approval to appoint Norman to be ambassador to Egypt and minister to Lebanon. Norman arrived in Cairo on 19 August, two months before the outbreak of the Suez crisis which caught him in Beirut where he was presenting his credentials. Returning to Egypt in November, Norman worked feverishly over the next several months to convince President Nasser to permit Canadian peacekeeping troops into the Sinai under United Nations supervision. Just as his efforts were proving successful, in mid-March 1957, several old allegations concerning his ties to communism resurfaced in U.S. Senate hearings.

On 4 April 1957 Norman committed suicide in Cairo. Four days later his body was cremated in Rome. The following day his ashes were placed at the base of a tree in an unmarked grave next to the poet Shelley's tomb in the Protestant Cemetery in Rome.

The Norman family, January 1917, Mitchell, Ontario
(Herbert is between his parents)

OPPOSITE Graduation, University of Toronto, 1933

With Douglas MacArthur. Canadian Mission, Dominion Day, 1947

TOP Speaking to assembly in Nagano at memorial service for
his father, 1947

With women who had associated with his mother. Nagano, 1947

Presenting his staff to Egyptian President Nasser, September 1956

With General H.D.G. Crerar (left) and General Chase (centre) at
Camp Drake, Japan, 4 August 1947

With his wife, Irene. Canadian Mission, Dominion Day, 1947

Greeting Minister of External Affairs, Lester Pearson, on his visit to
Tokyo, January 1950

Part One

Life

An immediate disclaimer: The five articles that follow do not constitute a biography. Rather, each is a very different sort of sketch of Norman from the author's point of view at a particular time in Norman's life. Two of the articles – Reischauer's and Kilgour's – are somewhat personal reminiscences that recall very short periods during which each of the authors enjoyed a direct relationship with Norman. For Reischauer it was several childhood years primarily, and for Kilgour the months just before Norman's death. Kiernan's contribution, by contrast, focuses less on the man and more on the milieu of Norman's Cambridge University days. Though less personal than the others, it is a valuable addition because Kiernan like no one else describes the political and intellectual climate in such matter-of-fact terms that Norman's decision to join the Communist party appears equally and altogether reasonable and appropriate.

Cyril Powles's 'E.H. Norman and Japan' falls somewhere in between the personal and contextual approaches. As the title of his essay suggests, and no doubt because Powles's own early life experiences parallel Norman's, the lifelong influence that Norman's early years in Japan had on his adult life are crucially important to an understanding of the 'Born in Japan' syndrome.

My essay is the most conventional of all the biographical sketches used here. It is a nuts and bolts account of Norman's activities between his student days and his death in 1957.

But even when taken together, these essays leave much about Norman's life unexplained, making very clear the need for a full-length biography. What these essays do provide, however, is valuable new information and perspectives about the man and the events that shaped his life. It is hoped that the short 'editor's introductions' to the essays in this section will help fill in those gaps in information which the essays do not cover.

In a great many respects, Edwin Oldfather Reischauer is E.H. Norman's only real American counterpart. Like Norman, Reischauer was born in Japan to missionary parents, was schooled during his formative years in Japan, was bilingual at an early age, was always very athletic and academically inclined, studied in Europe following an undergraduate education in his native land, received in the same year as Norman a Harvard doctorate in East Asian studies, wrote many books about Japanese history, and finally served his nation as its highest-ranking diplomat in Japan. Not only counterparts; some might say alter egos. They were also friends, as Professor Reischauer's essay title suggests and as some of Norman's private correspondence indisputably shows. It seems to have been a curious friendship, however, that bore the rather common burden of an ingenuously disguised envy and jealousy that is not at all unusual between friends competing in the same area of endeavour. Some of Norman's admirers have taken umbrage at the effects of the unspoken competition, pointing to the absence of mention of Norman's books in the bibliographies of Professor Reischauer's books. Those who criticize Reischauer, however, should read carefully the sincere words of praise that he has for his old friend (and competitor) in the essay that follows. Therein Professor Reischauer shows that, contrary to the laws of geometry, parallel experiences along different ideological and experiential paths might none the less intersect in a perceived bond of friendship.

Edwin O. Reischauer

HERB NORMAN: THE PERSPECTIVE OF A LIFELONG FRIEND

E.H. Norman is a name that does not come easily to my lips or pen. I cannot think of him except as Herb Norman, a person I have known since the beginning of my memory. There is a quality about a childhood friendship that makes it a matter of fact, expected to last forever, however little contact there may actually be in later life. That is the way I have always felt about Herb. We did in fact meet only very rarely past childhood, though our similar interests in Japanese history and our mixing of scholarship with government service kept us aware of each other. Our somewhat parallel careers as well as our common missionary background in Japan have always made me feel a special sympathy towards him to add to our childhood friendship.

Herb Norman was born on 1 September 1909 in Karuizawa, the mountain summer resort where most of our childhood contacts took place. His father had gone from Canada as a missionary to Japan in 1897, eight years before my father went from the United States. I remember Herb's father as seeming much older and more austere than mine. His career was also quite different. Where my father had followed the more usual work of an educational missionary – teaching in a seminary, becoming a scholarly student of Japanese Buddhism, helping to found a women's university (the now very prestigious Tokyo Women's University), and helping my mother in introducing the oral education of the deaf to Japan – Herb's father had gone to the countryside, concentrating on direct evangelistic work in rural mountainous Nagano Prefecture, where Karuizawa is located.

I believe that this rural background may have had a profound influence on Herb Norman's view of Japan and also of history. He saw less of the successfully modernizing parts of Japan in the big cities and the intellectual classes that were adapting to modern ideas. He was more aware of the poverty and problems of rural Japan and the deep roots of its traditional ways. This difference in perspective, I suspect, helped shape his later interests in Japanese history, giving rise to his deep concern and sympathy for the peasantry and moulding his views of the modernization process in Japan. His rural background also gave him a much stronger start in the Japanese language than we missionary children raised in cities enjoyed. We felt sorry for our underprivileged 'country cousins,' but they, without other foreign children to mix with and denied the divertissements of city life, learned the Japanese language much better from their largely Japanese playmates.

Herb Norman had a sister, enough older to have been only on the periphery of my consciousness, and an older brother, Howard, who was about the age of my brother Bob. Howard and Bob later in 1932 and 1934 had the advantage of being together in Tokyo as young married men and developed their boyhood contacts into a deep adult friendship. It was because of this bond that early in 1956, long after my brother had been killed in the bombing of Shanghai at the start of the Sino-Japanese War in 1937, Howard, then a missionary himself at Kwansei Gakuin University near Kobe, came to Tokyo to perform the marriage ceremony for me and my present wife. Six months later my new wife and I, together with my three children by my deceased wife, spent our last night in Japan in the home of Howard and his wife, Gwen, before embarking on a 56-day 'honeymoon cruise' by freighter to Europe on our way back to the United States.

But to go back to earlier days, Herb Norman and I were much together during our summer vacations in Karuizawa. Whenever the weather permitted, we were at the tennis courts, and we regularly were tennis partners, winning consistently the junior championship of our age group, and he consistently beating me in the finals for the singles championship. I do not remember any sense of resentment at his superiority in tennis. His greater age of a little more than a year probably made it seem natural. I have the feeling that we were tennis partners almost forever, but a check of the travel dates between North America and Japan of the Norman and Reischauer families reveals that this period could only have lasted from the summer of 1918 through 1922, when he was eight to twelve and I seven to eleven.

After that I saw little or nothing of Norman for many years. He successfully overcame a bout with tuberculosis and then went to Victoria College at the University of Toronto. After graduating from Oberlin College in Ohio, I went for two graduate years to Harvard to study early Chinese and Japanese history. We both happened to go to Europe on scholarship in the summer of 1933 for two-year periods of study, he in medieval history at Trinity College at Cambridge, and I in classical Chinese and Japanese studies at the University of Paris.

Before leaving Europe in the late spring of 1935, I visited Norman at Cambridge, staying with him at his lodgings for two or three days. I haven't the slightest idea of how, after all those years, I knew where he was. Those were grim times, when the whole world economy was in serious depression, Hitler was seizing control of Germany, France was swept by rioting, and the downward trend towards militarism started by the Manchurian Incident of 1931 was continuing in Japan. Norman and I must have discussed these matters of mutual interest, though I have no memory of what we said. I do remember, however, being struck by the fact that while I, an American in France, had been an outsider looking on at these unhappy events, he as a Canadian in

England had been taking part in political activities.[1] I gathered the apparently somewhat erroneous impression that he was engaged in supporting the Labour party.

I went from France to Japan for two years of study and spent a third year in China, returning to Harvard in the summer of 1938, where to my surprise I learned that Norman had spent the past two years studying under my own old mentor, Serge Elisséeff, and had just gone to New York to finish up his thesis under the auspices of the Institute of Pacific Relations. I saw him briefly when he came back to Harvard in the spring of 1939, but being only a teaching fellow myself, I could not have been formally on his PHD thesis examination board, though I remember reading his thesis, which was to become the basis of his famous *Japan's Emergence as a Modern State*, published the next year.[2] I received my PHD from Harvard at the same time as Norman in 1939, writing a thesis on ninth-century Chinese and Japanese history, which attracted interest in only very narrow scholarly circles when it was published in greatly expanded form sixteen years later.

We were both soon swallowed up by our careers – he with the Department of External Affairs in Canada, I at Harvard – and then by World War II. I spent four years in Washington in the War and State departments and the American army; he spent the war years in Ottawa, after repatriation from Japan. Unlike me, he found time to continue his scholarly work, writing *Soldier and Peasant in Japan* (1943) and producing for a conference of the Institute of Pacific Relations in 1945 a policy-oriented study entitled *The Feudal Background of Japanese Politics*, based on his earlier work.

After the war, Norman served for a while in the counter-intelligence service of General MacArthur's headquarters in Tokyo and became the official Canadian representative in Japan, residing at the somewhat palatial Canadian embassy. It was there that we met for the last time.[3] I was in Japan from September 1948 to January 1949 as a member of a five-man Cultural Sciences Mission, dispatched there by the American government at MacArthur's request and on the suggestion of the Japanese academic community. Some time during that period Norman asked me over for lunch. With our shared background and interests we had plenty to talk about, though all I can remember now is his telling me about his recent scholarly studies, which were to appear in 1949 as the impressive volume entitled *Andō Shōeki and the Anatomy of Japanese Feudalism*.

Thus, my direct contacts with Norman after childhood add up to very little, but we had much deeper indirect relations through our similar scholarly interests and many mutual friends. One was Shigeto Tsuru. In the thirties, Tsuru was a young leftist-inclined economist taking his PHD at Harvard and was one of Norman's close associates there.[4] Norman's searching for the papers Tsuru had left behind when he was repatriated to Japan in 1942 later figured in the inquiries about Norman's political loyalties, and Tsuru, invited back to Harvard as a visiting professor in the 1950s, underwent his own ordeal of unsubstantiated accusations and innuendo, though in a curiously reverse form of McCarthyism. Asked to testify to a senatorial committee of inquiry, he blithely set off for Washington to put the record straight, but found himself permitted to respond only to questions as to whether he knew a long list of alleged communists, most of whom he had never heard of. The committee aide then announced from the steps of the Capitol to an eager pack of Japanese newsmen that, in connection with the questioning of Professor Tsuru, the committee had a long list of names of communists who had served in the American government. The newsmen swallowed the statement hook, line, and sinker, with the result that the powerful Japanese press crucified Tsuru with sensational accusations of his having betrayed his former friends and associates. At this time it was as unfashionable in Japanese intellectual circles to be openly anti-communist as it was taboo to be pro-communist in the United States. Tsuru eventually survived the ordeal to become the president of prestigious Hitotsubashi University, and he is still one of my valued friends and associates.

John Emmerson, whom I had known since we had studied together in Kyoto in the spring of 1937 and who was to be my deputy chief of mission from 1962 to 1966 when I was the American ambassador in Japan, was also closely associated with Norman. Emmerson, as a Japanese language specialist in the American Foreign Service, had been sent during the war to Yenan to interview Japanese prisoners held by the Chinese communists. Because of this assignment, he came to know some of the future Japanese communist leaders, and after the surrender was designated by the occupation authorities to be the official contact man with the Japanese communists. For this reason he and Norman called on the imprisoned communist leaders Tokuda Kyūichi and Shiga Yoshio in October 1945 to tell them and other political prisoners that they were about to be released, and later drove Tokuda and Shiga from the prison to downtown Tokyo.

Emmerson himself has always been a completely non-political servant of great integrity, but because of these activities, in which he was involved as a result of his linguistic talents and not because of any political leanings, his career, if not completely blighted, came under a heavy cloud. Because of the relentless hounding of a best forgotten Senator Hickenlooper of Iowa, he was subsequently twice passed over for appointment as ambassador to newly independent African countries where, because of his current service, he was the obvious choice. The second time, an overly timid but none the less remorseful Secretary Rusk asked me if I would take Emmerson as my second in command, since deputy chief of mission in Tokyo was the highest and most important post Emmerson could be given without subjecting him to senatorial scrutiny. I was, of course, delighted to agree, though I was indignant that the stupidity of certain senators and the spinelessness of the State Department had put this cap on Emmerson's career.

Norman and I shared a host of other friends. My present wife knew him slightly. Her history professor at Principia College, Robert Peel, was one of his close friends in the counter-intelligence service, and her work as assistant to Gordon Walker, Tokyo correspondent of the *Christian Science Monitor*, also brought her into contact not just with Norman but with Tokuda, Shiga, and other Japanese communist leaders. Walker was often critical of MacArthur in his dispatches and fell out of favour with the occupation authorities. My wife believed that she was blacklisted by the counter-intelligence service at this time and, being a defenceless Japanese citizen, felt it safer to leave newspaper work between 1948 and 1950, seeking refuge through employment at the Swedish diplomatic mission.

Many other close friends of mine, such as the Seymour Janow, knew Norman very well in those early occupation years. Their warm memories of him as a deeply scholarly, thoroughly charming, and very kind man show me how much I missed by having had only sparse contacts with him after he had developed into the learned and altogether remarkable man he became.

Despite my lack of much contact with Norman as a man and scholar, I, as a fellow student of Japanese history and a contemporary in the experiences of the years surrounding World War II, do not have my own clear evaluation of him and his scholarship. His leftist views were a natural part of the times, completely understandable in terms of the intellectual spirit of the age and the terrible experiences that shook the world in the 1930s and 1940s. His harassment by the American government was unforgivable and, to the discredit of the United States, contrasts sharply with the sensible handling by the Canadian government of the security problem presented by his leftist activities during his student days.

Norman's scholarly achievements were truly outstanding. It seems almost miraculous that in three short years he was able to do the course work required for a PHD at Harvard, develop his reading skill in Japanese to the level needed for his thesis, and then write a work of such sweeping breadth and penetrating depth as *Japan's Emergence as a Modern State*. Almost equally remarkable was the fact that, while working full time for the Department of External Affairs, he found time and energy to write his stimulating *Soldier and Peasant in Japan*, which has always been my favourite among his writings, and his much larger and more deeply researched analysis of the life and thought of Andō Shōeki, an iconoclastic figure of the late Tokugawa era.

Japan's Emergence as a Modern State was not just an amazing scholarly achievement. It and his 1945 Institute of Pacific Relations paper on the 'Feudal Background of Japanese Politics,' which drew heavily on it, were probably the most influential scholarly works shaping American and all Western political attitudes towards Japan during the war and early post-war years. Ruth Benedict's *The Chrysanthemum and the Sword* has often been cited as the book that most determined American attitudes towards Japan during the occupation, but, however extraordinary an achievement it was and however much it influenced later interpretations, it was not published until 1946, long after the major outlines of American policy had been thought through before Japan's surrender and put into practice during the crucial early occupation period. For those key phases, *Japan's Emergence as a Modern State* was *the* book – by far the most important scholarly influence on American policy thinking.

Norman's interpretations in *Japan's Emergence as a Modern State* show a strong Marxian influence, traceable to his own political inclinations at the time and the prevalent Japanese scholarship of the day. Shifting through my wartime experiences from an almost exclusive interest in ancient history to more concern with modern times, I was myself much influenced by it. In the first edition of my first general history of Japan, entitled *Japan Past and Present*, which I dashed off in the autumn of 1945 and published in 1947, I incorporated a good bit of Norman's analysis of the transition from the Tokugawa period to modern times. In my current view, subsequent studies have shown that a Marxian analysis of this transition does not fit the actual events very well and creates an unduly negative picture of Japan's modernization. As a consequence, in subsequent editions of *Japan Past and Present* and in a series of later histories I wrote, I steadily modified my interpretations away from Norman's. My changing evaluation of the validity of Norman's early work, however, does not change the strength of his influence on me and on a host of other people during the important years around 1945. Moreover, however correct or mistaken his views may have been, I believe that they had on the whole a profoundly beneficial effect. Norman's gloomy views of the prospects for democracy and social justice in Japan undoubtedly contributed greatly to the strongly reformist and often radical nature of occupation policy.[5] Without this influence, the occupation, in the hands of a military force dominated by such an essentially conservative and often reactionary figure as MacArthur, might very well never have opened the doors in Japan very wide to healthy democratic growth and sweeping social change. Viewed in this perspective, *Japan's Emergence as a Modern State* must be seen as a book of truly great historical significance, substantially influencing developments at a crucial phase in the history of Japan and Japanese-American relations. For this fact alone, Norman's name should loom large in historical scholarship.

I believe Norman deserves credit for another great achievement, which is often overlooked. In the early post-war years he was virtually unique as a deep scholar of modern Japan among the occupation forces. As such, he renewed contacts with the Japanese historians, establishing in this way a valuable link between victor and vanquished. His interest and encouragement helped reinvigorate Japanese historical scholarship. His interpretations, being fundamentally based on Japanese scholarship, gave his Japanese friends self-confidence and a realization that among their conquerors were people who understood their fears and hopes about a new Japan. The fact that Norman spoke or at least understood their Marxian vocabulary helped further the dialogue. His role in re-establishing intellectual contact between Japanese historians and the outside world was a significant service often lost sight of in the later controversy over his career.

Norman's contributions to scholarship and also to shaping history were indeed substantial, especially for a diplomat whose life was cut off so early. It is a great pity indeed that recent controversy has grown up over his scholarly writings, and a shame that this fine man, who suffered so grievously in his career and personal life because he had become a controversial figure should now in death be subjected to new controversies.

The origins of the needless debate are not hard to describe. After the war, a new generation of Western scholars of Japanese history grew up, building on the language training in Japanese they had received during the war and specializing more deeply and at greater leisure than Norman had ever had a chance to do. They naturally took off from *Japan's Emergence as a Modern State* to look more closely at the various aspects of the great nineteenth-century transformation of Japan. In a way characteristic of all scholarly advances, they found much to correct or modify in Norman's more general and hastily drawn picture. Other more complex interpretations became the common wisdom of the day, and Norman's views came to seem one-sided and in part ill-informed.

Later, still another generation of scholars, motivated in part, it would seem, by their well-founded dismay over American policies in Vietnam, turned back to Marxian interpretations of Japan's modern development, attacking their own professors' less Marxian interpretations and making Norman their scholarly hero. Such an ebb and flow of scholarly interpretation is the heartbeat of healthy scholarship. I have written enough to have had a chance to see my own ideas and books dismissed contemptuously by younger scholars as 'the conventional wisdom' or 'textbook accounts.'

In the case of the controversy over Japan's modernization, however, some of the participants unfortunately made intemperate accusations against the intellectual honesty of those they were criticizing, and extravagant claims were put forward about the originality of Norman's views. This development led to angry rebuttals by some of those attacked and careful expositions to prove that *Japan's Emergence as a Modern State* was based on secondary sources. It had to be, of course, given the times and the period of work Norman had available to him. Writing a book of the depth and sweep of *Japan's Emergence as a Modern State* in the short time he had was an achievement few scholars could ever hope to match. The whole controversy has been quite pointless. On the one side, accusations against the honesty of scholars with whom one disagrees are an unfair and thoroughly despicable form of intellectual debate.[6] On the other, Norman's scholarly achievements were tremendous, and his subsequent work demonstrated fully his ability to use primary material in a scholarly fashion when the size of the subject and the time available permitted. It is a terrible disservice to his memory to have made his work the focus of this unseemly and ill-tempered squabble.

As a lifelong friend and admirer, I seriously hope that Herb Norman in death will not be made the controversial figure he was forced to be in life. He was a great and talented writer and scholar. He was a deeply learned, sensitive, thoughtful, and kind man. As man and scholar, he greatly influenced his time, and he deserves to be remembered as a significant figure, both as a historian and as a shaper of history.

NOTES

1 Now in France, of course, as an American, I never had any thought of engaging in French politics. I would probably have gotten thrown out of the country very quickly if I had done that, but he, as a Canadian, felt that he had a right to participate in British politics, which I am sure he did. [This and the following few notes are taken from the transcription of the author's keynote address.]

2 Herb's great work, most outstanding one, and one that will go on living in history as a very significant book.

3 We were almost thrown together at that time because General MacArthur sent word back that he wanted me for his counter-intelligence service out in Japan. It was something that I didn't want to get involved in, and I managed to protect myself from it and stay in Washington where I could work on policy – not that it did any good. Once policy had been determined and sent to MacArthur in 1945 there wasn't any point in anybody else trying to tell MacArthur anything.

4 Well, almost everyone was a Marxian economist in those days. This was a common thing to do; there was nothing special about it at all.

5 [His interpretation] is one of the reasons, perhaps the major reason, why American policy was as radical as it was.

6 [George Akita's critique of Norman is obliquely referred to by Professor Reischauer: 'The man who responded most strongly of all was not one of those attacked (by one of Norman's defenders, Professor John Dower). I think what he (Akita) was doing was trying to defend me.' For details of Akita's critique, see pp. 102–5 of this volume.]

Cyril Powles makes the obvious but sometimes forgotten point that the life experiences of an academic directly affect his scholarship. Professor Powles's primary concern is to show how this relationship between life-style and scholarship pertains to Norman's childhood family experiences in Japan and his later adult writings.

Norman's first sixteen years were spent in Japan, the first half of these years at home in rural Japan under the care and educational supervision of his parents. Rural values, life among Japanese farmers, many of whom were quite poor, and the Christian socialist principles of his parents, Powles argues, permanently conditioned Norman to see the world and its problems from the perspective of the rural dweller in particular and the disenfranchised in general.

Professor Powles's line of reasoning has special insight to offer, inasmuch as he was born to Canadian missionary parents nine years to the day after Norman in the same area of Japan, and he himself became a highly respected student of Japanese history.

Cyril Powles

E.H. NORMAN AND JAPAN

On 4 May 1957, just a month after Herbert Norman's death in Cairo, his Japanese friends held a memorial assembly at the Gakushi Kaikan in downtown Tokyo. In the presence of Prince Mikasa, the emperor's youngest brother, eulogies were delivered by Nambara Shigeru, president of Tokyo University, and around a dozen other notables and friends. Twenty years later, many of the same scholars showed that they had not forgotten their friend when they contributed to a special issue of the journal *Shisō* [Thought] that discussed Norman's significance for the study of history in Japan. Around the same time, others were writing recollections and tributes for the fliers that went out between 1977 and 1978 to announce each of the four volumes of Norman's collected works.[1]

Considering that Norman is hardly known in his own country, and that in the United States his reputation is a matter of hot debate, the almost universal esteem in which he has been held in Japan may seem difficult to understand. One might even say that Norman himself felt more at home in Japan, with his Japanese scholar friends, than he did in North America. Certainly the tone of his letters to Japan give the impression that he admired and depended on the opinions of Japanese scholars and friends in a way that few foreigners have done. It is this close relation of mutual interdependence which characterizes Herbert Norman's special status as a student of Japan. As this status in turn grew out of his experience as the son of a Canadian missionary in rural Shinshu (Nagano Prefecture), we shall attempt to examine the two together, using his writings, those of his friends, and his personal experiences to gain some insight into his intellectual development.

WHAT IMPRESSED JAPANESE SCHOLARS

In the West Norman has been judged as a historian – and sometimes found wanting – on the level of technical efficiency. But in Japan he has been valued for qualities that are different and more difficult to measure. In reading the literature on the subject one is struck by the number of references to his humanism.[2] But this is a broad term which requires more detailed definition. One writer has called it 'understanding with sympathy' or, as we might paraphrase it, empathy with critical insight. Although analysis is a poor tool for understanding qualities that are essentially personal and indivisible, we may look at several facets of Norman's thought.

The first is his love of common people. Maruyama's phrase, 'An Affection for Unknown People' (or, as Ronald Dore translated it, 'the Lesser Names') is of course famous. In its most obvious sense this term means an interest in the less well-known characters of history: in 'Epicurus and Lucretius rather than Plato or Aristotle, the Levellers rather than Cromwell. Mo-tzu and Chuang-tzu rather than Confucius or Mencius.'[3] But such interests in themselves might signify nothing more than a rather dilettante antiquarianism unless combined with some reason or purpose. Norman is a humanist because he is concerned for and involved with the struggle of ordinary people to live more human lives. His 'lesser names' represent the host of nameless human beings whose daily suffering and striving become part of the stuff of history.

The point is well illustrated in a lecture that Norman gave in 1947 in his birthplace in Nagano to commemorate his father, entitled

'People Under Feudalism.'[4] He concludes his speech by pointing to the farmers of Shinshū who, by going in for sericulture, were able to escape the burden of the rice-bound peasant and usher in a day of new economic activity. With pride he reminds his hearers that by so doing the people of Nagano had been able to achieve a level of independence of mind and progressive political activity that could be matched by few other regions. This advance in the life of the people provided the foundations on which the pioneers of Japan's democratic movement – men like Nakamura Tahachirō or Kinoshita Naoe – could build.[5]

Another side of Herbert Norman's humanism is his sympathy for the underdog, a feeling which he wisely tempered with understanding, breadth of learning, and critical insight. Maruyama Masao, in the same article whose title we have quoted, writes, 'He was a historian of the world before he was a historian of Japan, [and his profound erudition] was always there under the surface, gleaming like silver through the interstices of his conversation.'[6]

One of Japan's most eminent historians, Tōyama Shigeki, also refers to this aspect of Norman's historical writing, contrasting the often narrowly specialized nature of much modern Japanese scholarship with the expansive European tradition of Sansom, Bloch, Carr, and Pireene. Norman, he writes, in his ability to accept complexity and ambiguity without losing hold of meaning and purpose, belongs to this tradition.[7]

A third aspect of Norman's humanism was his unashamed aestheticism. Okubo writes, 'He was a lover of the good life,'[8] and reminisces about listening with him in his study at home to records of Bach and Handel while they talked of reading and the theatre.[9] In a letter to Maruyama, written in 1951 when the Japanese scholar was suffering from a serious illness, Norman discusses the various books and records he had recently accumulated, referring to the advantages of the newly appeared long-play records which were giving to the public such heretofore little-known composers as Rameau, LeGrand, Couperin, and Vivaldi.[10] As the Japanese tradition has always esteemed aesthetic accomplishments and combined learning with such attainments as calligraphy, poetry, and art, Norman's liking for drama, music, and novels struck a sympathetic chord.

Nevertheless, admiration did not mean adulation, and scholars did not hesitate to point out limitations in Norman's descriptions of the Meiji Restoration and of Japanese society in general. Kano Masanao, in his 1977 *Shisō* article, 'Serufu gabamento no kōkyōshi' (Symphonic poem on self-government), points to Norman's failure to carry his analysis of the Meiji state forward to include the concept of *tennosei*.[11] Ienaga Saburō, in an often quoted review of Norman's *Andō Shōeki*, wrote that 'the high level of scientific historical enquiry' which marked the book had been weakened by 'an excessively high evaluation of the *Kōzaha* line which sees in peasant rebellion the decisive factor in the break-up of feudal society ... The distinctively historic nature of Shōeki's thought consisted in the overall combination of an exceedingly modern and revolutionary aspect with an equally conservative and reactionary inertness.' Thus Norman's 'excessive admiration for Shōeki [which stresses only the radical aspect without accounting for the reactionary part] ... seems doubtful on historical grounds.'[12]

Such criticisms make the admiration come alive and help to clarify the real nature of Herbert Norman's relation to the academic world of Japan. It has been observed that Norman arrived in Japan at a critical juncture in the development of historical writing there, and that he was able to give his colleagues a sense of confidence in the new direction their studies were taking.[13] Although this is undoubtedly true, Japanese affection for his work and thought went beyond gratitude for a helping hand. It rested rather on a feeling of mutual interdependence between the two sides – Japanese and foreigner – in which each exchanged ideas *as equals*, neither side having a sense of getting less than it gave.[14] In this respect, as one scholar has acutely remarked, 'he was no foreigner at all.' As this sense of interdependence on Norman's side was related to his experience as the child of a missionary in rural Japan, we should now turn to examine the subject in some depth.

THE SIGNIFICANCE OF NORMAN'S MISSIONARY BACKGROUND

Near the beginning of his memoir of Herbert Norman, Okubo Genji remarks that the fact that Herbert spent the greater part of his first sixteen years in Nagano marked him out from the average child of a missionary, who grew up in 'some western-style house with green lawns inside the compound of a Tokyo mission school.'[15] It would be difficult to exaggerate the importance of the rural experience in the development of Norman's consciousness. The missionary who lived in the city dwelt apart from the life of Japanese society, associating for the most part with the fellow foreigners who lived on 'missionary row.' His children played with other missionary children, in English, and when they reached school age they went to the American school where they continued to study in English. They grew up with a basic sense of separateness from the Japanese community and of independence of its resources. But in the countryside, though some foreigners might often be present, they were a minority, and there was a basic sense of dependence on the local society.

In Nagano, a rural centre with a population of some 36 000 in 1912, there were two foreign families, the Wallers and the Normans. Although the former represented the Anglican church and the latter belonged to the Methodist mission, both were Canadian and both came from Ontario farms. The two families were good friends but they lived some twenty minutes' walk apart. Thus, going to visit was a special occasion. Normal playtime was spent with the Japanese children of the immediate neighbourhood who accepted their foreign companion as a member of the group. A story told by Okubo Genji (which I have heard related about other missionaries as well) illustrates this acceptance. Two children encounter Herbert's father, Daniel Norman, on the streets of Nagano. One says to the other, 'Look out, here comes a foreigner!' To which the other is supposed to have replied, 'Go on, that's no foreigner. That's Mr Norman.'[16]

This feeling of acceptance was reinforced by the recognition that the father was something of a personage in the region. Compared with J.G. Waller, a shy and rather stiff person, Daniel Norman was blessed with an ebullient and outgoing personality. Where Waller was not a good linguist, Norman became quite skilful in Japanese. Both travelled extensively in Nagano and Niigata prefectures, but Norman was able quite early to establish a special relation with the railroad workers on the Shin-etsu line. He organized study groups at several of the stations which became so popular that he was given a pass to enable him to travel freely up and down the line.[17]

A further example of their differences can be seen from two letters, one from Waller and the second from Norman. Waller was a convert from the Baptist Church to Anglicanism and graduated from Trinity College. In that sense, he opted into the Anglican ruling-class mentality, while Norman firmly belonged to the Victoria College Methodist tradition. In 1922 Waller, in writing about conditions following World War I, mentions workers' right to strike, but he says, 'A strange development, strange when we think of old Japan, is the spirit of unionism which became manifest during the war but was never prominent before the present financial depression. Thus faith that almost the only method adopted by all trades to maintain or restore former high prices is to limit entirely or to stop production to an amateur seems ridiculous and suicidal.' In contrast, Norman could write of the Great Depression and its effect on Japanese militarism: 'If this hapless system is not made over, changed, the outlook is dark indeed.' And at the height of anti-communist repression in Japan a few years later, he wrote to his home paper in Japan: 'I have long wondered why in many circles Communism should be thought of as something low or unworthy. Many of the best and noblest of men have been Communists. Jesus certainly taught Communism.'

Daniel's agricultural background, however, endeared him more than anything to the farmers of rural Shinshū. He had come to the ministry relatively late in life, having dropped out of school as a boy in order to work on the family farm. Thus he was twenty-five years of age before he returned to school, and his large, calloused hands remained with him all his life to reveal his working experience to those around him. He is reputed to have introduced cash crops like apples, tomatoes, and walnuts from Canada into the Nagano countryside. A Japanese associate writes of visiting the country with Daniel and of the apparent relish with which, even in later life, he would sit in a farmhouse *kotatsu*, drinking tea and eating pickled vegetables according to rural custom.[18]

Daniel Norman's firm base in the Shinshū countryside made him a valuable intermediary, when the need arose, between Japanese and Westerner. In later life he rejoiced in the nickname *Karuizawa no son-chō san* (mayor of Karuizawa) because, having retired to that town, he was sometimes called upon to represent the interests of the permanent Japanese community to the summer residents, and vice versa.

If consciousness of his father's secure position in Japanese local society provided one part of Herbert's sense of belonging, a further dimension was added by the nature of his life at home, with his mother and with books. His brother has spoken of the close tie between Mrs Norman and her youngest child; how the mother would come into the son's bedroom when he came home, 'to tuck Herbert in,' and how the custom hung on even after the boy had become an adult. Mrs Norman, a trained schoolteacher, gave Herbert all his education until he left for the Canadian Academy in Kōbe at the age of eleven. By that time, as the writer can testify from similar experience, basic habits of study and the motivation to learn came from a well-stocked family library. In an age without radio or television, long hours were spent with books, so that no clear demarcation existed, as tends to be the case today, between education and recreation. The present writer remembers vividly how, at the age of eight or nine, his mother would read him to sleep out of one of the historical works of Francis Parkman, or his father from the novels of Charles Dickens or Sir Walter Scott. Undoubtedly Herbert's experience would have been similar, though the books may have been different. Thus, some years later, when illness imposed leisure on a young and athletic man, it became natural to turn to books for solace and enjoyment.

Perhaps – although we need not stress it too much – there is the beginning of a conflict here between the sense, gained outside the home, of belonging to, and being dependent on, Japanese society and the sense, instilled at home, of being part of a different culture with different beliefs and values. The consequences, though, were not necessarily all negative. As we have seen, Herbert Norman attracted his Japanese fellow historians precisely because he refused to see the Japanese experience only in terms of its uniqueness and loved to discuss it in the context of a broader, world-wide view. The clash of cultures forced expatriates to see matters creatively, in relation to one another.

WHAT IT MEANT TO BE AN EXPATRIATE CANADIAN

The question is complex, forcing one arbitrarily to select certain aspects which seem to cast light on Herbert Norman's Canadianness and his relation to Japan. Most obvious of these would be the colonial, or as we might express it today, the 'third-world,' character of Canadian society. At the beginning of the twentieth century Canada was moving from a colonial to a neo-colonial status within the Empire, giving it an ambivalent relation to the mother country. Thus, on the one hand, Canadian culture was seen as an overseas extension of English society. This view was particularly true of English-speaking Ontario, former seat of the Family Compact and originally colonized by United Empire Loyalists.

To take just one example, when Herbert Norman began his higher education he enrolled at Victoria College in the honours classics course. The college had been founded to give the Methodist population of central Ontario an education formerly denied it by the establishment Anglican monopoly of King's College. The secularization of the latter institution permitted federation in 1890, so that by Norman's time Victoria had been thoroughly co-opted into the English style of the University of Toronto, with the wearing of academic gowns, dining halls complete with high tables, and the rest. That Norman should have considered classics as a proper discipline for a bright young mind represented a further reflection of British education, which saw the study of Greek and Latin as a fitting foundation for training in the humanities and the building of all-round character.[19]

Yet there was another side to this relationship. As victims of colonial policy and as people who had deliberately chosen a different kind of life in the New World, free from dead traditions and class distinction, Canadians felt antagonistic to British culture. At the same time, the nearness and economic superiority of the English-speaking United States, combined with continuous immigration from the British Isles, prevented Anglophone Canadians from developing a clear sense of identity, unlike their French-speaking compatriots in Québec whose distinct way of life had evolved over three centuries of isolation. Reaction against Britishness tended to be expressed by pro-Americanism, an inclination particularly evident among the Methodists who possessed strong ties of kinship and religious affinity with the United States. For a person like Norman, however, whose grandparents on both sides had immigrated from England, such sympathies would be relatively weak. It was this weak sense of identity, most characteristic of Canadians, which expressed itself positively abroad as openness to other cultures and manners.[20]

In the life of the expatriate Canadian, who represented a minority group sandwiched between the numerically superior Americans and English, this openness revealed itself as a positive affirmation of Japanese institutions. On the whole, the attitude to Japan of missionaries from Great Britian and the United States reflected the nature of their respective countries' overseas political and economic commitments. While the British, assuming their own society to have reached the pinnacle of human evolution, were quite content to leave Japanese society as it was, an exotic medieval culture, the Americans, moved by their manifest destiny, wanted to see a change, not only in the heathen faiths but also in political and economic structures, to become 'more modern' – by which they usually meant like their own country, democratic and capitalist.[21]

For Canadians, who had few national interests to uphold, Japanese culture could be perceived more openly, in all its complex and seemingly contradictory wholeness. Their early unwillingness to accept life in the foreign concessions – preferring rather to 'live with the Japanese' – insistence on the inclusion of Japanese representatives on mission boards, and seriousness in the study of the language and indigenous religion all represent marks of this cultural openness.[22] Herbert Norman's early memory was of a father who had protested against a plan to open a summer community at Lake Nojiri because Japanese residents would not be included; this experience may have played a part in influencing his attitudes in a formative period.[23]

This peculiarly Canadian refusal to be bound by a particular national interest did not mean that Canadians came to Japan free of all cultural baggage. For instance, they brought with them, along with their counterparts from the United States, the common Protestant aversion to alcohol which gave rise to what some wag has termed the first Christian creed in Japan: 'One God, one wife, no wine.' It has been remarked that the architecture of the Norman house in Nagano combined the worst features of both Daniel and Catherine Norman's Ontario farmhouses.[24] Nevertheless, the fact that cultural conditioning reflected itself in *personal* rather than in what might be broadly called *political* attitudes allowed Canadians to remain more open than their other Western colleagues to the social aspects of Japanese culture. Indeed, their very refusal to conform to the political ethos of the missionary movement resulted in many Canadians seeing themselves as 'against the established order,'[25] a mind-set which continued with the children, even after they had returned to Canada. Herbert Norman's experience as a student radical can be paralleled by the activities of dozens of other Canadian missionary children: Endicotts, Walmsleys, Willmotts, and Woodsworths, to name only a representative few.

Of course, belonging to a minority religious group within a non-Christian society reinforced the nonconformist mentality. Children grew up – particularly in the country – learning to depend on and think of their own family customs and values as in some sense absolute and of higher worth than the mores of the community at large. Nevertheless, one still has to explain why so many Canadian missionary children became radicals when their British and American companions, who share the experience of being a minority, did not. Here certain differences in the way the Canadians perceived their faith may help us to understand, along with the colonial experience, what made them stand out against the establishment.

In this connection, the Canadian literary critic Ronald Sutherland is helpful when he points out certain key variations in the way Protestants in Canada have been conditioned by their Calvinist heritage. For Americans, Calvinism reinforced the individualistic dynamism inherent in their mission to bring enlightenment to a backward country. In other words, the Protestant ethic and the spirit of capitalism went hand in hand. But for Canadians, whose society remained predominantly agrarian and pre-industrial, the Puritan ethos expressed itself more quietly, in a personal idealism untied to any established political messianism.[26] It was this 'agrarian' idealism which could be transmuted into radical opposition to capitalist industrialism when conditions (economic depression, 'imperialist' war) demanded.

In the end, though, Herbert Norman's effectiveness in the eyes of his Japanese colleagues resulted from his ability to combine an anti-establishment stance with a strong sense of identification.[27] Critiques of militarism coming from outside Japan could be shrugged off as foreign interference. Conversely, identification with Japanese culture that ignored the contradictions and injustices inherent in the society ended up as superficial romanticism. But for Norman, whose childhood had conditioned him to feel part of his adopted society, love of country involved the search from within that society for a better way ahead.

NOTES

1 *Shisō*, no. 634 (Tokyo: Summer 1977); Okubo Genji, ed. and trans., *Hābāto Nōman zenshū* (The Complete Works of E. Herbert Norman), 4 vols. (Tokyo: Iwanami 1977–78): hereafter *HNZ*. Many thanks for information throughout to W.H. Norman and Okubo Genji. The writer, who grew up in Takada, less than 70 km from Nagano, has drawn on his own experience to supplement the argument.

2 Tōyama Shigeki in *Shisō*, no. 634, 27; Kano Masanao in ibid., 7–9; Maruyama Masao in ibid., 91

3 Maruyama Masao, 'An Affection for the Lesser Names: An Appreciation of E. Herbert Norman,' *Pacific Affairs* 30 (1957)

4 Reprinted here, pp. 143–54.

5 *HNZ* I: 365–7
6 Maruyama, 'An Affection,' 250
7 Tōyama, 34–5
8 *HNZ* IV: 439
9 *HNZ* IV: 446
10 *HNZ* IV: 598, 439, 450
11 Kano, in *Shisō*, no. 634, 10. *Tennōsei* literally means 'Emperor system' and refers more broadly to the concentration of power during the Meiji (1868–1912), Taisho (1912–25), and Showa (1925–) periods by successive Japanese governments that derived legitimacy from the imperial institution.
12 Ienaga Saburō, *Shigaku Zasshi* 59 (1950), quoted in *HNZ* III: 458–9. *Kōza-ha* refers to one of two main 'schools' of thinking among Japanese Marxists.
13 H.D. Harootunian, 'E.H. Norman and the Task for Japanese History,' *Pacific Affairs* 41 (1968–69): 545
14 Tōyama, 30
15 *HNZ* IV: 562
16 *HNZ* IV: 561–2
17 *Missionary Bulletin* (Toronto 1920), 563, in Daniel Norman biographical file, United Church of Canada Archives, Victoria College, University of Toronto
18 *HNZ* IV: 562, quoting Mutō Ken, Introduction to *Nagano no Noruman* [Norman of Nagano] (Tokyo: Fukuinkan 1965). A *kotatsu* is a traditional form of heating; over a low-level fire, built in a specially constructed hole in the floor, is a table covered by a heavy blanket.
19 For this ideal, as represented by Thomas Arnold, see E.C. Woodward, *The Age of Reform*, 2nd ed. (London: Oxford 1969), 474.
20 Charles Taylor, *Six Journeys: A Canadian Pattern* (Toronto: Anansi 1977), ii–vi
21 C.H. Powles, 'Foreign Missionaries and Japanese Culture in the Late Nineteenth Century: Four Patterns of Approach,' *Northeast Asia Journal of Theology* (Tokyo: September 1969), 17–20, 25–8
22 C.H. Powles, 'The Development of Japanese-Canadian Relations in the Age of Missionary Activity.' Paper (in process of publication) read at Japan-Canada Conference, Hachiōji, Japan, 1 September 1979, pp. 24–7.
23 Conversation with Dr W.H. Norman
24 Conversation with the late Dr A.R. Stone, United Church of Canada missionary in Nagano, 1934–41

25 See, for example, the remark of J.G. Waller, *Canadian Church Magazine and Missionary News* 7: 234, re living in the foreign concession.
26 Ronald Sutherland, *The New Hero: Essays in Comparative Quebec/Canadian Literature* (Toronto: Macmillan 1977), 5. See also Richard Allen, *The Social Passion* (Toronto: University of Toronto Press 1971), 200–18.
27 Sutherland (*The New Hero*) refers to this combination of idealism with 'trust in authority and systems' as distinguishing Canadian Calvinism from the 'defiant individualism' of the American type.

The life in rural Japan which Norman had come to accept as normal was abruptly interrupted when he contracted tuberculosis shortly after his sixteenth birthday. The failure of medical treatment in Japan forced young Herbert, accompanied by his mother, to leave Japan in late 1926 for a sanitorium near Calgary where he spent one year regaining his health among a great many who had no chance of recovering from that dread disease. There he learned about the sobering experience of death; his heretofore unquestioned Christian faith was badly shaken. He wrote on 25 July 1927, 'I often feel conscience-stricken. Strange (or perhaps naturally) to say that even among society which one would call highly respectful, thoughtful, etc., there is [a] destructive, agnostic atmosphere that is impervious to reason, sentiment, or exhortation and acts as a wet sponge on one's beliefs unless he can rise above his own gift (or curse) of thought and doubt.'

Now fully aware of his gift (or curse), he entered Albert College in Belleville in the fall of 1928 to complete his college preparatory work at grade thirteen level. The next autumn he entered Victoria College in Toronto. By his senior year (1932–33) he was privately expressing strong and radical words of contempt for the Conservative Bennett government, calling it 'reactionary' for using the 'mask of democracy' to hide its attempts to protect 'capitalism in its decay.' He possessed the kind of condemnatory language common to radicals, but he had yet to discover an alternative vision which could offer hope for the future. He held little regard for the Russian example, saying that it is likely 'to drift into bureaucracy' and 'lose sight of the end, that the State is for Man, not Man for the State.' 'I fear,' he wrote during the final exam period in 1933, 'I am still much at sea when it comes to balancing the evils and possibilities of set-back in a revolution on the one hand, and the chances of gaining a more hopeful and equitable society on the other.'

Herbert latched onto a different sort of mooring that fall when he entered Trinity College, Cambridge University, on a scholarship in history. Norman 'found' Marx, and Strachey, and Dobb, and John Cornford. He also 'found' Victor Kiernan, the author of our next piece. Kiernan was a fellow student of Norman's at Cambridge in the years 1933–35, during which time they both joined the Communist party. Kiernan remained a Party member for twenty-five years; we do not know when Norman exited. But, regardless, we can reasonably suspect that their motivations for join-

ing were much the same. Kiernan's article provides a contextual explanation for joining – it speaks for itself – but he also gave a more direct answer in replying to a suggestion made by Professor John Howes, during open discussion, regarding the close relationship between socialism and religion. Kiernan remarked:

'I grew up as a Congregationalist, and I have no regrets about that. As a Marxist historian, I do feel more and more how important a formative influence, very often a bad influence, but sometimes a good one, religion has been.

'But when I went to Cambridge, at the age of eighteen, in 1931, I was still in a sort of twilight, I mean, in a sense a sort of secular Mish kid myself. My parents were quite religious. I was still in the twilight between religion and militant atheism, although remaining the college representative of the Cambridge Congregational Society.

'I joined the Communist party in 1934 and remained a member until 1959. Since then, I'd like to describe myself as an independent Marxist. And as I say, one of my main and ongoing interests is religion.

'Already drifting at Cambridge, the influence there, notably the books by Bertrand Russell, converted me from my youthful Congregationalism. The main point I would like to make here is whether or not the sort of change that I and others were going through was an irreversible, final stage in history, the world, or rather Western Europe, seemed to have reached the point where religion was decaying into something else. Was our political enthusiasm really a kind of liberation of energy from some kind of moral transmutation? If so, has this reservoir dried up now that there is no doctrinal left? Therefore, is it possible to recapture the kind of socialist enthusiasm of an organized and disciplined form that we had in those days?

'I have the feeling this process is not repeating itself, that the renewal of political life or social responsibility, or whatever it was, faded with religion, having lost one of its vital taproots. I am rather led to think that this feeling of ours, this approach, that we were committed to the party for life, was an inheritance from our religious background. Obviously, if you belong to a religion and take it seriously, then you are in it for life.'

At Cambridge Norman experienced, in words he wrote in 1935, 'an intellectual rebirth': he was reborn a Marxist. In many respects, as Professor Kiernan remarks, Norman was 'in it for life.' Nowhere else can we better gain an appreciation of how this happened to Norman than in Kier-

nan's description of the intellectual world in which Norman experienced his political rebirth.

Victor Kiernan

HERBERT NORMAN'S CAMBRIDGE

The most stimulating environment may be the one with the greatest mixture of elements, and the Cambridge of the inter-war years was full of contrast and incongruities. Today, by comparison, it is more uniform, academically on average more respectable, less intriguing or exciting. In those days it had room for curious personalities, even eccentrics. Seriousness and frivolity, brilliance and stupidity, cobwebs and novelties, were to be found side by side. It was still a haunt of the *jeunesse dorée*, who were there to amuse themselves in a playground of snobbery and upper-class lotus-eating. Edwardian self-indulgence was having its last fling. For college seniors, a luxurious mode of living was sustained by the genteel practice of underpaying overworked college servants. Newcomers from more modest social backgrounds reacted sometimes admiringly, sometimes critically. There was a growing influx of them, among students and more gradually among teachers. Meritocracy was coming in, and individuals from the humblest families might soar by way of Cambridge or Oxford to high posts, fortunes, knighthoods, even gaiters. Others were less easily assimilated (a fact that their tutors found exceedingly hard to comprehend); the establishment was apt to strike them as smugly self-complacent, pretentiously genteel, over-anxious to keep up the pose of 'effortless superiority.'

It often seemed as if the Great War had never happened. Yet in reality the old world of before 1914 was now hollow and brittle, the country was groping its way painfully towards a different existence. Cambridge was a microcosm of this process. The university was highly paternalistic, standing *in loco parentis* to undergraduates in a fashion no university nowadays dreams of. Gowns had to be worn at lectures, as well as in the evening in the streets, which were patrolled by proctors. Bedroom windows on the ground floor were heavily barred, and young men and women were kept as far apart as possible. No woman ever had a meal in the hall of Trinity College until the present queen was given lunch there after her coronation. Yet there were two women's colleges, and heated debate and controversy after 1918 led to partial incorporation of their students into the university. They were not regular members of it, and not entitled to wear gowns – it took another world war to shake the walls of Jericho as far as that – but they could attend university lectures, sit for examinations, and take degrees. There were dire warnings, eagerly denied by feminists, that once allowed university membership women would want to get into men's colleges as well – as they have lately been doing. Their unequal treatment must have helped to push a good many girl students towards the political left, and one campaign early taken up by socialists was for the admission of women to that celebrated Cambridge institution, a club and a debating society, the Union.

Religion was another area where Cambridge was in a state of flux. Howarth[1] quotes from the diaries of A.C. Benson, master of Magdalene College, an account of a Church of England service where he noticed dignitaries nodding or snoring all around him – 'A disgraceful scene of infinite futility and grotesqueness.' In the Cambridge Inter-Collegiate Christian Union (CICCU – pronounced 'kick-you') was preserved a simple evangelical creed, muscular Christianity of the Victorian empire-building sort. A newer, more unwholesome version of its non-intellectualism was Moral Rearmament, whose founder thanked God for Adolf Hitler. More reasonable, more sensitive to social problems, more open to what is now called 'dialogue,' was the Student Christian Movement.

In spite of much frivolity and mediocrity, there were departments of knowledge where what Cambridge was thinking was of importance to the whole world. There was a galaxy of talent, even genius – more than at any time in its history – and some awareness of this may have helped to sharpen the faculties of the rising generation. In certain sciences especially, startling advances were being made. In the Cavendish Laboratory the way into the atom was being explored, Pandora's box about to be opened. Mathematics was another very strong field; so was astronomy, as books for the general reader by Jeans and Eddington, and on relativity by that banished Cambridge philosopher Bertrand Russell, made the public conscious.

Equally significant in a different way was a new conception of the social responsibility of the scientist. It was emerging chiefly in association with fresh ideas in biology, the science of life instead of, as physics has come to be, the science of death. J.B.S. Haldane, who had been at Cambridge in the 1920s, was already well known, a fellow of the Royal Society and professor in London, when his book *Materialism* was published in 1932. At Cambridge, Needham and Bernal were the scientists most heard of among progressives. A recent writer has emphasized the influence such men were having on the young men round them. Laboratory life and its team-work facilitated such influence, and a number of young research workers of those days were to become distinguished scientists in their turn, and carry forward the social ideals they were imbibing. These found a kind of manifesto in Bernal's big book *The Social Function of Science*. It included sections on 'Science and Fascism' and 'Science and Socialism,' with warm praise for developments in the Soviet Union. It came out in 1939, just before the outbreak of a war that was to give the writer a social function of a sort he little expected, as scientific adviser on the preparations for the Normandy landing.

In arts subjects and social sciences, currents of change were making themselves felt from a diversity of angles. English literature was presided over by 'Q' – Sir Arthur Quiller-Couch – who had written novels once popular but by the 1930s forgotten. In Leavis it had a literary critic of a radically new species, but Leavis was something of an Ishmaelite, ill at ease in orthodox Cambridge; he went about defiantly, without a tie. In economics, the theories worked out by J.M. Keynes as an alternative to socialism were only very slowly making their way. He brought from Italy the Marxist economist Sraffa, who had fallen foul of Mussolini; and there was actually a communist lecturer, Maurice Dobb, who was not, however, given a fellowship at his college (Trinity) until many years later. Economic history had lately been recognized as an independent subject. Its first professor was Clapham, about whose book on modern Britain a reviewer made the joke that if Clapham ever found himself in hell it would not be long before he produced a report showing that it was not really so bad a place as it was made out; some localities were distinctly cooler than others. A more exotic figure was Postan, who came to Cambridge from far away, and knew more about Marxism than the home-grown conservatives.

At Cambridge and Oxford, life revolved around the colleges, though the more important lecturing was increasingly organized, like the laboratory work, by the university. Tuition was left to the colleges and followed an archaic pattern; a history student had to compose a weekly essay and read it aloud to his tutor, who might or might not know something about the subject. Trinity was by far the biggest and richest college, with the longest list of great men of the past, as various as Newton and Byron, and a quite long list of remarkable men among its fellows now, though some of these were old or aging. Sir James Frazer, the anthropologist, must have been the oldest of all; the master was Sir J.J. Thompson, who had been one of the atomic pioneers. A.E. Housman, the professor of Latin, was a remote, self-isolating figure, devoted to arid textual criticism, though the poetry he had written in youth was more widely read than any other English poetry of modern times. G.M. Trevelyan, the Regius professor of history, belonged to a worthy Liberal tradition of other days.

Among the other Trinity historians, none of whom did much writing, R.V. Laurence upheld a tradition of conviviality going back to the toping and ease of the eighteenth century. When one went to his room with an essay he would be found in an armchair, gouty limbs swathed in bandages, half the floor covered with empty bottles. A fellow Epicurean, Lapsley, lectured on medieval constitutional history – unaided by any notes – with ardour and gusto, but wrote nothing. His snobbery, unchecked or perhaps fostered by an American origin, was well known; it was understood that he did not much care to be visited by anyone below the rank of viscount. In addition, there was a Catholic priest, an Anglican clergyman – F.A. Simpson, so much in demand as a fashionable preacher that he acquired a private plane to fly him up and down the country – and an Anglican lay-preacher, G. Kitson Clark, at one time secretary of the county Conservative Association; he had a nervous horror of Marxism, or socialism in any guise.

To the censorious eyes of young people coming under the spell of socialism, this old Cambridge was part of an *ancien régime* about to be swept away – as it largely has been in fact since those days. At best its teaching seemed trivial, irrelevant, with no answers for enormous problems and perils weighing on the world, and with little show of even recognizing their existence. It was quite in tune with the government of the time, the self-styled National Government or right-wing coalition, mostly Tory, which began with a landslide election in 1931, following a financial crisis which, in the light of later research, seems to have been somewhat artificial, but which paralysed a timid Labour cabinet and pushed Ramsay MacDonald and other leaders into abandoning their party and joining hands with the Tories. In 1935 the National Government was re-elected, with a smaller majority; MacDonald had been replaced by the Conservative leader Baldwin, who was succeeded by the disastrous Neville Chamberlain.

Its policies, at home and abroad, were of a sort to inflame left-wing feeling. It had no cure for the massive unemployment brought by the Slump, the economic depression that suddenly descended on the capitalist world in 1929. Such a state of affairs was unfamiliar then, not taken for granted as it is coming to be nowadays, and unemployment was far more painful than now, when it is cushioned by the welfare state. Allowances were meagre, and the so-called Means Test made things worse, at a time when the rich were still living with their old prodigality. One of the experiences that did most to swell the Socialist Society at Cambridge was the sight of the Hunger-marchers, a contingent of whom passed through the town in February 1934 on their way from the north of England to London. Students joined them at Huntingdon, a dozen miles north, and walked back to Cambridge with them. At Girton College, on the outskirts of the town, some of the women students provided refreshments; they were lodged for the night in the Corn Exchange, and bus-loads of socialists went to London to join in their demonstration meeting in Hyde Park.

Between hungry unemployed and gluttonous college banquets the contrast was vivid. Something could be learned about living conditions in the town from college employees, porters and bedmakers. With about 80 000 people, it had always supported itself a good deal by working for the university, but was now developing some light industry. Trade unions were gaining ground, there were strikes, of busmen for instance, and in elections the Labour party was making a better showing in what had been a Tory stronghold. Left-wing students canvassed for it at election-times, at least those who were not too far left: to communists, in those embittered days, the Labour party was as much anathema as the Conservative. Within its national ranks there was a left-wing minority movement; one of its prominent figures was Sir Stafford Cripps, after the war a right-wing chancellor, but leader of a Socialist League within the Labour party (from which he was expelled for a while) at the time when he came to Cambridge to address a big public meeting. A bodyguard was provided to protect him from attack, thought to be meditated by Tory students; the meeting stirred up much excitement, applause from one side and heckling from the other. It was the same at another meeting where the speaker was Ellen Wilkinson, who had been a member of the Labour cabinet, Britain's second woman cabinet minister.

On this occasion some of the arguing was about foreign policy. Foreign horizons were overshadowed by the rise of fascism. The coming to power of the Nazis in January 1933 was quickly followed by the Reichstag fire, the Dimitrov trial, the 1934 purge, persecution of Jews, and before long rearmament and conscription. In February 1934 there was fighting in Vienna, with the clerical-fascist dictator Dolfuss using the army against the Social-Democrats. Nazism, like Italian and Austrian fascism, found many admirers in Britain – Tories, often in high places, who liked it because it put an end to socialism and trade unions, even if they had some decent minor objections to some of its other doings. Rather too sweepingly, all Tories were suspected by the left wing of sympathy with fascism and of thinking that it would be a wholesome medicine for Britain too. There had been a first attempt at a fascist movement in imitation of Mussolini, under aristocratic leadership, in the early 1920s; now a far more determined effort was being made by Sir Oswald Mosley.[2] Refugees from fascism abroad were numerous, a good many of them in Cambridge and the other universities, and some of them, chiefly those belonging to left-wing movements, politically active. Socialist students on holiday on the continent made contact with like-minded people in countries like France and Spain, where they breathed a headier atmosphere.

War was the darkest shadow falling across Europe and Britain. A deep anti-war spirit survived into the thirties from the Great War, and there was a conviction that with the new and terrible weapons that were rumoured, any fresh war could only be blindly destructive. For the left it would be the result of capitalist greed and plotting, as 1914 – there was an increasing realization – had been. A landmark in Cambridge politics was a protest one night early in November 1933, at the Tivoli cinema, against the showing of a film called 'Our Fighting Navy,' which was regarded as war propaganda; it led to a riotous counter-demonstration outside. This was followed by an event that made more stir, an anti-war procession through the town on Armistice Day to the war memorial. All left-wing and some religious groups took part. It was attacked by a swarm of conservative students, with eggs and tomatoes and other missiles, but in spite of a running battle succeeded in reaching its goal and holding an open-air meeting. In subsequent years a November 11 march became an annual event, never interfered with again. The Cambridge Anti-War Exhibition was an impressive endeavour to warn the public of the horrors another conflict would entail, very much like the warnings of anti-nuclear campaigners today against the atom bomb. 'Scholarships, not battle-ships!' was a favourite slogan of demonstrators.

All these feelings about the bad state of our world, and the possible nearness of doomsday, were brought into focus by events in Spain – the three years' civil war set off in the summer of 1936 by the rising of Franco and his fellow-generals against the liberal Republican govern-ment. The spectacle of an international fascist crusade, with German and Italian forces in Spain along with the Foreign Legion and a horde of Moors brought from Spanish Morocco; the farce of 'non-interven-tion,' sponsored by the British government; the improvised Inter-national Brigade fighting on the Republican side, in which a number of Cambridge and other British students served and several were killed – all this stirred up feeling that was all the more intense because of a conviction of Britain's and Europe's fate also being at stake. Tory prejudices in favour of the Spanish fascists and their aristocratic spokesmen were unconcealed, and added to left-wing detestation of the government. There was nearly as much indignation with the more backward Labour leaders, whose attitude over Spain was hesitant and shuffling. A good part of the time and energy of all progressives, not socialists only, went into organizing meetings and collecting funds for aid to Spain. Not far from Cambridge new refugees were living, a colony of Basque children.

All these pressures were multiplying socialists, and pushing many of them towards communism. This was already taking root in the university by 1930, and all through the thirties was gaining ground remarkably. Those who led the way at first were from well-to-do families, typically – as in John Cornford's case – of the academic elite. On the one hand, they felt ashamed of their comfortable place in soci-ety when so many in the country and in the world were so badly off; on the other, they felt secure enough to be able to take some risks with their future. In some families of the elite the whole younger genera-tion caught the flame; at Trinity for instance, the daughters of the dean of Chapel. As the movement spread, it drew in a cross-section of Cambridge students, undergraduates and researchers from every social background; it seemed to have answers to an equally mixed array of problems, at home and abroad, in face of which bourgeois thinking was bankrupt. ('Bourgeois' was a term habitually used to denote everything capitalistic, reactionary, or simply stupid.) In the gathering atmosphere of crisis, individual motives or psychology were felt to be of no account; only the practical collective result mattered. Freshmen began to arrive with political consciousness already acquired at their public or grammar schools. By the time the war came there were more than two hundred communists, when the Party nationally still had not very many thousand members.

In any such situation there are always some who are in a movement because it is in fashion, and they want to be in the swim. But in general, these communists were very much in earnest, dedicated to what they regarded as their mission. It was not a 'student movement' in today's sense, when the university population of the country is vastly greater and has its own trade union organizations. Cambridge undergraduates were mostly not suffering from economic hardships, and though the left wing might be critical of the way the university was run, its concern was far more with the way the country and the world were going. They organized themselves with an efficiency which, looked back on after many years and much other experience of people working together, was really remarkable. In those years when Europe was increasingly divided between rival camps, communist and fascist, each highly monolithic, discipline and uniformity seemed indispensable virtues. That capitalism was in its final stage appeared self-evident; the question was whether it would drag civilization down with it in its collapse, and the only way to avert this end was to build up rapidly a force and an ideology, based on the masses, which would be capable of replacing it. The Party was a twentieth-century Ark, designed not to rescue a handful in a perishing world, but all humanity.

It would be absurd of course to depict these communists as perpetually wrapped in such thoughts, never giving way to more cheerful moods or lighter occupations such as falling in love. All the same, the moral pressure of the collective on the individual was firm. All paid a yearly levy or 'income tax,' in the form of a regular percentage of their means, part of which went to subsidize the hard-up Party in the East

Anglia region; in addition there were always extra contributions wanted for causes like Spain. Each college had its own 'cell' (it was only after the war that the CP gave its local bodies the less foreign-sounding name of 'branches'); cells met weekly, as study groups, and to hear reports from representatives of the secretariat, and in a businesslike way checked up on the fulfilment of individual assignments. Among these 'contact work' always held a high place, the duty of keeping in touch with prospective recruits – who were often taken aback, when they became members in turn, to discover how systematically their shepherding towards the Party had been conducted. 'Aggregates' were periodical meetings of the whole body; there were special ones for 'activists,' though a good deal of activity was expected from all.[3]

Proceedings were rather more conspiratorial than they need have been, in emulation of Bolsheviks of Lenin's day working underground; but if they were not being spied on as persistently as some supposed, a number of college tutors were uneasy and inquisitive. In the practice of infiltration into other bodies, setting up 'fractions' inside them, manipulating unsuspecting liberals – in a style sometimes counter-productive – there was a certain pride in behaving in an un-British fashion, discarding conventions and good manners as bourgeois nonsense. In a more above-board way, speakers or speakers' notes were supplied for any meeting of any society where invitations could be got, as a means of 'putting the Party line': the Party had an opinion, actual or still to be worked out, on everything under the sun. Members went out into the town to deliver copies of the *Daily Worker* to subscribers, or distribute leaflets at factory gates. They took part in poster parades to advertise the *Worker* and in demonstrations in Cambridge or London, lobbied MPs, and turned out in force as hecklers at meetings of the Blackshirts, who had not much concrete support in the university or in the district, but were hopeful of winning it.

In all this the USSR was the grand inspiration. Communists looked up to it nearly as undiscriminatingly as their conservative teachers denigrated it. Most diatribes against it were so patently prejudiced and ignorant that they reacted with an opposite refusal to believe that anything could be amiss under Stalin. From 1928, the five-year plans were launching the first planned economy in world history, and they had enormous success on the industrial front, quadrupling production in a period when in the capitalist world it was falling by anything up to half. Of the leading countries, Russia alone was firmly anti-fascist. It alone was giving arms and diplomatic backing to the Spanish Republic; the national secretary of the CP, Harry Pollitt, had a powerful case to make when he came to speak on Spain, after a visit to Madrid, in a debate at the Union.

A bad side of all the seriousness, and the sensation of crisis, was the sectarianism which made it quite usual for communists to denounce Labour party supporters as 'social fascists,' and universal for them to view Trotsky as a fiend in human shape. It helped to provoke a breakaway of the more moderate wing of the Socialist Society, which was affiliated to a militant Federation of Student Societies set up in 1932; in 1934 a separate Labour Club came into being. This schism was overcome, and the two wings came together again in 1935 in a Socialist Club, though within it the communists maintained their own very definite existence. In the same year, the 7th World Congress of the Third International gave a call for cooperation with other parties in popular fronts against fascism, and on the international plane for collective security. But the legacy of sectarian division was not easy to overcome.

Communists were not seldom accused of being as fanatical about their creed as if it were a new religion, and there was no doubt something like a religious flavour in their make-up. To most of them, a combination of Christianity and socialism like Joseph Needham's seemed bizarre. Yet many of them came from a religious background; and in their sense of duty to be always diligently at work they could be said to have some resemblance to Milton, toiling in his great Taskmaster's eye, even if the eye was watching them from the Kremlin instead of from heaven. But established religion and churches – very different in those days from what they have since come to be – seemed to them mostly reactionary humbug, which Russia had done well to cast off. Most German Protestants welcomed or submitted tamely to Hitler; Italian Catholics applauded Mussolini's conquest of Abyssinia; the attitude of the Spanish Church during the civil war (for which many years later its national assembly was to express contrition), and of Catholic churches everywhere, was violently pro-fascist. All the same, in places like Cambridge there was a dawning recognition by each side of better features of the other side, and some friendlier exchanges were taking place.

Most of a left-wing student's political reading was sternly practical. A journal like *Inprecorr* ('International Press Correspondence') strengthened his consciousness of belonging to a world-wide movement, of having unknown comrades who were waging guerrilla war in Brazilian forests, as well as others who were building socialism in the USSR. The Left Book Club, launched by the publisher Gollancz, was in full swing. Progressive bookshops were sprouting up and down the country; one was started in Cambridge in the mid-thirties, surpassing sales of literature by the Socialist Club.[4] Of Marxist theory, however, there was far less available than today, when left-wing students are often surprisingly well versed in it. There was a 'Little Lenin Library' – cheap reprints of tracts by Lenin, of whom more was known than of Marx. Until about 1934 or 1935 a term like 'dialectical materialism' had a mysterious sound, like a conjuror's spell.

In the next few years things were changing. One reason was that Party students formed something of an intellectual as well as political cream. Their code included the principle that time had to be found for academic work too, and that one way to win collective respect was to be at the top of the examination lists. A good proportion did take first-class degrees, and in later life some of these reached the top of their academic trees. Especially among those reading subjects like history or economics, political interest and intellectual curiosity converged and set them trying to discover or work out for themselves approaches to their problems in Marxist terms. This was true of none more than the two leading spirits, those very remarkable individuals James Klugmann and John Cornford.[5] Already before the latter's departure to Spain, history students under his lead felt strong enough to try to create a forum for discussion of history on lines opposed to the prevailing orthodoxy, and to challenge a hostile set of lectures on the USSR by a very conservative scholar, Reddaway, who was obliged to agree to a debate with his critics. It was the first time such a thing had happened in Cambridge, perhaps in any British university.

In the country, Marxist ideas were beginning to be thrown up by a few writers like Ralph Fox or Christopher Caudwell, whose pioneer *Illusion and Reality* was only published in 1938, after his death in Spain. John Strachey – after the world war a Labour minister – was then very close to the CP, and was writing books on the economics of capitalism and socialism which many read. They helped to inspire a few ambitious learners at Cambridge, humorously known as 'the

Bible class,' to try to struggle through *Capital*. Dobb was an inspiration closer at hand. By this time there was a small CP group of dons, one of them a writer on German literature and history. Klugmann might have been the equal of any Marxist scholar Britain has produced. After graduating in modern languages, of course with distinction, he embarked on research into the social basis of French Romantic literature; but this was interrupted when he was drawn away into full-time work in Paris as secretary of the World Student Movement (*Rassemblement Mondial des Étudiants*), then by the war, after which he devoted the rest of his life to the Party's service, chiefly in its educational department. He died in 1977.

A good many on the Left were fond of music, in which Cambridge abounded, but they liked to think of themselves as practical, down-to-earth people,for whom the annual figures of coal and steel production in the USSR were more important than any number of symphonies in the decadent West. Anything progressive in the arts, however, was sure of a welcome. Paul Robeson drew many to London one year to see him acting in *Stevedore*. A small cinema, the 'Cosmopolitan,' showed foreign and experimental films; among its patrons was Herbert Norman, whom I remember saying that everyone needed some 'mechanism' as a safeguard against depression; for him, films seemed to have this function. Among Soviet films seen in those years were *The White Sea Canal* and Eisenstein's *Ivan the Terrible* and *Thunder over Mexico*. Novels of revolution or social protest found readers – works like Malraux's *La condition humaine* (Man's Fate), about the Chinese counter-revolution of 1927; or *The Cannery Boat*, by the Japanese writer Kobayashi, murdered by the police; or, a little later (1939), Steinbeck's *The Grapes of Wrath*.

Those with serious literary interest read *International Literature*, which was mostly Soviet and not always easy going. Several small left-wing journals were trying to blaze a trail towards a new, socialist kind of poetry and fiction; in memory they seem to have been carrying on an endless dissection of every fresh attempt and concluding that there was something amiss with it. One visiting speaker at a left-wing meeting was Stephen Spender, then in the very socialistic phase of his *Forward from Liberalism* (1937); a phase which, as with other writers admired at the time as progressives, like Auden and Isherwood, turned out to be only a flash in the pan. Like the poets of the Romantic era, they proved politically unstable by comparison with many other left-wing intellectuals. Cornford, more than most of the

Left, wanted to fuse politics with imagination, as well as with thinking. He wrote verse himself, even in Spain; and in one of his first
essays, written in 1933–34 for *Cambridge Left*, he found fault with
Spender as too much abstracted from life. Art and action should be
inseparable, the artist must throw in his lot with the people. He and
others were saying what Mao said a few years later at his writers'
conference at Yenan. Cornford predicted a 'revolutionary literature,'
which has not in fact got far, either in the West or in China; the
difficulty of turning art into propaganda, or propaganda into art, is
more intractable than it looked in the 1930s. But he was closely followed at Cambridge by two others who have since contributed to
Marxist theory, Raymond Williams and Arnold Kettle.

In the inter-war years, scarcely anyone guessed that the British
colonial empire was destined to disappear so soon. It looked majesti-
cally rock-firm. Its virtues were an article of faith with Tories (and
with many Labour leaders), and official Cambridge believed in it un-
questioningly. Yet unrest was spreading in many parts of the empire,
and it was deepened, and nationalist movements like those in India or
Egypt were invigorated, by the economic depression, which hit the
third world harder than the industrial countries. Of facts like these
very few in Britain were aware. Partly from insularity, partly because
colonial issues seemed remote compared with those close at hand in
Europe, only a few on the Left, even among its intellectuals and students, felt any close concern about the colonies. Occasional happen-
ings drew attention, like the sentences imposed in 1933 at the end of
the Meerut Conspiracy Trial in India, a prosecution of communists
and trade unionists on charges of sedition. Three of the accused were
Englishmen, one of them a former Cambridge student. The Socialist
Society collected signatures for a protest about the convictions. But the
imperial event that made the greatest impression on Cambridge students, socialist or other, was one unconnected with the British empire – the Italian invasion of Abyssinia in 1935. One morning, an
Abyssinian flag was seen flying from a pinnacle of King's College
chapel, hung there by some unknown climber, a difficult and dangerous feat. Honorary membership of the Union was conferred on the
exiled Emperor Haile Selassie, who received a prolonged standing
ovation from a packed house when he came to receive it.

Cambridge offered plenty of chances to meet an exotic array of students from Afro-Asia. There was a time in the 1920s when two Indians were passed over for the tennis captaincy because of their colour,

but in general race relations were good. One of Cambridge's better qualities was a sort of republican equality and fraternity. One or two efforts were made to start discussion groups with Africans about what socialism could mean to African countries. There was a Chinese society with forty-odd members, some of them from Malaya or Singapore, and the best-known of them tennis players; but the Japanese invasion of China was something that stirred them all, and there was some knowledge of the part being played in the resistance to it by Mao and the communists. For socialists, one of the great books of the 1930s was Edgar Snow's *Red Star over China*, about the Chinese Soviets and the Long March. There was an Anglo-Japanese Society too, at one of whose meetings the head of a college gave a talk, approving (as most British conservatives did) the occupation of Manchuria as part of a Japanese civilizing mission.

The Indian society, the 'Majlis' or Assembly, with a membership of something like a hundred, was one of the university's long-established bodies; Jawaharlal Nehru had been a member when at Trinity early in the century. Some of the Indians were well off, with a sprinkling of princes; most were from professional or official families, and there were a number of probationers for the high-ranking Indian Civil Service. But all were affected more or less emotionally by nationalism, and a good many were willing to take an interest in socialism or even communism. Gandhi's second civil disobedience movement in 1930 had led to the Round Table Conference in London; in 1935, after a protracted filibuster by the die-hard Winston Churchill, a new Government of India Act marked a further instalment of constitutional concessions, which the National Congress thought very meagre. Against this background, young Indians could see the force of what Nehru had long been saying, as leader of the progressive wing of Congress, that there must be a program for the benefit of the miserably poor workers and peasants to mobilize wider mass support. In other words, socialism was a necessary part of the struggle for independence.

Herbert Norman was already acclimatized to Cambridge when I got to know him, but his Canadian and Japanese antecedents put him in an exceptional position, from which he could view the world more broadly than most of us, immersed in our European cauldron, were able to.[6] He was of course following events in the Far East.[7] But his practical work consisted of trying to attract some of the Indians towards the Party. It was not easy; psychological barriers and mistrusts were strong. One of his converts told me later on that he had been suspicious of all white faces, but Herbert won his confidence with the clinching argument that he was not an Englishman, but a Canadian.[8] Indian students were under official watch, and the business of putting together a small group had to be gone about very discreetly. Another recruit had some experience of the need for secrecy, having been arrested in Calcutta as secretary of a student body suspected of terrorist leanings; his family was allowed to send him to England as an alternative to prison. His father had been a famous nationalist who gave away most of a large fortune to patriotic causes; a nephew of his, with a Scottish wife, is active in left-wing causes in India today.

I first learned of the group when Norman, its founder, before leaving Cambridge, invited me to take over from him the responsibility of liaison with it.[9] I was engaged in post-graduate work on Anglo-Chinese relations, which gave me more interest than most Party students had in Asian and imperial affairs. Similar groups were coming into existence in other universities, chiefly Oxford and London. The Party functionary in charge was Ben Bradley, one of the Meerut prisoners, who had been sent out to India to take part in trade-union organizing. Through him, and a young Englishman in the Indian Civil Service who had turned communist and come home to undertake Party work, there were exciting glimpses of the small outlawed Communist party of India struggling underground.

Herbert's strategy, in line with Party policy of the time, had been for the group to 'capture the Majlis,' by getting members elected to the committee. This was achieved without much difficulty, and the result was a more lively, stimulating program of discussions and lectures, in place of mere social gatherings, with stress on political issues. One of our friends was president of the Majlis when Nehru, in the autumn of 1935, was released from prison because of his wife's illness, and came to Europe. Hearing of Nehru's arrival in London, he took the initiative of telegraphing an invitation to him to visit his old university, and collected subscriptions to cover expenses. Over tea Nehru met the group, in my room, and discussed the Indian situation with them; in the evening, after dinner at the Union, there was a public meeting, at which he addressed a mostly sympathetic audience. It could scarcely be guessed that day that in a dozen years he would be prime minister of India. His daughter Indira, also to be prime minister, was with him, and stayed in England as a student at Oxford. She did not do much there in politics, but several women joined the Cambridge and other groups; for Indian women, socialism could appear a double emancipation.[10]

Groups like ours in Cambridge not only acquired a degree of influence over Indian students, but could do something to give British students and others comprehension of Indian national aspirations. One who became the first Indian president of the Union carried a motion in a debate that 'the continued existence of the British empire is a menace to world peace.' He was the son of a wealthy feudal landowner, and had been at school at Eton; he was one of two from the group who were imprisoned for a time on their return to India, and one of three who devoted all their time for a good many years to work in the Communist party there, under very spartan conditions. His sister, from Oxford, did the same, and is now a communist member of Parliament. One of his brothers, following a different track, rose to be commander-in-chief of the Indian army. Indians in London undertook work for the India League, run by Krishna Menon, later a cabinet minister under Nehru. He opened a conference in London, largely organized by the Cambridge group with much counsel from James Klugmann, which set up a federation of Indian student bodies in Britain. Marxists in London, Sajjad Zaheer and others, had the chief hand in planning the Indian Progressive Writers' Association (IPWA), which made a considerable stir in literary circles in India before the war. Zaheer, who died a year or two ago in Moscow, became in 1947 at the Partition secretary of a new Communist party of Pakistan and, not surprisingly, was very soon in prison. It was an Indian Muslim at Cambridge, a few years before our time, who invented the idea and the name of Pakistan, taken up after 1935 by Jinnah and regarded by us as highly retrograde. As socialists, Muslims and Hindus worked side by side.

In retrospect, it is clear to survivors of the thirties that their hope, or rather certainty, of a speedy advent of socialism in Britain was illusory; it might be compared with the faith of a minute Scottish sect a hundred and fifty years ago that its adherents would be translated to heaven while still living. It went with a very uncritical, almost mystic belief, instilled by the Party, in the working class and its mission to transform society. Things were seen too simply, too much in black and white. Some illusions may be necessary to any positive, active movement. Nevertheless, many of the fundamental issues confronting that generation of the Left – fascism, imperialism, Spain – really were in essence simple, and it was right about them. And it was, after all, the USSR that defeated the Nazi army and liberated Europe. Convictions formed at Cambridge in the thirties were often formed for life, whereas the student excitements of more recent years seem to leave little permanent trace on most participants. Not many communists of those days grew into conservatives; a notable proportion have continued to be associated with progressive causes, from within the Party or outside it. To them, the Cold War and American hegemony seemed evidence of a new menace, not unlike that of fascism, to be resisted. Vietnam came to be for them what the Spanish Republic had been.

As Marxist theorists, many of them, along with newer comers, were soon making much more headway than before the war, above all in history. Historical Marxism has made perhaps more progress in Britain than in any other country, east or west. Dobb's most original work, which came out in 1947, was an economic history of England. He took part in a Marxist historians' group formed soon after the war, divided into sections among which the one concerned with sixteen- and seventeenth-century Europe went furthest. Eric Hobsbawm was one of the Cambridge undergraduates of the thirties who figured in it, Christopher Hill one of those from Oxford. The group gave everyone the feeling that he was learning history over again. They began, in the prewar spirit, by wanting their work to have a very practical value to the Party, for instance through studies of local history and working-class struggles. These expectations were not fulfilled; the unity of theory and practice, that bedrock principle of the thirties, seldom finds a straightforward application. More generally, the ideas that were being developed, largely through collective discussion and sometimes heated argument, have had an appreciable influence both on other scholars and on readers of history. In this process, still going on, Herbert Norman might have found the place most congenial to him.

NOTES

1 T.E.B. Howarth: *Cambridge between Two Wars* (London: Collins 1978) (By a Cambridge historian. No sympathy with the Left, but well informed and well written.)

2 Mosley launched his British Union Movement in 1931. Aldous Huxley had depicted something very like it in advance, in his novel *Point Counter Point* (1928). H.G. Wells's fantasy of a dictatorship plunging Britain into war, first with the USSR and then with the U.S., *The Autocracy of Mr. Parham*, came out in 1930. An American parallel was *It Can't Happen Here* by Sinclair Lewis (1936).

3 I myself joined in November 1934, and remained a member of the Party until 1959; since then I have thought of myself as an independent Marxist. At Cambridge there was no special ceremony of admission; among London students (I learn from Professor John Saville) a new entrant had to present himself, in a somewhat cloak-and-dagger fashion, at a strange house.

4 I had been in charge of these sales for some time. The bookshop was run by a jolly Australian, Maclaurin, who had lost a teaching post at York through being caught by the headmaster in some tipsy frolic. He was killed in Spain. Norman, who knew him well, deeply lamented his death.

5 I am grateful for my good fortune in having had these two as my chief political mentors; they must have been well known also to Herbert Norman. Both were at Trinity, and Klugmann and I – and, incongruously, A.E. Housman – lived close together for a long time in a dingy college annex, Whewell's Court. See N. Wood, *Communism and British Intellectuals* (New York: Columbia University Press 1959), 85: 'A large number of the intellectuals were centred, during the thirties, at Trinity College, Cambridge'; and Samuels in P. Rieff, ed., *On Intellectuals* (Garden City, NY: Doubleday 1969), 215: 'The centre of communist activity was Trinity College, and its leaders were James Klugmann and John Cornford.'

6 I do not remember being conscious that he was four years older than I was, but these years must have made him a degree more mature than most of those he was with.

7 He was in touch with a variety of Japanese, and I was impressed by the fluency with which he conversed with them in their own language, sometimes in a small Chinese restaurant at Tottenham Court in London where he taught me how to eat with chopsticks.

8 There is a hint in this incident of the skill he deployed later in diplomacy. With his quietly engaging manner, and fondness for company and conversation, he was ideally suited to the task allotted to him.

9 Norman had to be careful not to advertise his own political doings. An unlucky accident was his being visited in his lodgings, when unwell,

by Kitson Clark, a conscientious tutor, who was plainly shocked by the left-wing books he noticed there. When Norman was leaving Cambridge, and had to ask for a testimonial, Kitson Clark gave him a very unfavourable one, which he showed me; it included a slighting reference to his having acquired 'a certain amount' of knowledge of the classics at Toronto – Toronto clearly was not Cambridge. He decided to remonstrate, and Kitson Clark eventually substituted a rather more useful certificate.

10 Through such channels Herbert Norman's political work, even if confined to a brief span of his life, and of course mingling with many other influences, can be said to have had some lasting positive results, like both his academic and diplomatic work.

*A question that continues to be asked by many is whether Norman re-
mained a communist after he left Cambridge in 1935 or, otherwise put,
did he ever exit from the Communist Party? The following article by
Roger Bowen tries to suggest that such a question totally misses the point.
Bowen argues that from the time Norman joined the Department of External Affairs in late 1939 until his death in 1957, Norman did nothing in
either his official capacity or as a private person to indicate an ongoing
loyalty to the Party. In fact, as Bowen shows, during the last two decades
of his life, Norman's activities and behaviour seemed to be motivated entirely by career considerations, qualified only by an abiding sense of loyalty to his government and to long-held humanitarian principles.*

*After briefly outlining Norman's student politics, Bowen proceeds to
explain the series of events and circumstances that led to his death. He
concludes his essay with an interpretation of the meaning of Norman's
death.*

Roger W. Bowen

COLD WAR, McCARTHYISM, AND MURDER BY SLANDER: E.H. NORMAN'S DEATH IN PERSPECTIVE

Probably no event in recent years involving Canadian–United States relations aroused such a wave of indignation and resentment in Canada as the
suicide on April 4 in Cairo of Canadian Ambassador E. Herbert Norman.
The general belief was that charges of communism against Mr. Norman,
which were revived by the Subcommittee of the United States Internal
Security Committee, were directly or indirectly responsible for his death.
Canadians were indignant because the charges were regarded as false, as
well as because the tactics employed by the Subcommittee were considered reprehensible and unwarranted interference in Canadian affairs.[1]

So reads a 'confidential' dispatch sent to the State Department by the American ambassador to Canada two weeks after Norman's fatal leap from a nine-story Cairo apartment building in April 1957. Concerned exclusively with the 'Canadian Reactions to the Suicide of Ambassador E. Herbert Norman,' this dispatch catalogued the plethora of charges which Canadian newspapers levelled against the American government, ranging from 'guilt by association' and 'character assassination' to 'trial by smear.' Extensively quoted was a Toronto *Globe and Mail* article which claimed that 'the smear of Norman was just one more example of a long series of insults and injuries [inflicted] by the Americans' on Canada.[2] The highly emotive cries of 'witch-hunt' and 'murder by slander' that issued forth even from the halls of Parliament were similarly recorded in the dispatch to State. Yet the Americans fully understand that while the moral outrage expressed by press and public was no doubt genuine, it could not be sustained, particularly as the moral issue involved was being transmogrified into a political one.[3]

During the first week after Norman's death, Secretary of State for External Affairs Lester 'Mike' Pearson said nothing to indicate that the charges of communism levelled against Norman by the American Senate subcommittee might be grounded in historical fact, but instead remained silent as press reports recalled Pearson's 1951 defense of Norman when the same subcommittee had first alleged Norman's previous association with the Communist party. Pearson had then, on 9 August 1951, reported that the 'security authorities of the Government' had given Norman 'a clean bill of health' and personally praised Norman for being 'a trusted and valuable official of the department.'[4] Seen in this light in 1957 after Norman's death, the expressions of moral outrage by the press seem altogether reasonable. Equally reasonable, and much applauded by the Canadian press, was Pearson's 10 April official note of protest to the American government that threatened to cease providing security information on Canadians unless the American executive branch could guarantee that future congressional investigatory bodies would be denied unrestricted access. But two days later, and following repeated reaffirmations by the Senate that its information on Norman was correct, the man who could hardly wait to be prime minister, John Diefenbaker, turned the 'Norman affair' into a political football in this election year.[5]

Diefenbaker asked Pearson in Parliament whether the American allegations were 'untrue, unjustified, and had no basis in fact.' Pearson finally came clean on 12 April, replying: 'To say there was no truth in statements about Mr. Norman's past associations would have deceived the country.' Pearson was then pummelled by the press. A typical response to his admission was a 15 April editorial in the Montreal *Gazette* which accused him of having exercised bad judgment in 1951 by giving the public a 'misleading impression' about Norman's involvement in the Communist party. Pearson tried defending himself in an article in the same newspaper two days later. Referring to the 1950–51 RCMP investigation of Norman, Pearson said, 'I concluded that he had had, as a student, ideological beliefs which were close to some brand of Communism. I also concluded, 'Pearson went on, 'that he regretted these earlier associations and beliefs and had voluntarily abandoned them by the time he entered the Canadian Foreign Service.'[6]

Yet despite his attempts to offer a defence of his position, Pearson's credibility had been damaged. Mr Low, leader of the Social Credit party, summed up Opposition sentiment, and perhaps public sentiment as well, when he said to Mr Pearson, 'The Minister is letting us know something that he has withheld ever since 1951.'[7] A 'confidential' American dispatch from Ottawa to Washington at this time further explains the effect of Pearson's truth-telling: 'The opposition position on the Norman case has undergone a fundamental change in the last few days. From a position of supporting the Government in its defense of Mr. Norman and in its protests to the United States, it has now accused the government of using the protests for political purposes and of withholding information on the case.'[8] In the more personal terms of how these disclosures affected the way Norman would be remembered by the Canadian public afterwards, the image of Norman as martyr for Canadian nationalism was replaced by Norman the communist.

A secondary but by no means less important consequence of the politicization of Norman's death was the impact it had on Canada's foreign policy. As James Eayrs suggests, some of Canada's more prominent Anglophiles began to call into question the Liberal government's policy under Pearson of volunteering Canadian military forces for peacekeeping purposes in the Middle East.[9] Norman after all had been Canada's ambassador to Egypt until his death. Now critics could point to a one-time communist negotiating with a suspected pro-Russian Egyptian President (Nasser) towards the undoing of Mother England's noble attempt to prevent the Suez Canal from being nationalized. Moreover, now that Pearson's credibility had been damaged by the Norman affair, evidence suggesting that Pearson had also seemed to be all too sympathetic towards Egyptian nationalism (and, conversely, prejudiced against Israel) took on a new light, especially as Pearson himself was being attacked by McCarthyite innuendo. Arthur Blakney reported in the *Gazette* that 'there have been veiled suggestions that the Subcommittee [on Internal Security] could – if it were bent on causing trouble – release secret testimony by ex-communist Elizabeth Bentley tagging Mr. Pearson as a man who was far too close to the inside of wartime communist espionage rings.' The same report also asserted that Pearson could have been 'a source of information to communist espionage rings during the war.'[10] State Department records from this period show that the Americans took these allegations seriously. That the allegations against Pearson, as well as against Robert Bryce for that matter, were not made public by the Senate subcommittee can likely be attributed to pressure placed on the Senate by the State Department, which wished to avoid another Norman affair.[11]

In this sense, the reputations of Pearson and Bryce were not assaulted by the Americans *because of* Norman's death, or rather because of the politicization of Norman's death by both the Americans and the Canadians. But because Norman's death was so politicized, his life was in the process stripped of all meaning. For with Pearson's admission that Norman had once been 'some brand' of communist, the McCarthyites, who had tried him for his past associations, seemed vindicated and the public's memory of Norman formed unidimensionally around the ideological imprint of 'communist.' Only recently have North Americans started to rethink Norman's death in terms of his life and scholarship. Initiated first by a scholarly study of Norman's Japan-related writings by the American 'New Left' scholar John Dower and then a sensitive but excessively psychological treatment by Canadian journalist Charles Taylor,[12] Canadians seem more prepared today to consider Norman's life in the complex terms it deserves. Yet just as political events in 1957 seemed to conspire to obfuscate the meaning of his life and death, so too does the rise of a new 'red scare' threaten once again to distort the real meaning of the Norman tragedy.

Over the past several years, it seems, every reported espionage case in North America or Britain invariably refers to Norman. Most recently, Norman's name re-emerged in the context of the Hambleton case which 'proved,' says the popular weekly magazine *Maclean's*, 'that Canada is enmeshed in the international espionage game.'[13] Similarly, when in March 1980 Sir Roger Hollis, chief of British counter-espionage from 1956 to 1965, was accused of having been a 'mole' for the Soviets, Norman was again mentioned by the Canadian press. So too in 1979 was he mentioned in the context of the discovery that Anthony Blunt might have been the 'fourth man' in a Soviet spy ring consisting of Guy Burgess, Donald Maclean, and Kim Philby, all of whom were Norman's contemporaries in Cambridge in the 1930s. And for those swept away by what *Maclean's* calls Canada's 'mood of paranoia,'[14] the publication of Chapman Pinscher's *Their Trade Is Treachery* in 1981 put to rest any lingering doubts about Norman. Therein Pinscher states unequivocally that Norman, along with John Watkins, Canada's ambassador to the Soviet Union between 1954 and 1956, served as a spy for the Soviets.

Old questions have therefore been asked with renewed interest in recent years: Was Norman the long-sought 'fifth man' in a Soviet spy ring? Was he simply a vanquished traitor rather than a victimized martyr? Was he accurately labelled by the Senate subcommittee and just poorly protected by Pearson? Or rather, from an entirely different perspective – one that is supportive of Pearson's 1951 judgment – are not these accusatory questions, offered as they are during a period of heightened political conservatism and fear of communism, simply old grist for neo-McCarthyite mills?

The latter is a rhetorical question and the abbreviated account of Norman's adult life which follows is an attempt to substantiate the claim of Norman's 'innocence.' I emphasize 'innocence' now so there will be no misunderstanding. For some people, belief in Marxism will always remain a 'crime,' albeit of a lesser order than membership in the Communist party. Norman was 'guilty' of both prior to joining External Affairs in 1939, and probably for a good while after that time he still subscribed to a Marxist-humanist vision of historical change. Let it also be mentioned now that after surveying over eight hundred pages of FBI documents, over a hundred pages of State Department material, hundreds of pages of External Affairs files, and all the material held by U.S. Army Intelligence and U.S. Navy Intelligence, I can quite confidently assert that there is not one shred of evidence to suggest that Norman ever served the Soviets or any other foreign country as a spy. Instead, as I shall try to show, this heretofore classified material reveals only that a great many Americans suspected disloyalty on Norman's part because of the people with whom he associated and the ideas he professed. Of course, to believe that any American had the right to attribute 'disloyalty' to any individual Canadian suggests a presumptuousness and arrogance that some Canadians, especially Lester Pearson, saw at that time and decried as a violation of Canada's sovereign rights. As much as anything, the terrible lesson of Norman's death is that he was prosecuted in America by Americans who were ideologically trapped by Cold War, McCarthyite fears. But the deeper meaning of his death can only be captured by looking at his life. To this account, in dangerously abbreviated form, I now turn.

STUDENT YEARS

By the time Norman was sixteen years old he was already a serious student of Karl Marx. His early correspondence shows that while he, the son of a missionary, could in no way accept Marx's 'unchristian spirit,' he none the less found Marx's condemnation of 'ironfisted capital' appealing. In justifying to his older brother his attraction to Marx's ideas, he quoted an epigram attributed to the King of Sweden: 'If a man under 30 had never been a socialist, he had no heart, and if a man over 30 was a socialist, he had no head!'[15] Still under thirty in 1933, six years later Norman was quoting Marx and Reinhold Niebuhr with equal facility in order to justify revolution in capitalist society. 'Capitalism,' he wrote, 'is now pure stupidity; its historic role has long been finished and is acting contrary to civilization.' 'Reason and Humanity,' he told his brother, 'cannot come about without revolution, so tightly and firmly will the acquisitive society in power fight to preserve its privileges.'[16]

Such was Norman's state of mind when he left Canada with a Victoria College B.A. in the autumn of 1933 for Trinity College in Cambridge, England. Within a month of enrolling, Norman attached himself to the liveliest young socialist group then active in England. He noted in one letter that once he mentioned to other students he had read John Strachey's *The Coming Struggle for Power*, 'you are granted a sesame into their company.'[17] The company to which Norman was admitted was the Cambridge University Socialist Society, then dominated by the young and brilliant radical John Cornford. A class list shows that Guy Burgess, Donald Maclean, Anthony Blunt, and James Klugmann were among Norman's classmates. Kim Philby had already graduated that spring. But it was under Cornford's political guidance that Norman wrote of experiencing an 'intellectual rebirth' upon renouncing 'infantile Canadian Marxism.' 'Under his [Cornford's] tutelage,' Norman proudly wrote four years later, 'I entered the party. I not only respected him and his gifts, both intellectual and political, but loved him.'[18]

He returned to North America in 1935 and the following year entered graduate school at Harvard. Besides working for a doctorate in Asian studies, he involved himself in collecting money and goods to be sent to the anti-Franco Spanish rebels; he helped organize a Canadian affiliate of the American Friends of the Chinese People, an organization supporting Mao's forces; he joined a Marxist study group that included Robert Bryce, later to become an Ottawa mandarin, and Tsuru Shigeto, today a well-known economist in Japan; and he aided Phillip Jaffe, who in the mid-forties was indicted for communist spy activities during the time he headed *Amerasia*, a magazine openly sympathetic to what are now known as 'national liberation movements.' According to Jaffe, Norman was at this time a member of the Canadian Communist party.[19]

By late 1939 Norman was in the process of completing his doctoral dissertation, entitled *Japan's Emergence as a Modern State* and published under the same title in 1940 by the Institute of Pacific Relations. Regarded by most Japanologists today as a pathfinding effort,[20] his book was singular for its heavy reliance upon secondary histories by Japanese Marxist writers; and remarkable for its unabashed use of Marxist terminology in explaining Japan's transition from the feudal epoch to an exploitative capitalist era. This work was followed by another IPR publication, *Soldier and Peasant in Japan* (1943), an unpublished monograph called 'Feudal Origins of Modern Japan' (1944), and in 1949 a biography of Tokugawa period utopian rebel Andō Shōeki, whom Norman likened to seventeenth-century English egalitarians John Lilburne and Gerrard Winstanley. All these later works shared with *Japan's Emergence* a striking left-leaning, anti-authoritarian message that was embellished by an iconoclastic radical tone and analysis.

Norman's first writings had a political relevance and impact too important to overlook. His first two books particularly brought him a tremendous amount of acclaim and notoriety in the field of Asian studies. Owen Lattimore, for instance, wrote in 1945 about Norman: 'Widely read in Japanese sources, this young Canadian is already the most authoritative contemporary analyst of Japan's economy, society, and government. He is to some extent a disciple, and in a sense the successor, of Sir George Sansom.'[21] In October, 1945, this very quotation was incorporated into a memorandum to General Thorpe, counter-intelligence chief of the occupation forces of Japan, recommending Norman to the general's attention. A handwritten postscript was added, interestingly, noting that 'Dr. Norman would be too modest to bring this evaluation of his own work to anyone else's attention. Owen Lattimore is, of course, one of the outstanding American writers on China, now a professor at Johns Hopkins University.'[22]

Norman's writings, in other words, earned him the attention and respect of scholars and military people alike. But this prominence was a mixed blessing. Once Thorpe was replaced by General Willoughby, who turned his office into a 'loyalty board' (as we shall see), and people like Owen Lattimore became a target of McCarthyism – or in other words as political power shifted to right-wing forces – Norman's writings and the fame they earned him were turned into evidence of infamy and disloyalty. Should this be difficult to believe, one has only to look at the 17 April 1957 'Summary of Bureau [FBI] Files Re Egerton Herbert Norman' which cites 'Norman's Published Writings for IPR and *Amerasia*' and 'Owen Lattimore "Impressed" with Norman's Work' as two major pieces of evidence against Norman. Ironically, except for one section on 'Norman's Participation in Marxist Discussion Group at Harvard, 1937,' there is nothing in this 'top secret' document about Norman's involvement in Marxist groups during his student years.[23]

FOREIGN SERVICE YEARS

Shortly after joining External Affairs in late 1939, Norman was sent to Japan to serve as a language officer in the Canadian embassy. After the outbreak of war, he and the other embassy officials were interned until June 1942, when through a prisoner exchange with the Japanese government they were repatriated to Canada. It was right after the trip home that the FBI first intruded into Norman's life. Upon disembarking from the SS *Gripsholm* he was interviewed by an FBI agent regarding information he might have to offer about 'other passengers.' As he had none to offer, says the 5 September 1942 report, the interview was brief, and the report concluded with the words: 'failure to develop any derogatory information through a personal interview with the subject.'[24] Norman's FBI file was started.

It was added to in 1946, though the event which prompted the newest report occurred in November 1942 in Cambridge, Massachusetts. On 9 November, Norman had contacted the FBI in Boston for the purpose of 'securing from them the property of Tsuru [Shigeto],' Norman's graduate school friend of several years earlier. According to the FBI report, Norman produced a calling card of Tsuru as evidence of his authority to take possession of the property. The report read, 'Norman first claimed to be on an official mission for the Canadian government to obtain the books of Tsuru for the use of the Canadian government in a special investigation. He indicated that he held diplomatic immunity. Norman stated that he was on a highly confidential mission and could not divulge the details of the mission.' Norman likely had only a vague idea about what Tsuru's property comprised, and probably did not know that the FBI had already completed a thorough inventory of Tsuru's possessions. In fact, they consisted of Senate reports on munition hearings, communist propaganda materials, correspondence on the Young Communist League, and so on. Norman most likely gained some appreciation of the sorts of materials involved during his conversation with the FBI agents from whom he was trying to secure Tsuru's possessions. The agent's report reads: 'Later on, during the conversation, Norman changed his story and indicated that he did have a personal interest in the possessions of the subject [Tsuru] and that he was not actually on a special mission for the Canadian Government to obtain this material.'[25]

Norman had been caught in a lie – one, moreover, that made him look all the worse because of the sort of communist materials involved. Without going into details, suffice it to say that this incident followed Norman for the rest of his life. Several hundred pages of FBI reports on this episode appear periodically in Norman's file over the next fifteen years. As late as 1957, interest on the part of the U.S. Senate subcommittee in Tsuru and the Tsuru-Norman connection remained strong. In fact, on 27 March 1957, a week before Norman's death,

Japanese citizen Tsuru *voluntarily* testified before the Senate subcommittee regarding his relationship with Norman (and Robert Bryce) in the Harvard Marxist study group.[26] For Norman, this must have been the ultimate betrayal. A generous interpretation might have it that in 1942, the thirty-one-year-old Norman, who was after his repatriation involved in a very sensitive intelligence work aimed against imperialist Japan,[27] risked a great deal to help his Japanese friend by retrieving materials the content of which, if reported to the Japanese wartime government, would most certainly have put Tsuru in prison.

It is easy to imagine that Norman felt compelled to dissemble before the FBI agents precisely because his job in Ottawa from late 1942 until the end of the war involved security and intelligence matters concerned with the war against Japan. Assisting a Japanese national, even a leftist, at this time could have seriously compromised his position with External. Regardless, it must be concluded that this run-in with the FBI was not reported to Ottawa because Norman kept his security job until the end of the war.

Norman's duties at External changed within a month of Japan's surrender when Norman Robertson, under-secretary of state, gave Norman a new assignment to assist in the work of assembling and repatriating liberated Canadians in the Far East. He was sent first to the Philippines, and then to Japan, and was expected back in Ottawa by late September or early October. 'There could not be a better man for the assignment,' wrote Owen Lattimore upon learning of Norman's Far Eastern duty.[28] Apparently the American occupiers thought the same, for in late September or early October the supreme commander for the Allied powers in Tokyo sent a request to Ottawa, asking that Norman be permitted to remain in Japan and serve as a civilian head of an American army counter-intelligence unit. 'We were particularly asked to leave him there awhile, and I agreed rather reluctantly,' wrote H.H. Wrong, acting under-secretary, in late October 1945.[29]

The young thirty-four-year-old Norman was clearly enthusiastic and thrilled with his new assignment; he wrote his wife at this time: 'You have no idea how terribly busy I have been the last two weeks, yet never so excitingly busy in my life. My present position is head of the Research and Analysis Branch of the Counter-Intelligence Section of GHQ – and it is every bit as interesting as it sounds. My boss, the head of CIS, is General Thorpe – a frank, blunt, rough-tongued soldier but so accepts suggestions with so much ease and affability that sometimes it quite astounds me.'[30]

His assignment, as it later became clear, was a precarious one. A major part of his task, defined by the Americans, was first to help arrange for the release of long-imprisoned Japanese radicals who had opposed Japan's war effort – some were communists and Norman was later slandered for assisting in their release – and secondly, to interrogate them. Among those working with him was John K. Emmerson, who himself was later a victim of McCarthyism. A few years later their duty came to be regarded as a 'crime' when Eugene Dooman, who during the war had served as chairman of the Far Eastern subcommittee of the State-War-Navy Coordinating Committee, testified in 1951 that the official attention given by Norman and Emmerson to these Japanese communists served to enhance the public regard for the communists to such an extent that they were able to recruit '100,000' new members. But for Norman, in that job of releasing the imprisoned Japanese communists he was simply following the orders of General MacArthur. Innocently, he wrote of the experience: 'I have never enjoyed anything so much as being able to tell them [the prisoners] that according to General MacArthur's orders they were to be released within a week ... Later we had the opportunity to interview them at greater length and after a few days at liberty they were able to give us political information on current affairs of the utmost interest.'[31]

The work was exhausting, he wrote, often necessitating ten-hour days. What pleasures he enjoyed during this period, he told his wife, came from the occasional tennis game, conversations with Japanese intellectuals, and the close personal associations he had with noted Asian specialists then in Japan such as T.A. Bisson, Bill Holland, Owen Lattimore, John K. Emmerson, and Shigeto Tsuru, all figures who later figure prominently in the McCarthyite witch-hunt directed at the Institute of Pacific Relations. In another letter (25 November 1945) Norman mentions seeing Jack Service as well, one more Far Eastern expert whose career was badly damaged by the infamous 'China Lobby.'

During this very early phase of the occupation, when the essential policy was to demilitarize and democratize the Japanese state, Norman was enamoured of the MacArthurian radical messianic zeal that prosecuted militarists and protected democrats. Norman easily accepted MacArthur's judgment that the occupation was a 'spiritual revolution' wherein 'freedom is on the offensive, democracy is on the march.'[32] In his own words, Norman believed that MacArthur was 'following a course designed to give the Japanese the maximum opportunity to develop their own democratic institutions.'[33] At the same time, Norman retained a healthy scepticism about the possibility of imposing democracy from above, a view reinforced by his superiors in Ottawa. Dr Hugh Keenleyside, Norman's superior at the Far Eastern desk during the war, believed in late 1945 that 'there is nothing in MacArthur's record to lead one to think that he has any serious interest in democracy and all that should mean.' Keenleyside worried that the 'enlightened policy' towards both China and Japan of men like John Carter Vincent – later victimized by McCarthyism – in the State Department would be undercut by MacArthur who could not 'know just where the convenience of supporting the old order should be sacrificed to the *necessity* of encouraging a growth of economic as well as political democracy.'[34] Although early on in the occupation Norman tried to dispel such doubts held by Ottawa ('No one is more fully aware of the need for the Japanese to take hold and to perform the task [of democratization] than General MacArthur'),[35] he later echoed doubts similar to those of his superiors once MacArthur 'reversed course' and partially 'de-democratized' Japan. Nevertheless, by the end of his first tour of duty, his pro-occupation views and actions had earned the genuine respect of his commander, General Thorpe, Mac-Arthur's first chief of counter-intelligence. Upon Norman's departure from Japan, General Thorpe wrote the prime minister of Canada, MacKenzie King, on 31 January 1946: 'I should like to express to you my personal appreciation of Dr. Norman's services. His profound knowledge of Japan, his brilliant intellectual attainments and his willingness to give his utmost to our work has made his contributions to the success of the occupation one of great value. During his tour of duty with us, Dr. Norman has won the respect and admiration of all who have been associated with him. It will be difficult, indeed, to fill the vacancy left by his departure.'[36]

In January 1946, given a respite from the occupation, Norman was assigned to the office of Canada's ambassador to the United States, Mike Pearson, who also was serving as Canada's chief representative to the Far Eastern Commission (FEC), the Allied powers' organization that was *nominally* in charge of overseeing the occupation of Japan.

Norman was Pearson's first secretary and the alternate Delegate to the FEC. But when by mid-1946 it had become clear that Norman's talents were being wasted by serving on the powerless FEC, on Pearson's initiative he was reassigned to head Canada's mission to occupied Japan. Pearson wrote to the secretary of state: 'As Mr. Norman is a distinguished Japanologist and served for a time on General MacArthur's staff in Tokyo and later as Canadian delegate on the FEC during its tour of Japan, it was felt that it would be easier to get SCAP's cooperation if Mr. Norman was named head of the mission, and that he was the best man we could send.'[37] MacArthur personally accepted this argument. On 2 August 1946, Norman departed aboard the SS *General Meigs* from Vancouver and arrived in Yokohama on 14 August as Canada's head of the liaison mission. There Norman remained until October 1950 when, in the words of Arthur Menzies, until recently Canada's ambassador to China, he was recalled 'following certain inquiries undertaken as a result of allegations concerning Norman's communist connections.'[38] Thereafter began the nightmare that ended only with his death.

The political atmosphere of the occupied Japan to which Norman returned in August 1946 had changed from the early period which was so evangelically democratic in tone. Occupied Japan of late 1946 can best be characterized by quoting General MacArthur's 'Statement on the First Anniversary of Surrender.' MacArthur made it clear that occupied Japan had become enmeshed in the emerging Cold War, which he depicted as 'dread uncertainty arising from impinging ideologies which now stir mankind.' MacArthur asked, 'Which concept will prevail?' The choice for the Japanese was clear: 'principles of right and justice and decency' or the evil of 'the philosophy of an extreme radical left' that could prove seductive to a nation afflicted by 'generations of feudalistic life.'[39] As far as Norman was personally concerned, once MacArthur began yielding to Cold War rhetoric, his chief witch-hunter, General Willoughby, was permitted to conveniently forget that the Japanese communists whom Norman and Emmerson released in 1945, in order to serve as a countervailing force to rightist tendencies in Japan, had been freed and encouraged to organize political parties and labour unions by MacArthur himself. Unknown to Norman, General Willoughby began investigating Norman as a 'security matter' in October 1946, two months after Norman's return to Japan.[40]

None the less, from all accounts Norman and MacArthur enjoyed a healthy, mutually respectful relationship during much of Norman's last four years in Japan. Though critical of some of MacArthur's policies, Norman admired the general for the missionary zeal he still brought to this crusade for democratization, and MacArthur for his part seemed to have genuinely respected Norman's expertise as a Japanologist. Charles Kades, then a high-ranking functionary in Government Section (G-1) and one of the architects of Japan's constitution, wrote:

So far as General MacArthur is concerned, I know of my own knowledge that they [EHN and MacArthur] were on excellent terms ... It is my recollection that the first person in GHQ General MacArthur spoke to after the Emperor visited him in the Embassy was Herb Norman, which perhaps is some measure of his closeness to the Commander-in-Chief, and in my opinion Mr. Norman's memoranda and oral advice were very favourably received and influential ... There is no doubt Herb Norman influenced me ... and I frequently turned to him for advice ... When I needed additional personnel for the Government Section who were experts on Japan, he recommended that I try to secure the assignment of then Captain (U.S.N.) Sebald.[41]

Sebald later became America's ambassador to Japan.

For his part, Norman no less admired MacArthur, and seemed to enjoy an intimacy with the General that few might expect. Some of Norman's letters to the general began with 'My Dear General MacArthur,' even as late as July 1950, after the Korean War broke out. One of Norman's then junior advisors in the Canadian mission recently told me the story about MacArthur's personal appearance at Canada's Dominion Day celebration in 1947. MacArthur, who on record was a teetotaller and non-smoker, accepted both a drink and a cigarette from Norman before the two men retired onto the veranda of the legation for a private chat.

Norman's private communiqués to Ottawa, a few of his public speeches, and his private correspondence with the general, however, clearly show that Norman was not uncritical of the man and many of his policies. In a confidential memo to External, dated 28 January 1948, and in response to MacArthur's second anniversary message, Norman wrote: 'The ideas which he stressed in the message were not new and could be criticized for not admitting the slightest possibility that any grounds of criticism of the occupation existed.'[42] He further observed, in referring to emerging Cold War realignments, that MacArthur's policies were designed 'to tie [Japan's] economy to that of the United States.'[43] In a different communiqué of the same year to Ottawa he warned that democratic reform was being undone because of MacArthur's policies aimed at 'de-purging' war criminals: 'Some of the most powerful political forces in Japan today are those commanded by former leaders who have been purged but still exert an indefinable but nonetheless potent influence behind the scenes.'[44]

Publicly, Norman was saying to Japanese audiences that 'there would seem to be dangers inherent in the tendency of the occupation to think of democracy as something institutional.' Institutional reforms, he said, 'were imposed on Japan from the top. These reforms, admirable in themselves, were not initiated by the Japanese, hence they could scarcely command the deepest loyalty ... It is safe to say that not all the changes of the occupation will remain.' In the same speech Norman questioned MacArthur's pronouncement that Japan had by 1948 undergone a 'spiritual revolution' in the name of democracy. He queried, 'If democracy can be measured by written laws, he [MacArthur] was right, but can it be?' The mistakes of the occupation authorities, he said, grew out of the Cold War which prompted policy that would 'favour the interests of the conservatives in Japan who could be counted upon to be anti-communist.' The result was a 'watering down' of most progressive reforms undertaken earlier on.[45]

Privately, in his letters to MacArthur, Norman also raised questions about the wisdom of certain occupation policies. One of the best examples was his questioning, on humanitarian grounds, of the sentences imposed on two Japanese 'war criminals,' Shigemitsu Mamoru and Togo Shigenori. In pleading for commutation of their sentences, which MacArthur had personally endorsed the day before (22 November 1948), Norman defended his recommendation by saying, 'This may not be legal reasoning but I think at least it has in it a quality of common sense and humanity.' Reduction of their sentences, he further argued, 'will reveal to the Japanese public in a practical manner that the victorious powers are not motivated by a general and indiscriminate sense of revenge.' Norman ended his letter saying, 'I feel that I am carrying out my obligations to my government and also following the dictates of my conscience.'[46] Though MacArthur did not heed

Norman's advice on this issue, neither does it appear that he bore Norman a grudge for questioning his wisdom, for three months later MacArthur personally recommended to Ottawa that Norman's rank be upgraded to minister. Lester Pearson, by then secretary of state, immediately endorsed MacArthur's recommendation, adding in a note to the general, '[Norman's] cordial relations with you have resulted in benefits to your Headquarters, as well as to the Government of Canada.'[47] In thanking the general for this vote of confidence, Norman sent MacArthur an autographed copy of his new book, *Andō Shōeki*, and MacArthur responded to this gesture of goodwill by urging Norman to write a general article on Japan, past and present.[48]

But outside the relationship of mutual respect, goodwill, and cooperation between MacArthur and Norman, suspicions regarding Norman's 'loyalty' to the occupation were being voiced. As mentioned earlier, General Willoughby, head of counter-intelligence (G-2) and a notorious right-winger who reputedly said of Franco of Spain that he was 'the second best general in the world,' began investigating Norman for his past communist sympathies. Why Willoughby chose Norman as a target can easily be guessed. One reason stems from Norman's strong criticism of many in MacArthur's staff whom he accused of incompetence or indifference. Norman bemoaned what he termed the loss 'of the old crusading zeal that characterized the earlier phase of the occupation,' and the emerging, 'rather blind and unquestioning faith in all the policies that have emanated from SCAP and a somewhat intolerant impatience with any doubts as to whether there is a discrepancy between the theory and implementation of occupation policy.'[49] He especially regretted the reversal in land reform policy – these democratic advances had been reversed by American 'disinterested officials' and the 'very mediocre and in some cases painfully inept performance of an increasingly conservative Japanese bureaucracy.'[50] In large part the cause of these problems could be found, Norman wrote in a report of February 1950, in the contradiction inherent in the occupation: 'A brief review of the fate of the post-war government of Japan will show that a parliamentary democracy is scarcely compatible with a military occupation.'[51] Shortly thereafter, Norman's assessment was, if anything, even more negative: 'As the year wore on it became more and more evident that GHQ, SCAP, believed it could secure the economic and political stability of Japan by placing its confidence in, and giving support to, the more conservative social forces at work here. This development cast before it a shadow over the future of liberal democracy; it gave hope to the "old guard."'[52]

If Norman's official expression of such sentiments was not responsible for Willoughby's investigation of him, then some of Norman's activities and associations were, once Willoughby began organizing his 'loyalty boards' in order to search for 'leftists and fellow-travellers' working for the occupation. And, of course, once America 'lost' China to Maoist communism, the 'loyalty boards' began operating at a feverish rate. Suddenly, all Far Eastern experts, especially those who advised the State Department, came under suspicion. FBI reports, among which there was one on Norman, were sent to Willoughby from Washington. It was then remembered that Norman had earlier in the occupation worked with Japanese communists; that he was a friend to such Japanese socialist scholars as Hani Gōrō, and to American Far Eastern experts Owen Lattimore, Bill Holland, T.A. Bisson, Emmerson, and others. Subsequently, it was also learned that Norman had involved himself in organizing a Japan branch of the Institute of Pacific Relations, which for Willoughby was 'a spy ring for Russian Communists,' and 'heavily weighted with known leftists in control positions.'[53] And in 1947, Norman brazenly travelled to an IPR conference in England. The 'evidence' began mounting: he wrote four articles for *Amerasia* in 1937 and 1938, six for *Far Eastern Survey* (1939–45), and six for *Pacific Affairs* (1943–49). These were allegedly 'communist-inspired' journals. Then, after the outbreak of the Korean War, according to speculation in the press, Norman criticized Willoughby's faulty intelligence reports which rejected the possibility of Chinese intervention in Korea. But the *coup de grace*, according to one U.S. security report, was the discovery by the Government of Canada of 'certain communist connections, especially with Israel Halperin,'[54] a Russian-Jewish *émigré* who had been implicated by Igor Gouzenko, the Russian embassy cipher clerk who defected in Ottawa in 1945. Halperin had once shared a dormitory room with his friend Norman in the early thirties when both were undergraduates at the University of Toronto, and later kept in touch it would seem; Norman's phone number was found by the RCMP in Halperin's personal notebook.

The Gouzenko-Halperin-Norman connection had not been made until August 1950 when the FBI asked Counter-Intelligence (G-2) to initiate an investigation of persons listed in the address book of Israel Halperin. The investigation showed, or rather the connection was made for the first time, that in addition to Norman's name appearing in the address book, so too was Tsuru Shigeto's. Suddenly, the 1942 interrogation of Norman by the FBI over his attempt to secure Tsuru's possessions took on renewed relevance. This information was communicated to the FBI, which in turn sent it on to Ottawa. With little advance warning, Norman was abruptly recalled from Japan on 19 October 1950 on the basis of a 17 October report compiled by the RCMP and most certainly based largely on the G-2 and FBI information.[55] On the basis of these reports, Norman was subjected to intermittent interrogation by the RCMP over a six-week period, ending in late November.

'A pile of bricks does not make a house,' to cite one of Norman's favourite quotations: the evidence against Norman, though considerable, was insufficient and inconclusive. And so the RCMP 'cleared' Norman, noting in a 1 December 1950 report that the original 17 October RCMP report that prompted his recall and which had been sent to the FBI, was no longer valid. The newest report said: 'Of the numerous points supplied at the time, the majority have been absolutely determined to be in error. The remaining few have not been confirmed nor does there appear to be any answer to them.'[56] The most damning comment to appear in the second RCMP report read: 'The worst possible conclusion we can arrive at is the very apparent naivete in his relationships with his fellow man.'[57] The December report also concluded that the October report's findings should be discounted; this too was communicated to the FBI.

But for Norman's sense of well-being, the judged validity or invalidity of the early report mattered little. By all accounts, from both friends and family members, the experience had been terrifying and emotionally exhausting. Though one of his interrogators told me not long ago that Norman had 'stood up' well to the questioning, Norman's close associates say he was still recounting the nightmare years later, especially after the second Senate attack came in 1957.

Shortly after the interrogation ended, he was made head of the American and Far Eastern division, a position he held until July 1952. It was unfortunate that External Affairs retained this archaic combination of American *and* Far Eastern affairs in one division, for in August 1951, when Asianist and ex-communist Karl Wittfogel testified before a Senate subcommittee that Norman was a communist, American State Department figures expressed alarm that a communist was in charge of American affairs in the Department of External Affairs, entitled as he was to inspect 'top secret' material. Ottawa was outraged by this public disclosure and immediately issued a protest, claiming Norman had been 'given a clean bill of health' and remained 'a trusted and valuable official of the Department.'[58] Unofficial Canadian reaction to the McCarran committee disclosures was no less swift and angry. Harold Greer, writing for the *Toronto Daily Star*, suggested that the 'smearing' of Dr Norman was the result of 'vendetta' on the part of Major General Willoughby who had been angered by Norman's objections to the increasingly undemocratic policies of the MacArthur occupation of Japan. The Toronto *Globe and Mail* demanded that 'the Federal Government protest strongly to Washington against the manner in which the Canadian diplomat was smeared with the allegations of Communist sympathies.' The *Globe and Mail* further asserted that in this instance 'the Washington witch-hunt' had insulted Canadian national integrity by not working quietly through regular diplomatic channels; Washington, the newspaper claimed, was treating Canada like a 'poor relation living in the porter's lodge on Uncle Sam's estate.' The *Ottawa Citizen* echoed these remarks, saying that 'the U.S. Congressmen show as much contempt for Canada's sovereignty as the Soviet Union does for Bulgaria's.' The *Citizen* attack ended: 'U.S. Senators would do the cause of world freedom a great service if they confined their star chamber procedures to their own citizens.'[59]

Pearson sought to erase the smear by discrediting the 'unimpressive and unsubstantiated statements by a former Communist [Wittfogel],' before announcing at the conclusion of a press conference on 16 August that Norman would serve as his chief advisor to the 4 September San Francisco Conference on the Japan Peace Treaty.

Politically, however, a 'clean bill of health' only serves to remind the 'once-afflicted' of the disease. Norman confided to a friend in the aftermath of the 1951 publicity, 'You can't wash off the poison of a smear from your emotions.' 'How can you,' he asked in desperation, 'fight back against this sort of thing?'[60] Deeply depressed at losing the sine qua non attributes of a successful diplomat, his private anonymity and his public reputation, Norman passively resigned himself to unattractive and out-of-the-way foreign service positions during the next few years. After a closet post in Ottawa, Norman went off to New Zealand in 1953 as high commissioner for, in the words of one high-ranking Canadian diplomat still in service today, 'a rest and cure.' 'For someone of Herb's calibre,' this same diplomat remarked, 'New Zealand was exile.' Norman, of course, knew this, and suffered diplomatic convalescence passively. Hence, his hopes were renewed when in 1956 Lester Pearson told him of his political resurrection, namely that he was being sent to a diplomatic hot spot, Egypt, as ambassador. According to many who were closest to him at that time, this new and promising assignment served to lift the cloud of depression still troubling Norman, sending him into Egypt filled with enthusiasm and high hopes of being able to make an important contribution to the cause of world peace.

And contribute he did by establishing a relationship of trust with President Nasser following the invasion of Egypt by Israel, England, and France in October 1956. From Norman's dispatches to Ottawa during this period of the Suez crisis, it is clear that his intervention with Nasser was crucial in securing Egyptian acceptance of a United Nations–Canadian peacekeeping force to be stationed in the Sinai. As late (in his life) as 14 March 1957, Norman's personal intercession with Nasser, in this case a late night visit to Nasser's holiday retreat, had the effect of clearing the way for additional Canadian troops to occupy the battle zones.[61] It is something more than mere historical irony that at the same time as Norman was meeting late at night with Nasser to work for peace in the Middle East, in Washington Norman's old American friend from the early days of the occupation, John K. Emmerson, was undergoing congressional hearings before being appointed to serve as political counsellor in Paris. It was in the course of those hearings that Emmerson mentioned something that members of Congress had not known, that E. Herbert Norman was then serving as Canada's ambassador to Egypt and minister to Lebanon. Emmerson also remarked that he had had the opportunity of meeting with Norman during his stay in Beirut in the fall of 1956. In Emmerson's words, 'the statement was like a shock wave: the sharp investigators [Senators Jenner and Watkins, and Counsel Robert Morris] had not known where Norman was and what he was doing. Both senators asked me to repeat it. Morris asked the senators if they would like to see the evidence in the security files that Norman was a communist. He proceeded to read into the record reports about Norman's communism, laying stress on statements by a former communist, Karl August Wittfogel, that Norman had been a member of a summer

Communist study group in 1938 and that he had been identified as a member of the Communist party in 1940.'[62]

Clearly, the record from which Counsel Morris read was the October 1950 RCMP report, the one discredited and superseded by the December 1950 RCMP report which also had been sent to Washington. But no matter; the full text of this meeting between Emmerson and his Senate interrogators was released to the press at 4:30 PM on 14 March. 'Senators Probe Canadian Envoy,' newspaper headlines read, the same 'Canadian Envoy' who was at the very same time meeting with President Nasser in order to ensure peace in the Middle East. Old charges, old evidence, but inserted into a new situation: Would internal saboteurs, 'stab-in-the-back' leftists cause the 'loss' of Egypt from the 'free world' as they had with China? The McCarthyite defenders of freedom, the architects of a new kind of organized stupidity, answered a resounding 'No!' Norman had to go. And thus began the public persecution of Norman that led to his jump from a downtown Cairo apartment building.

CONCLUSION

But was it 'murder by slander' as some have alleged? Was Norman guiltless of the charges of 'communism'? Had he been slandered?

The answer to these questions, according to official Canadian records, is a yes qualified only by the admission of youthful left-wing sympathies. According to official American records, the answer is an unqualified no. There is, as we have seen, support for both positions. Norman was undoubtedly a communist during his early years, but there is no evidence to suggest he remained a communist during his time as a foreign service officer. Yet there is evidence to suggest he was something of a radical-liberal who believed in, among other things, non-intervention, self-determination for all peoples, popular democracy, and the value of 'national liberation movements.' He supported, for example, what he called 'emergent Arab nationalism,' as a popular struggle for independence, even as he criticized Nasser for demagoguery. Before that he supported the rise of the Japanese Communist party and the labour movement because he saw them as positive countervailing forces to lingering fascist tendencies in the Japanese body politic and as the bearers of a historical, verifiable democratic undercurrent in Japan's past. For similar reasons, earlier in his life he was drawn to support democratic forces in Spain's civil war and communist forces in China's struggle. History, he believed, was on the side of the forces of liberation, and as a historian of transnational background he felt compelled to back those whom he believed were struggling for principles that transcended petty nationalism. That his conception of freedom conflicted with the ahistorical and ultranationalistic McCarthyite conception can be of no surprise to anyone.

Finally, as a Canadian diplomat in a world dominated by American power and U.S.–USSR ideologically based schisms, Norman was especially vulnerable to McCarthyism. Nor was he alone. A secret U.S. Foreign Service dispatch and other sources recently released under the Freedom of Information Act show, as we have seen, that other Canadians were similarly being targeted by McCarthyism at this time, the three most prominent names being Robert Bryce, clerk of the Privy Council; Arthur Menzies, until recently Canada's ambassador to China; and Lester Pearson himself. Bryce had once shared with Norman involvement in a Marxist study group at Harvard and had introduced Tsuru to Norman; Menzies had along with Norman joined the Canadian Friends of the Chinese People in the late thirties; and Pearson had helped prevent the Americans from getting Igor Gouzenko to testify in Washington. It may very well be that the international furor raised by Norman's death actually served to protect these other distinguished Canadians from McCarthyism.

But perhaps the more important point to be made about Norman's death was made by Lester Pearson: 'The issue before us, is not only the tragedy of one man, victimized by slanderous procedures in another country and unable to defend himself against them. There is the broader question of principle involved – the right, to say nothing of the propriety, of a foreign government to intervene in our affairs ... Such intervention is intolerable.'[63]

Norman's tragic death can be understood in similar terms, perhaps no less appropriate, as defined by George Grant in his influential *Lament for a Nation*.[64] Grant's book is a lament for the loss of his nation's identity to the all-consuming American leviathan to the south. Norman's story is in a very real sense a story of Canada's loss of one of its own to this same giant, the story of how one Canadian fell victim to the American behemoth run amok.

The imagery is apt, for it reminds us that giants may be both gentle and savage. Canadians no doubt benefit when the giant is gentle and protective, but they will suffer when it feels threatened and strikes out, blindly, even at its friends. Norman was the giant's victim, not really its target as some advocates of a conspiracy theory might suggest. Norman was a victim of its blind fear, albeit a fear expressed in a slow, methodical, organized, though sensibly stupid manner, much in the fashion of a blind person searching for his cane. That the blind giant struck out in fear, hurting friends in the process, might be forgiveable except for the fact that the blindness was self-inflicted.

NOTES

1 Department of State, dispatch no. 875, 18 April 1957, file no. 601/ 42274/4-1857. All American records cited in this paper were obtained through the Freedom of Information Act.

2 Appearing in the *Globe and Mail* on 11 April 1957.

3 Hence, we read in a 17 April 1957 telegram from the American ambassador to Canada to the secretary of state: 'Believe strong Canadian line re exchange security information motivated by domestic political considerations as well as by widespread bitter feelings resulting from Norman suicide. Pearson's detailed statement in Parliament and publicity given to exchange of notes [between U.S. and Canadian governments] would appear aimed at meeting political exigencies rather than at solving basic problem. April 16 speech by conservative leader Diefenbaker indicated intention conservative opposition use Norman affair as political ammunition in election campaign already underway' ('Confidential' telegram, file no. 601.4274/4-1057).

4 Quoted in a U.S. 'Confidential' memorandum, 14 August 1951, State Department document file no. 742.001/8-1451.

5 See note no. 3; and Department of State dispatch 892, 25 April 1957, file no. 601.4274/4-2557.

6 The *Gazette* editorial and Pearson's reply appear in their entirety in 'The Strange Case of Mr. Norman,' *U.S. News and World Report*, 26 April 1957, 153–54. See also 'The Pearson Case,' *Globe and Mail*, 19 April 1957.

7 Reported in 'Confidential' dispatch, 18 April 1957, American embassy in Ottawa, file no. 601.4274/4-1857.

8 The American ambassador's assessment in ibid.

9 See James Eayrs, ed., *The Commonwealth and Suez* (New York, Toronto: Oxford University Press 1964), 382–8, 416–21.

10 Blakney's article was quoted extensively in U.S. embassy dispatch (Ottawa) of 18 April 1957, file no. 601.4274/4-1857.

11 Department of State, file nos. 601.4274/4-1557; 601.4274/6-958; 601.4274/5-2658. See also 'Intolerable Incident,' *Newsweek*, 22 April 1957, 64. FBI Chief Hoover stated in a secret memorandum of 10 April 1957, 'I want complete summaries of all we have on Norman and Pearson.' FBI file no. 100-346993-73.

12 John W. Dower, *Origins of the Modern Japanese State: Selected Workings of E.H. Norman* (New York: Pantheon 1975); Charles Taylor, *Six Journeys: A Canadian Pattern* (Toronto: Anansi 1977): 107–51

13 *Maclean's*, 13 December 1982, 29

14 Ibid.

15 Personal correspondence to brother Howard Norman, 11 July 1927

16 Ibid., 15 May 1933

17 Ibid., 21 October 1933

18 3 March 1937; Cornford had recently been killed in action in the Spanish Civil War.

19 Personal correspondence, from Jaffe to the author, 25 February 1978

20 See the articles by John W. Hall and George Akita in *Journal of Japanese Studies* 3, no. 2 (Summer 1977), and Herbert Bix's rejoinder in the same *Journal*, vol. 4, no. 2 (Summer 1978).

21 Owen Lattimore, *Solution in Asia* (Boston: Little, Brown and Company 1945), 38, n. 4

22 No. 201 miscellaneous file, Department of External Affairs, no. 53038440; memorandum dated 22 October 1945

23 FBI file no. 100-346993-73

24 FBI file no. 100-346993-X; the interrogation actually took place on 25 August 1942.

25 FBI file no. 100-346993-2, dated 16 October 1946

26 Tsuru's testimony is quoted at length in the FBI's 'Summary of Information,' file no. 100-346993-73.

27 It appears that Norman's work between 1942 and the end of the war involved the translation and interpretation of captured and/or intercepted Japanese war documents. In the summer of 1943 or 1944 he arranged for security clearance for such work for his older brother who also read Japanese language material with facility.

28 Owen Lattimore to Hugh Keenleyside, 5 September 1945; External Affairs file no. 50061-40 (hereafter External Affairs will be rendered EA)

29 H.H. Wrong to Hugh Keenleyside, 20 October 1945, EA no. 104-C-34

30 Correspondence, 26 October 1945
31 Ibid.
32 Supreme Commander for the Allied Powers (SCAP) *Political Reorientation of Japan* II (Washington, DC: U.S. Government Printing Office), 737, 756
33 Correspondence to his wife, 26 October 1945
34 Correspondence, Hugh Keenleyside to Norman Robertson, under-secretary of state, 4 September 1945; EA 104-CD-34
35 From his speech on 'Japan in Evolution,' given in New York on 16 March 1946 to the Foreign Policy Association
36 EA 50061-40, vol. 3/4-1
37 Ibid., 30 May 1946
38 Personal communication to the author, 20 February 1978
39 SCAP, *Political Reorientation of Japan* II, 756
40 The case remained open until 11 March 1947 and was reopened in May 1950; FBI file no. 100-346993.
41 Personal communication to author, 18 January 1979
42 EA 4606-F-2-40
43 Ibid.
44 EA 4606-E-8-40, vol. 1, 19 January 1948
45 'Japan since Surrender' (unpublished typescript, 13 pp, 1951?)
46 23 November 1948 (This letter can be found in the MacArthur Archives, Norfolk, Virginia.)
47 9 February 1949
48 Norman letter to General MacArthur, 28 February 1949 (MacArthur Archives)
49 EA 10848-10, 26 October 1949
50 EA 10463-B40, 11 August 1949, 4
51 EA 10463-B40
52 Annual Review of Events in Japan for 1950, EA 4606-F-40, part I
53 See note 2 in the 'Conclusion' to this volume.
54 Department of State, 20 March 1957, file no. 601.4274/3-2057
55 Correspondence between G-2 and the FBI between August and October 1950, and references to communication with Ottawa by both, lend credence to this conclusion. Memo from GHQ, Far East Command, to G-2, Washington, 30 November 1950; reference to CIA involvement noted in 30 November 1950 memo from Lt Col Roundtree to Willoughby, G-2, GHQ, inter-office memorandum; and FBI file memorandum, 1 November 1950, file no. 100-346993-6.

56 This finding is one of several incorporated into a review of the Norman case by the American embassy in Ottawa, dated 25 April 1957, file no. 601.4274/4-2557.

57 Quoted in memorandum from U.S. Department of Justice, Ottawa, Liaison office, 7 December 1950, from Glenn H. Bethel to director, FBI, file no. 100-346993-24.

58 See no. 4.

59 All of the above newspapers' remarks are found in a 'restricted' dispatch from Ottawa to Washington, dated 20 August 1951; file no. 310.342/8-2051 XR 742.001.

60 Quoted by Sidney Katz, in *Maclean's*, 28 September 1957.

61 EA, 15 March 1957, file no. 50366-40 (A thirty-year rule restricting quotation prohibits specific citations.)

62 John K. Emmerson, *The Japanese Thread: A Life in the U.S. Foreign Service* (New York: Holt, Rinehart, Winston 1978), 334–5

63 House of Commons, 10 April 1957

64 George Grant, *Lament for a Nation: The Defeat of Canadian Nationalism* (Toronto: McClelland and Stewart 1965)

Arthur Kilgour's contribution to this volume is really a reminiscence of Herbert Norman the ambassador during his final few troubled weeks in Egypt. Kilgour at the time of Norman's death was the number two person in the embassy and therefore was in a position to have almost daily contact with the ambassador. His official position also provided him with the vantage point of a tested diplomat who could fully appreciate the tense political context in which Norman had to operate. As Kilgour very ably relates, Norman simultaneously had to contend with the problems of Canadian domestic politics impinging on a new and bolder Canadian foreign policy; with a young and uncertain United Nations attempting to define its police powers in a post-war climate no longer suited to the kind of big power intervention undertaken in Suez in late 1956 by France and England; with a strong-willed, highly nationalistic President Nasser of Egypt who could only reluctantly extend his trust for safekeeping his country to British Commonwealth member Canada; and, most important, with the damaging accusations of being a communist levelled against him by an American senate subcommittee at a time when his integrity as a non-political, impartial negotiator could least afford it.

Arthur Kilgour

ON REMEMBERING
HERBERT NORMAN

This article recalls some of my experiences working as the senior staff member to Herbert Norman at the Canadian embassy in Cairo during the six weeks prior to his untimely death on 4 April 1957. Mr Norman had arrived in Cairo as Canada's ambassador in September 1956, a month prior to the international crisis provoked by the Israeli invasion of Egypt on 29 October and the Anglo-French attack two days later. The United Nations–sponsored ceasefire had been obtained on 6 November. The ensuing three months saw the withdrawal of the United Kingdom and French forces and the organization of the United Nations Emergency Force (UNEF). Throughout the immediate crisis of the hostilities and the establishment of UNEF, Canada had been intimately involved. The UNEF in fact had been proposed in the UN General Assembly by Canada. All these events had placed new responsibilities on the Canadian embassy and had created a heavy workload for Mr Norman.

I arrived in Cairo on 17 February 1957. The overall situation at that time continued to be tense and uncertain. I perceived a number of circumstances that would keep us on edge.

Although UNEF was almost fully up to the approved strength, its presence had to be considered somewhat tenuous. Israeli forces remained, adamantly, in Gaza and in vital areas of the Sinai, including the strategic Sharm El Shaikh, despite considerable international controversy, resolutions of the UN General Assembly, and U.S. pressure to withdraw. (President Eisenhower made his famous television address on 20 February; and Israel announced compliance on 1 March.) The United Kingdom, France, and other nations were pressing for a quick start on clearance of the Egyptian blockade of ships in the Suez canal. Egypt was tying clearance to Israeli good faith in facilitating the operation. The Egyptian relationship with the USSR, indeed the Egyptian freedom of diplomatic manoeuvre, was subject to considerable speculation. The Egyptian land forces, although defeated at Gaza and Port Said and having suffered from air attack, still possessed considerable strength, including armour. The possibility of a resumption of hostilities over some incident or misunderstanding could not be ruled out. World attention remained focused on the Sinai and Suez problems. This situation was reflected in the continued presence in Cairo of a number of eminent correspondents from the United States and other countries.

Secondly, the Canadian government had committed itself to an unprecedented peacekeeping experiment. A contribution of Canadian troops – they were the largest national contingent – was a major responsibility for Ottawa. The government was committed to the success of the experiment. Moreover, the Canadian role in the Suez crisis had been controversial in Canada, the government having been bitterly criticized – in particular, for not supporting the United Kingdom – and, with an election pending, every decision the government made or did not make tended to be highly political.

Finally, the Egyptian government, while appreciative of the Canadian role, was suspicious of Canada's sympathies and intentions. It carefully scrutinized statements of Mr St Laurent, the prime minister, and of Mr Pearson, the secretary of state for external affairs, for indications of partiality, particularly of support for the Israeli point of view. Bias did, on occasion, show through on specific issues such as Israeli withdrawal from Gaza and Sinai and the question of a civil administration for Gaza.

It was in this difficult situation that Herbert Norman had been working with exceptional distinction. I had not known Mr Norman previously, but I was aware of his considerable accomplishments in diplomacy and in academic scholarship on Japan. I looked forward to the experience of working with him. It was known that he had played an important role during the Suez crisis, particularly in obtaining President Nasser's acceptance of UNEF and a Canadian presence in the force.

The first significant impression of my new ambassador came not from personal contact with him but rather from an encounter with a well-known American correspondent. Spotting a new face in the Semiramis hotel where I was staying, the newspaperman inquired about my business. Upon learning that I was at the Canadian embassy he commented, 'Well, I'll tell you something. As far as I can make out, there are only three ambassadors who count in this town. There's the American; there's the Indian; and there's yours.' That stimulating remark was confirmed on my first morning at the embassy when Mr Norman's callers included General Burns, the Canadian commander of UNEF, Mr Raymond Hare, the American ambassador, and Mr Aly Yavar Jung, the Indian ambassador. Diplomacy was conducted in style at the Canadian embassy. Subsequent experiences in working with Herbert Norman reinforced these initial impressions.

Herbert Norman was an exemplary practitioner in the art of being an ambassador and head of a diplomatic post. Without delay he took me on a series of calls on the people whom he judged should be known by his new deputy. These visits were completed in my first two weeks. I recall the evident appreciation of others in receiving a call from Herbert Norman, the respect they had for his insight, and the enjoyment of his easy style and manner. Somebody remarked to me that for every call Mr Norman made he received two.

Within the embassy, Herbert Norman shared his views with all diplomatic officers. In spite of the demands on his time, he saw to it that we all had the opportunity to learn and benefit from his experience. Surprisingly, perhaps, his technique was not the formal morning meeting, but close one-to-one contact with his colleagues. As well, he took an active interest in the welfare of all members of the mission. There was no pretence about Herbert Norman. Devoted to the diplomatic service, he was a diplomat's diplomat.

A few weeks after my arrival, on or about 12 March, a cable arrived from Ottawa with a personal message from Mr Pearson. I recall the opening words. 'A major political storm,' the message said, had arisen in Canada over a delay on the part of the Egyptian authorities in approving a United Nations request for the admission of a Canadian armoured reconnaissance squadron for UNEF. Mr Norman was instructed to obtain the desired Egyptian permission. I need scarcely say that any cable commencing with these words would be more than enough to start an ambassador's adrenalin running. The real significance of the instruction was of course that it reflected the extreme political aspect of the work falling on Mr Norman. He was involved in activities for which the government at home was liable at any time to come under sharp criticism from its political foes. [What I am saying is that all the work that Herbert Norman was involved in then was, in a sense, highly political, involving the reputation of the Canadian government, of Canada, and in some ways the political fortunes of the Liberal party which was then in power in Ottawa. The Conservative party, the Opposition, held a doubtful attitude towards Canada's international role, whereas the Liberals were committed to the success of the experiment. So, whenever Mr Norman received instructions from Ottawa, he knew that the matter was of vital interest, not only to Canada but also to his political masters in Ottawa.][1] The reported difficulty over the admission of additional Canadian troops was seen by critics as yet another insult to Canada, there having been a previous difficulty over the nature of the original Canadian contribution. It was clear that assent for the additional troops was wanted quickly and without qualification.

Herbert Norman sought and obtained an appointment with President Nasser for that evening. We waited at the offices to send a reply to Ottawa. I recall Mr Norman's return. In good spirits – it was obvious he had had success – he described the interview in detail, with his lively humour, dwelling in particular on the difficulty of conducting negotiations not face to face but, at the president's request, and meant as a friendly gesture, sitting together on a French empire settee, a piece of furniture especially designed for tête-à-têtes.

A few days later, on 14 March, the U.S. Senate Internal Security Sub-committee released testimony taken two days before which included the charge that Herbert Norman was a communist. This allegation had been made in hearings of the subcommittee six years previously in 1951. At that time, the Canadian government had stated that it had conducted a security investigation into this charge in 1950 and that as a result of its inquiry it had full confidence in Mr Norman. The testimony on 14 March 1957 added nothing new to what had been said before. The release of this testimony provoked a sharp and angry reaction in Canada. We heard somewhat later that President Nasser had commented, 'If they [the subcommittee] even attack a person like Mr Norman they must be a bad lot.'

A stimulating but trying event for Mr Norman was a visit to Cairo about a week later of Mr Hammarskjöld, the UN secretary-general, with a group of UN officials including Dr Ralph Bunche. The purposes of this visit were to discuss with Egyptian authorities problems having to do with the modus operandi of UNEF, particularly how it should deal with infiltrators in the Gaza area, and how the UN could facilitate clearance of the canal. Mr Norman entertained the secretary-general and members of his party at dinner at the Canadian residence. This building was a modest rented house, inadequate for anything larger than an intimate dinner party. Nevertheless, Mrs Norman successfully and in style grouped the large number of officials in the small dining room. Almost everyone, including Mr Hammarskjöld, appeared tired and preoccupied. The strain on Mr Norman by this time was apparent. His obsession with the attacks on him was reflected in his close and persistent questioning of members of the UN party about what was being said about him in the American press.

The departure of the Hammarskjöld party from Cairo a few days later marked the beginning of Herbert Norman's most trying days. For my part, the stimulation of the first weeks gave way to perplexity, unease, and a remoteness from Mr Norman. On 28 March the U.S. Senate subcommittee released more testimony, much of it relating to Mr Norman.

By this time Mr Norman was attending the office only intermittently. He was tired and weary. When in the office he passed much of his time resting on the couch. On only one occasion did we discuss at any length the proceedings of the subcommittee. Typically, the subject came up as Herbert Norman apologized for his behaviour, the absences and the lack of daily contact. It was then that I learned that whatever comments I made, he was unreassurable. Herbert Norman believed that there were people out to destroy him. The renewal of the old charges while he was in Cairo confirmed for him that efforts to discredit him had not been abandoned.

I assured Mr Norman that no responsible person took campus left-wing activities of the 1930s as having any significance; I recalled that even a United Kingdom cabinet minister had been well known for such sympathies; and I reminded him that the Canadian government had given him unequivocal support. Mr Norman listened but made no comment on these assurances. The name of Alger Hiss came up as a victim. The demoralization of a possible second prolonged security investigation became apparent.[2] Herbert Norman described the trauma of question after question after question, many being irrelevant and inept. My reference to a relative killed fighting for the Republican cause in the Spanish civil war provoked the advice – a statement which I considered to be the only irrational behaviour that I witnessed during those trying days – that I would do well not to provide this information to the Department of External Affairs. Mr Norman's inference was that such information could provoke an inquiry. Altogether, I found this encounter perplexing and depressing. At that time I considered that Herbert Norman had a melancholic imagination. I supposed that the episode of the subcommittee's renewed activity would in due course fade away.

Not many days later, on 3 April, Mr Norman asked me to come to the residence for lunch so that we could prepare a cable to Ottawa proposing a short period of leave for him in western Europe. The cable would be sent the following morning. That evening was passed in a socially pleasant occasion with Mr and Mrs Norman and another couple. We watched a brooding film sponsored by the Japanese embassy, 'Mask of Destiny,' the theme of which was the self-destruction of the principal character. We concluded the evening with some refreshment at my hotel and at a late hour the party broke up. My impression had been that Mr Norman had enjoyed the evening. He appeared relaxed and composed.

Early the following morning a telephone call came to the embassy from a detachment of the Cairo police requesting that a representative of the embassy come to their station. They said that a note on Canadian embassy stationery had been found in the pocket of a man who had taken his life by falling from a building in the street nearby.

The question of course is still asked, 'Why?' Can this tragedy be explained in terms of the stresses arising out of the responsibilities and uncertainties during and after the Suez crisis? Did the renewal of the old charge provide the final stress that provoked the psychological collapse of a man who, in the exercise of his professional duties, already had plumbed the depths of his inner resources? Certainly, the mental and physical exhaustion was there. Most of the principal causes for a state of extreme weariness have been described in these reminiscences. And, I recall a remark made subsequently to me by the number-two man at the Indian embassy. 'This post has broken our ambassador.' Yet, this subjective evidence does not seem to provide a fully satisfactory explanation. I believe that an objective yet sympathetic observer of Herbert Norman's career instinctively knows that, although life had become a torment, the ultimate decisive motive remains hidden.

NOTES

1 [Comments made by Mr Kilgour during the panel discussion on 20 October 1979]
2 [The first took place in Ottawa in late 1950.]

Part Two

Scholarship

All five of the contributors to this section of the book are widely published Japanologists of international reputation. They also share with one another a significant intellectual debt, which they themselves best describe, to E.H. Norman's historical scholarship on Japan. Beyond these two facts, however, the five authors have little in common. Ideologically speaking, the distance between them is vast, ranging from the British conservatism of Richard Storry to the Japanese Marxism of Tōyama Shigeki. That Norman's scholarship, and in two, perhaps three, cases his personality as well, could appeal to such different sorts of historians on Japan bespeaks the strength of his scholarship and the breadth of his historical vision. No doubt for this reason they, and other historians of Japan, use the term 'classic' to describe the timelessness of Norman's writings and particularly his Japan's Emergence as a Modern State.

Why this books especially warrants the professional judgment of timelessness is best dealt with by the contributors to this section. Yet perhaps a few preliminary remarks on those attributes of Norman's scholarship which give his writing an enduring quality are in order here as well.

First, *virtually all specialists in the field, even his detractors, agree that the beauty of Norman's prose sets his work apart from that of most Japanologists and further serves to prime the interest of non-specialists. Secondly, Norman's writing is infused with a sense of humanity that is impossible to miss. He seems to give both the socially high and the socially low near equal attention (though not always equal weight) in explaining the complex political, economic, and social change experienced by Japan in the nineteenth century. Thirdly, Norman's acute sensibility for the intricacies of change meant that after treating discrete events and personalities separately, he then placed them into the 'seamless web' of historical totality in a way that permitted comprehension without undue simplification. One senses that he did this as much for reasons of aesthetic judgment as for historical ones, but for whichever reason, even if for both, the effect is to give the reader a sense of the interrelatedness of historical personalities, events, and change that is missing in the writings of all but a few Japan historians. And finally, Norman's writings teach rather than merely lecture. Through the use of cross-cultural comparisons and finely drawn generalizations, Norman compels his reader to confront those lessons which the Japanese experience has for his or her own culture and historical experience. Thus, he places Japan into the stream of world history; Japan lost her insularity once Norman began publishing.*

As the five eminent historians in this section implicitly or explicitly acknowledge, these are rare attributes, seldom found in the work of other historians of Japan. Though several of the contributors also discuss weaknesses and limitations in Norman's scholarly writings, they are quick to point out that in many respects the pioneer quality of his work still serves to lead newer researchers in the field in directions that will serve the same goal that Norman set for himself – to enhance the West's understanding of Japan.

Maruyama Masao

AN AFFECTION FOR THE
LESSER NAMES:
AN APPRECIATION OF
E. HERBERT NORMAN[1]

It is a full week since the *Mainichi*[2] asked me to write a few words
about Herbert Norman. I still have not climbed out of the valley of
shock into which their telephone call plunged me that evening in an
Izu hotel. For days afterwards I seized every newspaper I could lay
hands on and searched greedily for one thing only, almost oblivious
of any headlines that did not concern Herbert Norman. Even now, as I
take up my pen to write, layer upon layer of mental images defy all
efforts to be brought into focus, washed as they are by ceaseless tides
and cross-currents of emotion. These will, I fear, be somewhat dis-
ordered reflections.

We last met in May two years ago. Norman was on a brief visit to
Japan and I had just returned from a sanatorium to convalesce at
home. Before leaving to take up his new post in New Zealand, he came
with Okubo Genji to call on me. They picked up Nakano Yoshio on
the way and we spent a few pleasant hours talking of this and that. He
was stouter than when I had last seen him and seemed in sparkling
health. It was obvious that he was enjoying his present work. When
we asked about his writing he claimed that he was slipping off into
dilettantism. He regaled us with a few of those crumbs of history of
which he was so fond: anecdotes of Lucretius, a few sidelights on
some of the heretics of the Renaissance. We laughed at his reflection
that it was the diplomat who was receding into the ivory tower and
the university professors who were getting more and more readily
involved in administrative work. But when he said that his Japanese
was gradually losing its fluency for want of practice, I thought I
detected a trace of saddened resignation in his smile.

We asked about his prospect of making a long stay in Japan. Uncertain, he said. How little any of us dreamed that this brief, hurried visit would be the last time he would set foot in a Japan he had loved so well. As a parting gift he left with me E.M. Forster's *Abinger Harvest* which he recommended warmly. I must admit that much of its excellence is lost on me, but it seems a fitting symbol of Norman's last days that he should have been fond of Forster, a man who continued the best traditions of European liberalism and had, moreover, a humane affection and understanding for the East.

Acquaintance with foreign students of Japan tends from the very nature of the case to be a somewhat one-sided affair from which one gets less than one gives – at least as far as scholastic interests are concerned. Consequently, being somewhat indolent by nature, I tend to keep a respectful distance from them. But no one would ever think of classifying Herbert Norman with that steady post-war stream of scholars 'specializing' in Japan and the Far East who are generally ignorant of anything of the history and culture of Europe. He was a historian of the world before he was a historian of Japan. If one could lead the conversation skilfully enough, there was almost no limit to what one could learn for his inexhaustible fund of scholarship. And the thorough classical training he had acquired at Toronto and at Cambridge was always there under the surface, gleaming like silver through the interstices of his conversation. It is no fulsome exaggeration to say that in him one could see what J.S. Mill meant by his complete 'man of culture.'

As a historian Norman had a never-failing interest in the crooked by-ways off the main road of history and in the wild flowers – the casual records and episodes – which bloom unnoticed in their hedgerows. He could hold a room in rapt attention with a rich profusion of historical anecdotes. He was less interested in the politicians and the generals and the orthodox scholars who stride boldly through the main streets of history than in the heretics, the slightly cynical, withdrawn satirists, the wing-players who tend to be pushed aside in the over-hasty business of teaching history. Epicurus and Lucretius rather than Plato or Aristotle, the Levellers rather than Cromwell, Mo-tzu and Chuang-tzu rather than Confucius or Mencius, Li Cho-wu rather than Chu Hsi or Wang Yang-ming – such was his consistent choice of personalities. His early discovery and appreciation of Andō Shōeki came not simply from the appeal of Shōeki's logic and views; it sprang, I think, from the fact that Shōeki was (as the title of Norman's book[3] has it) 'forgotten,' and from the very unorthodoxy of Shōeki's thought. John Aubrey, who appears in his book *The Face of Clio*,[4] was another of Norman's favourite characters whom he frequently brought alive in conversation at the dinner table.

Norman had a reputation for courteous and gentle straightforwardness. There was nothing hypocritical in him. He had, for instance, a fair store of *risqué*, and always witty, stories. I have mentioned his fondness for the Epicureans; and indeed he might himself be called in the true sense an Epicurean. In music, for instance, he preferred to the emotionalism of the Romantics or the strong rhythms of the moderns, the classical delicacies of Baroque music. In a letter from Canada he once told me that he was enjoying the scant leisure of his busy life collecting records of Rameau and Vivaldi and the lesser-known pieces of Mozart – here again an affection for the lesser names.

Like Clio, his Muse of History, he had a sensitive and receptive mind. But one would have called him the very reverse of introverted. He always liked a cheerful and sociable atmosphere. Had he been a solitary melancholic or someone like Stefan Zweig, who at once exuded an unmistakeable atmosphere of 'le néant,' or even had he had a more doctrinaire side to his character, this last news of him would not have been such an unbearable shock to his friends. It is because we knew him as a 'quiet optimist,' as someone determined never to overlook the brighter side of human life or the forward-looking movements of history, that the thought of that thing which tortured his mind as he hovered on the cliff-edge of death makes one hide one's head in horror.

This is not the place to attempt a discussion of Norman's view of history or his view of the world; nor indeed was he given to propounding anything as abstract as a generalized view of history. Instead of 'entering the lonely halls of philosophy,' it was rather to his taste to slip 'through the more hospitable portals of history' (see his *Andō Shōeki*). He was, of course, not the type of 'positivistic' historian so often found in academic circles who clings like a moth to his materials and obstinately refuses to flap the wings of his imagination. Nor was he one to chop history up in terms of Procrustean 'laws' – he too much loved to fondle its richness, he had too great a regard for its variety for that. 'History,' he says in *The Face of Clio*, 'is like an endless seamless broadcloth in which every thread is somehow meaningfully joined with every other thread. There is always the danger that a single careless touch might break this delicate network, and it is fear of this which must always strike at the heart of the true historian whenever he approaches his work.' When he tackles the 'large unifying themes,' however, the historian must learn to select, from the constantly interlocking strands, the more essential from the subsidiary, the decisive from the incidental, or he will run the danger of losing the wood for the trees. One whose senses are too coarse to feel within himself the pangs of this dilemma, the agony of 'ripping the seamless broadcloth,' is one unqualified to serve the Muse of History. Such was the teaching that Norman had drummed into him by his tutor Maitland in his Cambridge days; it was also the outlook natural to his temperament.

This sensitive consideration for the subject matter of history carried over, too, into his concern for the style of a thinker or a philosopher: 'To assay a literary style is to search and pluck flowers among thorny bushes ... When the blossoms are picked and held forth for display they may not appear as beautiful as when they were growing against the shaded background of the shrubbery. So with style; when we are asked by an enthusiastic acolyte of some author to savour the latter's felicitous turn of phrase, to appreciate the poetic imagery, the nuances in choice of vocabulary, we are sometimes not so prone to admire as if we were left to discover for ourselves the special flavour of an hitherto unknown writer' (*Andō Shōeki*). If, for over-concentration on the brilliant skill of his major historical work as represented by *Japan's Emergence as a Modern State*, one fails to understand his nostalgia for those odd frayed ends which spill over from the tears in the seamless broadcloth, one will surely never understand Norman the historian, still less Norman the man.

In historical research, as in his thinking on political questions, Norman was always on his guard against, even had a sharp hatred for, the over-simplification that paints everything in blacks and whites and claims to solve all problems at a single stroke. He describes how, when he was young, he bristled at the story of Alexander cutting the Gordian knot. 'It is like looking up the answers at the back of the book in order to solve a difficult problem of algebra. The essence of algebra lies in the very process of solving the problems' (*The Face of Clio*). It was for the same reasons that he disliked such insensitive phrases as 'the judgment of history.' Nevertheless, he knew how to catch the atmosphere of a society in a single penetrating phrase. Thus, for instance, he epitomizes the decadence of the Tanuma period: 'Not all officials took bribes, but what honest officials there were had little to recommend them beyond their honesty.' There is a touch of the French Encyclopaedists in this – and indeed they occupied a not inconsiderable place in the catalogue of his cultural debts.

Just as his historical outlook was firmly rooted in English and French historiography, so through his political thought ran the red empiricist blood of the Lockean tradition. Once when he, Shigeto Tsuru, and I took part in a magazine discussion he said, comparing the differing courses of development of England and Japan, that the Japanese situation at the beginning of the modern period offered less diversity and flexibility; there was a narrower range of possible choice. Consequently, there was 'no point in criticizing the Meiji leaders on moral grounds for not being democratic.' From his point of view, he said, 'the chief question was whether a given political decision was appropriate to its situation.' So he would make no general judgment of, say, feudalism – that it represented absolute evil, or that it brought a dark age. It was just that 'it lasted longer than necessary,' and thence various evils arose. Following the same line of thought he says, quoting Burke and de Tocqueville, that the ironies and tragedies of history arise 'from using violence in an attempt to hold back changes which have become irresistible.' It would, I am sure, be no insult to his spirit to assume that, amid the turmoil of Asian-Arab nationalism and at a time when the proud Anglo-Saxon tradition of political wisdom and mature judgment was in danger of being clouded over in fear and hate, Norman turned every ounce of his energy to the task of bringing the West back to an ability to adapt to 'changes which have become irresistible.'

To consider Herbert Norman's suicide as an 'incident' and to attempt to analyse its background and causes seems to me at this moment an unbearable piece of abstraction and I have no wish to link his death directly with the Senate subcommittee's report. Nevertheless, no one would deny that the long years of persistent and devious attacks by McCarthy and his tribe seriously damaged his reputation and left him with deep personal wounds. I think my feeble attempt at a portrait is at least enough to show just how absurd it would be, whether one considers his temperament or his ideological outlook, to label him a communist. But the question is not what, objectively, a communist is.

The question is: what do men like Morris and Jenner imply when they call a man a communist? They mean, first of all, a man incapable of ordinary decent human intercourse. Communist, that is, equals outlaw or criminal. Secondly, they mean a spy for Russia. It is difficult to express what a vile personal slander such an accusation is to anyone who appreciates the normal decencies of human conduct, let alone to one who represents his country as a diplomat. There was a time when it would have been cause for a duel. But consider who his adversaries are – men who, in Pearson's phrase, can only be treated with the contempt they deserve ... whom one would not stoop to challenge.

And if Herbert Norman, who so loved the good in men, and who had such faith in the power of reason to persuade men, has ended his short life in the midst of fanaticism and prejudices and intolerance, what should we do – we who remain behind?

NOTES

1 This essay first appeared in English translation in *Pacific Affairs* 30, no. 3 (September 1957): 249–53. Professor Ronald P. Dore was the translator. Reprinted here with the permission of *Pacific Affairs*.
2 One of Japan's best national newspapers.
3 *Andō Shōeki and the Anatomy of Japanese Feudalism*, in *Transactions of the Asiatic Society of Japan*, 3 ser., vol. 2, December 1949. Translated and published in Japanese as *Wasurerareta Shisōka* (The Forgotten Thinker) (Tokyo: Iwanami Press 1950).
4 *Clio no Kao* (Tokyo: Iwanami Shōten 1953)

Richard Storry

SOME REFLECTIONS ON
E.H. NORMAN:
A HISTORIAN IN THE
ENGLISH TRADITION

The memory of my only meeting with Norman, in August 1949 when he headed the Canadian mission in Japan, is still quite fresh. My diary records that I was 'very taken with him.' There was something a little larger than life-size about his personal aura. For he was not only extremely intelligent, but also totally free from any touch of self-importance or spurious official dignity. Having read *Japan's Emergence as a Modern State* with enormous admiration, I found that meeting the author face to face was in no way a disappointment. He was clearly, in his own way, a great man as well as an outstandingly able writer of history.

Japan's Emergence as a Modern State remains, in my opinion, a classic. The fact that certain of Norman's interpretations, notably his view as to who were the entrepreneurs of early Meiji Japan, have been challenged means very little. It is the *humanity*, the broad sweep combined with the eye for detail, of his book – not the theoretical underpinning – that is important.

In this respect Norman is in the class of Sir George Sansom, and of Sansom's forerunner, Murdoch. It is in fact a decidedly English (or, rather, British) tradition. And one cannot but suppose that his years at Cambridge University (England) played some part in shaping the structure of Norman's thought and the style in which it found expression. Which historians are likely to have been formative influences? I think one might not be wrong in believing that among them was G.M. Trevelyan, Regius professor of modern history and fellow of Norman's own college, Trinity. A telling phrase in his *England under the Stuarts* – it is part of Trevelyan's introduction to the book – records his view that the 'Glorious Revolution' of 1688 was to show the world 'how liberty could mean not weakness but strength.' Notably influential, too, in those days were R.H. Tawney and J.L. and Barbara Hammond. In their preface to *The Town Labourer* the Hammonds wrote: 'A civilisation is the use to which an age puts its resources of wealth, knowledge, and power, in order to create a social order.' They go on to remark that the Industrial Revolution in England, although it brought a great extension of material power, produced at first 'the degradation of large masses of people' – which the English people did not accept 'as its final contribution to the order and freedom of the world.' Such views are very similar in tone and sentiment to Norman's own outlook as a historian of Japan. Trevelyan, Tawney, and the Hammonds and other social historians of that time display that concern for ordinary people, the anonymous commonalty, which shines through everything Norman later wrote. Nor is that all. Those historians wrote in a clear, muscular style not characteristic of many scholars writing at the present time.

The critic Cyril Connolly once observed that 'literature is the art of writing something that will be read twice.' Like most epigrams, that is a half-truth. But it is certainly the case that everything written by Norman can be read a second time with enjoyment, whether or not one happens to accept the particular point he is making. Thus, two basic virtues in Norman's work are, first, a profound, unsentimental regard for the importance in a nation's history of the 'unsung millions'; and, secondly – and this is something which Norman shares with Sansom – a seemingly effortless mastery of style.

In his preface ('The Shrine of Clio') to the Japanese edition of his historical essays *Kurio no Kao* (The Face of Clio), published in 1956, Norman pointed out that in this age of increasing specialization he could not escape 'the feeling that historians tend to lose the grandeur and pathos which the great masters, no matter how intractable their raw material might appear, can convey to the reader.'[1] It is also true that in the world today the sense both of grandeur and pathos has been diminished.

In terms of pathos, at any rate, that could not have been said of the 1930s. Norman was at Trinity College, Cambridge, from 1933 to 1935; and it has been suggested that 'his interest in more radical politics presumably developed at this time.'[2] Those particular years may have lacked the overwhelming, passionate political fervour that pervaded university life in England after the outbreak of the Spanish civil war in 1936. Nevertheless, the early 1930s were of course full of shocks for students who took any interest in foreign affairs, and especially perhaps for those who happened to have been brought up, like Norman, in the Far East. Precisely at that period I was an undergraduate reading history at Oxford; and I recall the immense prestige and popularity of the League of Nations Union, which had an active membership in all the colleges. It must have been much the same at Cambridge. On the international scene, until the outbreak of war in Abyssinia in the autumn of 1935, the 'villain' or 'erring brother' for the league was above all Japan. For although there was peace of a kind in North China, following the Jehol campaign and the Tangku Truce, much feeling was aroused by reports of narcotics smuggling and other machinations by the Japanese army and its minions. So in those days Japan, in the eyes of Oxford and Cambridge undergraduates (even those on the Right in politics), occupied a position of rather low esteem, comparable with that of South Africa (or even Amin's Uganda) in the 1970s. For someone like E.H. Norman, with so many links in Japan and many Japanese friends, the sense of the 'dark valley' (*kurai tanuma*) could only have been sharpened by his contact with the liberal traditions of his English university.

If Norman acquired in his Cambridge days a conviction that he must always be firmly, whether openly or in private, on the side of those in Japan who resisted the tide of assertive nationalism, that would have been only natural and indeed, from a liberal and Christian point of view, wholly admirable. He was, after all, the son of a missionary; and the children of the clergy, whether they are conformists or rebels, are usually serious-minded and above the average in intellectual gifts. In the English tradition at any rate, the clergyman's household, containing few luxuries but many books and an atmosphere of altruistic commitment, has been the seed-bed of talent in every kind of field, from war (Nelson and Montgomery) to literature (the Bronte sisters, Matthew Arnold, and Cecil Day Lewis). Research might well reveal a similar pattern among the offspring of North American missionaries in the Far East.

What will be the place of E.H. Norman in the pantheon of English-speaking historians of modern Japan? The first thing that has to be said is that his output – his published work – was not voluminous. It will be on quality, not quantity, that Norman's fame must rest. In this respect he reminds one of the writer E.M. Forster, whose output was small but superb. Clearly, Norman's tragic death cut short what could have been a wonderfully productive scholarly engagement with late feudal and modern Japanese history. As it is, he belongs to a select company, headed (to mention only two British historians of Japan whose work he admired) by Sir George Sansom and Professor C.R. Boxer. Like them, he was steeped in European culture and therefore brought to his work a knowledge of the European past that enabled him to make all manner of fruitful comparisons. For example, in the introduction to *Japan's Emergence as a Modern State*, when writing of the transition from feudal to new Japan, Norman remarks that 'the autocratic manner in which the transition was carried out permitted the leaders to apply the brakes promptly so as to stop short of a leveling democracy.' He goes on: 'To make a hazardous parallel, it were as if the French Revolution had terminated with the triumph of the Gironde and the Feuillants, with a reformed monarchy supported, in the first instance, by the more liberal aristocrats, such as Mirabeau, and even more typically Lafayette, together with such respectable burghers as Barnave and Roland.'[3]

Norman proceeds in the next sentence to admit that this comparison 'distorts history,' because the strength of the French merchants in the eighteenth century was far greater than that of the Japanese merchants in 1868. But by the use of that admittedly 'hazardous parallel,' Norman stimulates our imagination, forces us to think, and at the same time enhances the pleasure with which we read his book. It seems inconceivable, whatever drastic reassessments are made about his conclusions, that Norman's work could be ignored by any serious student or teacher in the Western world concerned with Japanese history in the nineteenth century. Yet it has been alleged that such conscious neglect has occurred in certain academic circles. If this is true – and I find it difficult to believe – those guilty of such *mokusatsu*[4] (by the deliberate omission of Norman from a bibliography, for example) only damage themselves and their reputations. No one should be allowed to forget that E.H. Norman, the scholar, was also, in the practice of his craft, an artist. This is why he won the affection and lasting loyalty of so many Japanese friends; and this is why Western historians of Japan, scholars and amateurs alike, should respect his memory.

NOTES

1 Quoted by John W. Dower, ed., *Origins of the Modern Japanese State: Selected Writings of E.H. Norman* (New York: Random House 1975), 105.
2 Ibid., 469
3 *Japan's Emergence as a Modern State* (New York: IPR 1940), 7
4 To destroy through neglect.

Kenneth B. Pyle

E.H. NORMAN AND THE NEW STAGE IN WESTERN STUDIES OF JAPAN

It is noteworthy that at this time of the twentieth anniversary of E.H. Norman's death (1977) there is a renewed interest among Western scholars in his scholarship. This interest is not the result simply of an effort to commemorate him, but rather grows out of new developments in the Western approach to the study of Japan's history.

The spark that rekindled this interest was the publication in 1975 of a collection of Norman's writings under the title *Origins of the Modern Japanese State: Selected Writings of E.H. Norman*.[1] The collection is edited by John W. Dower and is prefaced with a long introductory essay by Dower in which he raises a series of provocative issues about Norman's scholarship. Dower is a young scholar who received his doctorate several years ago at Harvard and is now associate professor of history at the University of Wisconsin. He is regarded as one of the ablest of the so-called New Left historians writing about Japan. Dower's 108-page introductory essay to the collection of Norman's writings is, to my mind, perhaps the best statement of New Left positions on modern Japanese historiography. It presents a strong statement in behalf of the continuing relevance of Norman's scholarship and mounts a sharp attack on those he calls 'Norman's successors,' whom he also refers to as the 'modernization theorists.' This essay has been widely discussed and debated among Japanologists in the West, and has been the subject of a number of lengthy book reviews and several critical essays in the *Journal of Japanese Studies*. As a result, there is an unusual ferment in the field of Japanese studies and a renewed interest in the scholarship of Norman.

Compared to our colleagues in Sinology, those of us working in Japan studies in the West have been relatively little disturbed by harsh political antagonisms and debates within our field. For decades now, China studies have been beset by intense polemical battles and personal animosities, usually growing out of disagreements over the nature of contemporary China and over what should be the proper foreign policy towards China. These animosities in turn became deeply embedded in scholarship. From missionary days, China has always stirred deep emotions, particularly in the United States. In contrast, Japanese studies in the United States have been quieter. There have been debates and disagreements, to be sure, but they generally were scholarly and restrained and did not evoke the strong emotions that political polemics can arouse. Our colleagues in the China field, particularly since 1949, have been riven with bitter political controversy which the McCarthy period embedded in the scholarship of the post-war era. Again during the Vietnam War, China scholars became enmeshed in polemic and controversy in a deeply divisive way. If one analysed the content of the *Bulletin of Concerned Asian Scholars*, which has been the primary vehicle for revisionist scholarship among young Asian scholars of the New Left, one finds substantially less writing about Japan than about China. Japan simply has been less controversial as a scholarly issue.

Perhaps the closest the Japan field came to the kind of debate that the China field has experienced occurred when E.H. Norman became an issue in the Senate Internal Security Subcommittee hearings in 1951, and then again in 1957. I know that many observers believed that the charges brought against him and the McCarthyist atmosphere of the 1950s resulted in the polite shelving of his writings and the decline of his influence in the Japan field in the United States. To some extent this is true. For example, it has been pointed out that two recent works by young American scholars on the origins of Japanese militarism have unaccountably overlooked Norman's *Soldier and Peasant in Japan: The Origins of Conscription*. Others of his works, the study of the Genyōsha, for example, have not received the attention they deserved in the years since his death.

At the same time, I think it is accurate to point out that Norman's scholarship in many ways served as the point of departure for much of the post-war study of Japan. Above all, it was Norman's classic synthesis, *Japan's Emergence as a Modern State*, that several important works of post-war scholarship either built on or reacted against. Thomas C. Smith's *Political Change and Industrial Development in Japan*,[2] for example, was clearly inspired by *Japan's Emergence*. Smith's study of government's role in fashioning an industrial policy during the early Meiji traced in detail many of the issues Norman had briefly raised in his chapter 'Early Industrialization.'

Other works prompted by Norman's writing ended up disagreeing with him. For example, Albert Craig's *Chōshū in the Meiji Restoration*[3] had the effect of revising some of the basic themes of *Japan's Emergence*. He was critical of Norman's lower samurai – merchant thesis as too narrowly conceived; he stressed the importance of *han*[4] loyalties rather than class orientation, which Norman emphasized; and he concluded that traditional values had motivated the overthrow of the Bakufu[5] rather than the evolution of a new political consciousness. For these and other major works of Western scholarship on modern Japan Norman's writings were the point of departure, either for more detailed studies, consequently more refined in their conclusions, or for revisionist studies which sought to correct Norman or to express disagreement with his major themes. Whichever, I think it is not accurate to say that Norman was ignored. Quite the contrary.

It was a tribute to the breadth and authority of Norman's work that so many writers in the last generation sought to revise or build on aspects of it. *Japan's Emergence* has been referred to as a 'classic synthesis' in that it brought together a great diversity of secondary works in English, French, German, and Japanese and skilfully summed up and synthesized the understanding of Japan in 1940. It was natural that scholarship in the post-war period would try to go beyond Norman, and that as a sizeable literature grew up on Japan's nineteenth-century transformation his works lost some of their previous authority. Undoubtedly, if Norman had lived a full life he would have been at the centre of this process of elaboration and revision.

Like any active historian writing over time, Norman refined and revised his own ideas and interpretations. A particularly striking example is the evolution of his views of the Meiji oligarchy. In the conclusion of his chapter on the Restoration in *Japan's Emergence*, Norman lavishes praise on the Meiji leaders, emphasizing their 'brilliant leadership' which he says 'merits the highest praise of their countrymen'; and he adds that 'the machinery for the epochal changes accompanying the Restoration was a government formed from the ablest, most self-sacrificing of clan military bureaucrats who utilized to the full and with remarkable dexterity those autocratic powers which they steadily strengthened.' Moreover, Norman here goes on to see the use of these autocratic powers as justifiable and inevitable. Because of the foreign menace, he writes, the Meiji leaders 'had to concentrate on military problems at great sacrifice to social and political reform.' He goes on to say that 'the government had no choice but to retard the tempo of anti-feudal consciousness' and concludes that 'it was only through an absolutist state that the tremendous task of modernization could be accomplished.'

In his later writings Norman clearly retreated from this approval of the 'enlightened absolutism' of the Meiji leaders. For example, in *Soldier and Peasant* he places his emphasis on the burdens and restrictions that the new leadership put on the Japanese people: 'Any possibility of a steadily rising standard of living, a broadening out of popular liberties (all of which would have directed Japanese energies into channels other than those charted for her by the rulers of those days, channels which led to expansion, aggression, and wars) was resolutely blocked by the calculating Japanese Metternichs of the autocratic Meiji Government. As soon as the people of Japan could stand upright and breathe the intoxicating air of freedom, following the overthrow of the Bakufu, they were burdened with fresh exactions and taxes; their relative advance in terms of social and political freedom was soon drastically checked.'

Between the publication of *Japan's Emergence* in 1940 and *Soldier and Peasant* in 1943 Norman had clearly changed his interpretation of the character and effect of Meiji leadership. Whether it was his reflecting on the wartime experience, his thinking ahead about the need for democratic reforms in post-war Japan, his continued work with historical documents, or some other factor that changed his interpretation is difficult to say. The point is Norman's own views of modern Japanese history were evolving. How might his views have changed after 1957 if he had lived out a normal life of scholarship? We shall never know, but it is safe to declare that they would not have been the same as those he expressed in the 1940s. Together with other Western scholars in the 1960s he undoubtedly would have been involved in the elaboration and refinement – perhaps even revision – of his earlier interpretations.

At the same time, Norman most likely would have contested the mainstream of American scholarship on Japan in the 1960s with its emphasis on the 'amazing success' of Japanese modernization. His wavering interpretation of the work of the Meiji leaders – at first emphasizing their brilliance in having saved Japan from national disaster such as was experienced nearly everywhere else in Asia, and later stressing the repressive nature of the modern Japanese state – was indicative of the ambiguities he saw in the modern history of Japan. The new technology proved creative but also destructive; it offered new opportunities but at a high cost in human suffering and dislocation. Some students of modern Japan treat the militarist era of the 1930s and 1940s as an aberration, a temporary deviation from the path to becoming a modern industrial democracy. Norman had devoted much of his scholarship to searching out the origins of Japanese militarism and it is unlikely that he would have accepted such a view. He most likely would have agreed with other writers who argue that many of the same factors that promoted Japanese economic growth were also intrinsic to the rise of militaristic expansion, in short that industrialism and militarism were inextricably linked.

There are signs that the field of Japanese studies in the West has entered upon a new stage. In trying to assess this new stage, it is appropriate to return to a consideration of Norman, since in many ways, as we have seen, his scholarship was the point of departure for much of the post-war study of Japan. In contrast to the mainstream of American scholarship in the 1960s, which emphasized the relative smoothness and the non-traumatic character of Japan's transition to an urban industrial society, more recent scholarship is concentrating on the high cost at which rapid industrialization was brought – the tensions, the antagonisms, and the seamier side of life in industrial society. Any number of examples could be cited of this new scholarly concern. First of all, a number of recent biographical studies of Japanese socialists by American scholars have called attention to these aspects of industrial society. These studies include Fred Notehelfer's *Kōtoku Shūsui: Portrait of a Japanese Radical* and Gail Bernstein's *Japanese Marxist: A Portrait of Kawakami Hajime*.[6] The repressive activities of the Japanese state have been the subject of other books including Henry Smith's study of the *Shinjinkai*[7] entitled *Japan's First Student Radicals* and Richard Mitchell's study of the effects of the Peace Preservation Law of 1925, *Thought Control in Prewar Japan*.[8] A study of the effects of militarism on the villages is found in Richard Smethurst's book on the *zaigō gunjinkai*,[9] *A Social Basis for Prewar Japanese Militarism*.[10] The spring of 1975 issue of the *Journal of Japanese Studies* contains a symposium on the Ashio Copper Mine pollution case which treats this famous incident as part of an effort to understand the costs of Japanese industrialization. Another example of this new direction in Japanese studies is the organization of fourteen younger historians concerned with problems of conflict and dissent in modern Japan. The organization is chaired by Tetsuo Najita of the University of Chicago and is sponsored by the Social Science Research Council. Many other examples of the new direction of Japanese studies could be cited, but the point is already sufficiently clear. It is certain that Norman would have approved of this attempt by younger scholars to provide a more balanced picture of the course of modern Japanese history.

One aspect of modern Japan that Norman singled out as essential to study and to understand was the bureaucracy. 'The key to understanding Japanese political life,' he wrote in *Japan's Emergence*, 'is given to whomever appreciates fully the historical role and actual position of the bureaucracy.' He pointed out that the bureaucracy 'has scarcely brooked any interference from such lowly quarters as the Diet [parliament] or even from ministers who try to reform or ignore its corporate will.' There are many observers who might argue that this statement is scarcely less true today than it was when Norman wrote it. Nevertheless, the workings of the Japanese bureaucracy, its various forms of pervasive influence, remain poorly understood and little studied outside of Japan. It is probably not too much to say that our comprehension of the power of the bureaucracy has advanced very little in the period since Norman's death.

Another theme whose importance Norman stressed for understanding prewar Japan was the influence that German social policy thought had on Yamagata and Itō[11] as they drafted reforms of local government and the Meiji constitution. Western scholarship has generally not picked up Norman's suggestion that it is critical to see the way in which these political reforms were motivated by explicit concern with the social problems likely to be created by industrialism. Already, at the early stage, Itō and Yamagata sought to find ways to defuse social disruption, which German social policy taught them was inevitable unless preventative measures were taken. In his essay 'Feudal Background of Japanese Politics' Norman wrote: 'Policies of such administrators as Itō and Yamagata reveal that in Japan local government was made to serve two purposes: first, to absorb the heaviest blows of social discontent and so fracture these attacks as to spare the

Central Government from meeting the full brunt of an organized widespread agrarian movement; and secondly, to divert the political interests and activities of the people away from the central to the prefectural government.' Such commentary as this reveals how well Norman grasped the working of the *tenno-sei*.[12] Western scholarship has yet to recognize fully the importance of local government reforms in the building of the *tenno-sei* and in the bureaucracy's efforts to contain and deflect the social antagonisms created by industrialization.

These are merely two examples of important themes for future research suggested by a review of Norman's writings. As Western studies of Japan move into this new, more critical appraisal of the process of industrialization, it is altogether fitting and appropriate that it be accompanied by a reconsideration of the ideas of this pioneer historian.

NOTES

1 New York: Pantheon Press 1975
2 Stanford, Calif.: Stanford University Press 1955
3 Cambridge: Harvard University Press 1961
4 Feudal domain
5 Tokugawa government (shogunate)
6 Cambridge, Mass.: Cambridge University Press 1971 and Harvard University Press 1976, respectively
7 The New Youth Society of the Taisho (1912–25) period
8 Cambridge: Harvard University Press 1972 and Ithaca, NY: Cornell University Press 1976
9 Military Reservist Association
10 Berkeley: University of California Press 1974
11 Yamagata Aritomo and Ito Hirobumi, two leading oligarchs after 1868
12 Emperor system

Gary D. Allinson

E.H. NORMAN ON MODERN JAPAN: TOWARDS A CONSTRUCTIVE ASSESSMENT

For my purpose I shall look to an Oriental Clio, a Clio of partly Buddhist inspirations but whose features are surely Japanese. I recall her in the form of that miracle of grace carved in wood – the figure of Kwannon (Miroku) in the Chuguji Nunnery at Nara. Her right hand is raised lightly against her cheek; her lips are half-parted in the merest suspicion of a smile; her expression is serene rather than melancholy. She looks out upon human striving, both its follies and its greatness, on the passions and ambitions of this world, with an expression neither indifferent nor disdainful, but rather infinitely patient and compassionate. I can imagine the face lighting up with humour untinged with mockery ... Whatever of historical imagination or significant awareness, particularly of Japanese history, may appear in my work I owe to that Clio of Japan, to the memory of her smiling lips and pensive face.

E.H. NORMAN, 'The Shrine of Clio'

'Smiling lips and pensive face.' It is an elusive, almost ambivalent image, but from my readings, it appears to capture E.H. Norman's personal attitude towards his craft as a historian. He tried to summon feelings of serenity, concern, tolerance, and compassion for his task. These are surely qualities no historian would disparage, least of all those still influenced by the humanistic tradition of Western scholarship.

Norman also referred in the quotation above to 'humour untinged with mockery,' and to 'the merest suspicion of a smile.' This imagery is yet more elusive. Norman seems to imply that, however serious the historical enterprise might be, it should be undertaken with some detachment; the historian should attempt to see human folly and human greatness for what they really are. Such detachment – also tinged with a sense of bemusement? – undoubtedly lent his research and writing essential perspective.

I believe the recent debate over E.H. Norman's role as a historian has strayed both from his sense of serious purpose and his attitude of pensive amusement. It is difficult to find in the essays spread over the pages of the *Journal of Japanese Studies* much sense of serenity, tolerance, or compassion. The prose is harsh, the arguments biting, and the tone spiteful. In this essay I will try to suggest why I think this is unfortunate.

My own objectives are limited. The focus of my evaluation will be E.H. Norman's first study, *Japan's Emergence as a Modern State* (hereafter *Japan's Emergence*).[1] Owing to the time of its appearance, the breadth of its coverage, and the centrality of its topic, *Japan's Emergence* has been by far the most important work he published. My evaluation falls into three parts. First, I will look at three sets of direct, scholarly reactions to the study. These occurred in the 1940s (following its publication), in the late 1960s (a decade after Norman's death), and in the 1970s (following re-publication of some of Norman's writings). In a second part of the essay I will attempt an explanation of the fate of Norman's work among American historians of Japan in the 1950s and 1960s. Finally, I will assess the prospects for continuing interest in Norman and suggest how his writing might still aid our research. The intent of my remarks is to steer the present debate away from its destructive course and to set us on a more constructive tack.

When *Japan's Emergence* appeared in 1940, the field of Japanese studies was, of course, much smaller than it is today. Norman's book thus did not attract extensive attention from scholarly reviewers. The journals of the major disciplines, such as history, economics, and political science, did cite the work. But usually they offered only short notices or brief, ten-line reviews. Journals directed at area specialists gave the book lengthier coverage, though belatedly in some cases. *The Far Eastern Quarterly* did not publish its review of *Japan's Emergence* until 1943, and the review in *Pacific Affairs* did not appear until 1947.

No review that I have found disparaged the study in any way. Some offered simple descriptions with virtually no evaluative overtones.

And a few, usually longer ones done by established Asian specialists, bestowed the warmest praise. Cyrus H. Peake called it an 'important contribution' and 'one of the most significant volumes in the Institute of Pacific Relations Inquiry Series.'[2] G.F. Hudson commended Norman for having 'a keen analytical mind and an outstanding capacity as a social historian.'[3] And John Maki wrote confidently that 'this book will be one of the classics in the field of modern Japanese history.' He applauded the work because 'the very core of Mr. Norman's work is thought, bold and imaginative thought that seeks the motivation that is the activating breath of history.'[4]

Beyond the praise offered, reviewers agreed that *Japan's Emergence* demonstrated three unusual achievements. Many were struck by Norman's extensive use of Japanese secondary sources. One can almost detect a sense of envy in some reviewers, awed by the evidence of language ability that permitted Norman to treat deftly so much Japanese material. Virtually all reviewers who had the space to do so also commented on the remarkable sweep of Norman's analysis, and on the incisive manner of its presentation. Finally, several reviewers acknowledged that, with the appearance of *Japan's Emergence*, foreign scholarship on Japan had reached a new level of attainment. Norman's study signalled the passing of the refined amateur, dabbling superficially in many fields, and the arrival of the disciplinary expert, applying sharply honed skills to produce authoritative works.

On the whole, the initial scholarly reaction to *Japan's Emergence* was highly favourable. Reviewers recognized a path-breaking study, commended its author's acumen, and praised his achievement. Indeed, one gets the impression that readers were so overwhelmed they felt incapable of quarrelling with the author's arguments. Such attitudes shielded the book from close, critical scrutiny, and perhaps postponed an adverse reaction.

Following nearly a quarter of a century of extensive growth in American scholarship on Japan, the next direct assessment of Norman and his work took place in 1968. At the annual convention of the Association for Asian Studies, four younger scholars presented papers in which they discussed E.H. Norman. Three were historians who had been trained as graduate students in the early 1950s, when Norman's study was one of the few major works of modern historical scholarship available on Japan. They were Harry Harootunian, Bernard Silberman, and David Abosch. The fourth panel participant was Kozo Yamamura, who examined *Japan's Emergence* as an economic historian.[5]

All three historians expressed obvious respect for Norman in their essays. They remarked principally on the sweep of his vision, the power of his analysis, and the unique value his work had had for them, at least during their apprenticeships in Japanese history. But each in his own way was also critical of Norman. Harootunian, for example, recognized that 'we are beginning to reach beyond his own modest limits,' and indicated clearly at the end that he believed Norman took on too large a task and fell short of achieving his goals. Silberman, too, was critical. He pointed out that subsequent scholarship had illuminated mistakes, and he placed emphasis on the questions yet to be answered and the arguments that were suggestive but not sufficient. And one sensed in Abosch, as well, a dissatisfaction with Norman. He objected to Norman's emphasis on socio-economic change at the expense of political ideas. On balance, the three papers offered rather gentle criticism in a mood of sympathetic affection.

The fourth paper was of a different character. While conceding that Norman had had a salutary influence on Americans writing Japanese economic history, Professor Yamamura fairly excoriated Norman in his role as an economic historian, mainly, it seems, because Norman failed in 1940 to anticipate the questions that economic historians would be asking in 1968. At one point Yamamura wrote that 'Norman's observations are too general and empty in content to elicit a meaningful and testable hypothesis' (23). With the confidence born of hindsight, Yamamura thus tattered Norman's reputation as an economic historian.

Seven years of virtual neglect passed before E.H. Norman again entered the eye of American scholars. In 1975, Professor John W. Dower, a young historian at the University of Wisconsin, edited and composed an introduction to selected writings by Mr Norman under the title *Origins of the Modern Japanese State*. In addition to a full version of *Japan's Emergence*, the Dower volume also contained a long essay called 'Feudal Background of Japanese Politics,' a short essay entitled 'The Shrine of Clio,' bibliographical materials, and a lengthy introduction by Professor Dower himself. The book had two effects: it made many of Norman's writings readily available, and it made some of America's Japan historians very angry.

Professor Dower's essay, rather than Norman's work itself, seems to have stirred people's ire. Dower strived to do three things: rehabilitate appreciation of Norman, analyse the fate of Norman's works among his American successors, and suggest an agenda of research in line with Norman's concerns. Having once assessed Dower's essay, however, I will not dwell on it again here, where I wish only to draw brief attention to one element in his argument.[6]

In a section covering nearly a third of the essay and bearing the subtitle 'Politics of Scholarship: Norman and His Successors,' Professor Dower offers his interpretation of the fate of Norman's work among American scholars. The crux of the interpretation is that Norman's successors 'shelved' or denigrated his work principally out of partisan, ideological motives. Dower asserts that 'much American scholarship in Japan has tended to be congruent with the objectives of the American government' (33) and that 'it is also naive to underestimate the concern with creating a counter-ideology or counter-theory to Marxism which had preoccupied many of those who have been in a position to shape the general course of postwar Japanese studies' (44). Professor Dower singles out for special examination the work and ideas of four prominent American scholars – two historians, a sociologist, and an economist. Perhaps for this reason, or perhaps out of an aversion to the ideological tenor of the interpretation itself, many scholars have responded critically to the Dower essay.

The most direct, passionate, and unvarnished reaction arose two years later when a lengthy article appeared in the *Journal of Japanese Studies* under the title 'An Examination of E.H. Norman's Scholarship.'[7] Written by Professor George Akita, a senior historian at the University of Hawaii who was trained during the 1950s at Harvard University, the article set forth the most damning indictment of Norman's work that I have seen. Akita begins by noting that scholars have praised Norman's writings because he employed primary sources, was highly original, had analytical and conceptual strengths, and was a well credentialed scholar. The essay then states briefly Akita's 'conclusions,' which might be termed more accurately allegations. Akita asserts that Norman did not employ primary sources, that he was reliant on secondary sources in English (rather than Japanese), that his work lacked originality, and that he worked hastily and distorted sources. Near the end of the essay Akita writes that 'Norman, in his haste forcibly to dramatize his theses, ignored basic rules of historical scholarship and produced a work, *Japan's Emergence*, that is seriously flawed, flaws which the brilliance of his narrative skill cannot redeem' (418). And in a final sentence he says, 'By their [for which the antecedent is unnamed 'maturer scholars'] support of Norman, they are helping to create a mystique around Norman, a mystique which is not even being put to the test of the most elementary principles of historical scholarship' (419).

Although the field of Japanese history often witnesses one practitioner chipping away at the reputation of another, it is unusual to encounter a frontal assault quite like Professor Akita's. Without using the term itself, he strongly implies that Norman plagiarized the work of others, that he was sloppy in his use of sources, that he manipulated his data, and that his work was derivative. Each accusation is analysed and supported with lengthy quotations. At first glance, the essay appears to deal a devastating blow to Norman's reputation.

However, close scrutiny of the essay casts doubts on Professor Akita's claims. Many of his accusations are buttressed with data drawn from footnotes that have a marginal bearing on the book's theses. While it does seem that Norman was occasionally guilty of mis-citing a source, neglecting to mention all his references, or brushing over a hair-splitting point, the specific examples Professor Akita cites do not often challenge the major premises of Norman's arguments. Furthermore, many, although not all, of the assertions made about abuse of secondary sources are not entirely plausible, because ambiguities remain. In addition, some problems that Professor Akita characterizes as a misquotation of sources actually stem from imprecise use of vague terms, such as 'official' or 'gentry,' which are subject to at least two and often more interpretations. Finally, one of Professor Akita's points is simply moot. Few if any scholars have alleged that the value of *Japan's Emergence* rests on its use of primary sources; virtually everyone has recognized Norman's heavy reliance on the work of Japanese predecessors.[8]

Space does not permit my replying to each and every point that Professor Akita raises. He has found and demonstrated some cases of imprudence and error, but the minutiae of the charges do not, in my estimation, add up to impugn either the overall integrity of *Japan's Emergence* or Norman's reputation as a scholar. That reputation rests, after all, on Norman's ability to evoke a broad conception of historical change and to depict salient trends vividly and incisively. However damaging the Akita attack may seem, it largely skirts this issue, because it avoids extended confrontation with the series of interrelated arguments that lend *Japan's Emergence* its analytical force. Professor Akita's assertions burrow away at decaying timber in some weak foundation points, but the grand structure of *Japan's Emergence* survives his assault largely unharmed.

Finally, I think it needs to be said that younger historians are not engaged in creating a 'mystique around Norman' (419). Dower concedes that 'Norman's work can no longer stand alone or unrevised' (32) and Harootunian has noted that 'we are beginning to reach beyond his own modest limits' (552). Virtually everyone who has written about Norman has acknowledged that all his work, and *Japan's Emergence* in particular, suffers weaknesses. Some are intrinsic to the study, others have been exposed by later scholarship. Even in the face of these weaknesses, however, many of us remain impressed with the merits that shine through. They underscore the lasting value of a sometimes brilliant work of synthesis and historical analysis produced by a remarkably young man under difficult circumstances. It is a work that will probably long exercise a special attraction for scholars of a certain cast of historical mind, a point to which I shall return momentarily.

Exactly one year after the appearance of Akita's article, the *Journal of Japanese Studies* published a second.[9] Apparently it will be the only reply to Akita's charges to appear in that journal. The author of the rebuttal was Herbert P. Bix, a young historian trained at Harvard then working as the Fulbright scholar at *The Japan Interpreter*. The thrust of the Bix essay is that 'Akita's analysis is all of one piece and never once rises above the level of footnote excavation' (393). By examining a few charges in detail, Bix demonstrates the ambiguous nature of many of Akita's points. He closes his piece by referring to the Akita article as 'a minor and unfortunate incident in the growing body of literature on Norman,' and 'a fruitless intervention which failed to deepen awareness of any issues or ideas' (410).

This brief review of direct reactions to E.H. Norman's work over the past forty years reveals a depressing decline both in level of discourse and degree of admiration. There are many reasons why this might be the case, but I will not entertain them now. Rather, in an attempt to put behind us what has become a rancorous controversy, I wish to turn to a more detached analysis of Norman's influence on post-war American scholarship. I hope, thereby, to provide a useful first step in promoting a constructive assessment of E.H. Norman's writings.

I believe it will help us to understand the fate of E.H. Norman's work if we look at what might be called the cast of historical mind. Other terms that convey a sense of the intellectual posture I wish to portray are 'philosophical disposition' and 'methodological preference.' There are, and should be, in a society like ours, alternative ways of studying the past. The questions posed, the materials examined, the techniques employed, the perspectives adopted, and the purposes sought differ from one historian to the next. They produce a diversity of approaches and findings that our society can harbour and should welcome.

I believe we can find in the response to E.H. Norman's work a fundamental split between adherents of differing modes of historical inquiry, possessing different casts of historical mind. To demonstrate this point, I wish to turn to new materials. An article published in 1956–57 by John W. Hall (co-authored with Sakata Yoshio of Kyoto University) offers an excellent, explicit defence of one school of historical inquiry whose practitioners have not, by and large, celebrated Norman's work.[10] For purpose of comparison, I wish to examine an essay written shortly afterwards by Thomas G. Smith.[11] While the Smith essay is less explicit about its methodological premises, it does offer a counterpoise to the Hall essay, and it suggests by example the kind of work that an alternative school of historical inquiry might prize.

Before embarking on this comparison, I should confess where my own sympathies lie. I believe one can only understand historical change adequately by appreciating the social and economic context in which it occurs. For this reason, my cast of historical mind is, I believe, much closer to Norman's and Smith's than to Hall's. However, I do not wish to portray my own odyssey through the profession, or to praise one method of inquiry at the expense of another. I want to offer a sketch that is as objective as reasonably possible. But it should be recognized that personal inclinations, experiences, and relationships are bound to influence my analysis. While this modest confession will not ensure objectivity, I hope that it at least places you on your guard for what follows.

The purpose of Professor Hall's 1957 essay was to examine the Meiji Restoration as an event in political history and to explain the motivation of its leadership. 'For the political historian, then, the study of motivation becomes a primary concern ... The study of motivation is both a key to the larger problems of causation and more germane to the political phase of this history of the Restoration' (35). Whether one poses such questions because certain types of material are available or seeks out certain types of material owing to one's question is not made clear. But there is certainty about one point: 'The historian encounters as his primary data a large body of information concerning specific events and incidents' (33). Out of this body of information, one of the historian's 'primary concerns will be to identify as precisely as possible the participating agents in the political process' (34). Although the techniques one employs in this procedure are not made wholly explicit, the perspective on such historical inquiry is. 'The historian has still to answer the question of how and in which combination these conditions affected the human events which led up to the Restoration.' And later, 'a general picture of structure and process is most often not sufficient to explain the behavior of the agents of political action ... The context of action of these individuals was indeed something more limited, something confined to the actual areas of their private experiences.' In closing, Hall writes: 'Individual behavior was conditioned in the final analysis by personal motives exercised in a limited sphere' (35).

In a nutshell, Hall offers a resolute defence of one methodological preference. It is a method that endorses the role of individuals as the principal objects of historical inquiry. Their motives are the preeminent causal force in history, and they are to be sought in a 'limited sphere,' one that is 'confined to the actual areas of their private experiences' (35). To fathom individual motives and the personal experiences that shaped them, the historian examines materials that come to light during critical events or incidents in a nation's history. The implication is that official documents, letters, personal diaries, reminiscences, biographies, and similar materials are the real stuff of history. From .these materials the historian intuits how man shapes events and his world.

This brief, and perhaps overly crude, précis fails to do justice to the subtleties of Professor Hall's argument. But it does suggest how his philosophical disposition endorses a firmly humanistic view of history. Men as individuals, or acting in groups, occupy centre stage, and their activities and behaviour shape history's course.

Historians cannot, however, be content to examine only individuals and groups. They must also be alert to the necessity for examining other 'levels of the historical process' (33). The political acts of the Meiji Restoration took place, Hall notes, 'within a wide context of social, economic, and intellectual conditions. It is the conviction of the historians that these aspects of the historical process are somehow interrelated. The first level, largely the province of political figures and their actions, provides the answer to how history happened. The other levels, in which are made to appear the patterns of stability and change within the culture, help the historian understand why it happened as it did' (34). Thus, there really are two realms of inquiry, one that focuses sharply on individuals in limited spheres of action, and another that looks 'at broad social, economic, and intellectual conditions as background. But the essay leaves little doubt which one is paramount. As noted above, Hall contends that a 'general picture ... is more often not sufficient to explain the behavior of the agents of political action.' For this purpose, one must focus on individuals. General studies, if undertaken at all, are clearly a subordinate task. They offer material to flesh out the background, but they are not sufficient.

The views that Professor Hall articulated in 1957 found further reinforcement in two major studies that appeared shortly afterwards. One study, by Albert M. Craig, seeks to explain why the Chōshū domain played a major role in the Meiji Restoration.[12] Another, by Marius Jansen, explores the role of Tōsa in the Restoration by focusing on one of its most famous activists, Sakamoto Ryōma.[13] Both studies rely on the device of local history to illuminate the motives of the leaders of the Restoration and its causes. Both authors, therefore, adopt a philosophical and methodological tack that accords nicely with the one Professor Hall defended. Shunting aside a concern with broad social and economic issues, America's Japan historians grew preoccupied with narrow questions that focused on individuals, their ideas, and their political behaviour.

Students being trained in this academic atmosphere were probably not inspired or influenced by E.H. Norman's studies.[14] Norman dealt at length, after all, with the broad social and economic background whose neglect scholarly trends were endorsing. He dealt with individuals, too, especially in his chapter on the Restoration. But often those individuals were not the vivid, flesh and blood figures that Professor Hall's approach celebrates. If we accept the fact that the kind of thinking – the methodological and philosophical preferences – exemplified by the Hall essay did have an influence of America's Japan historians, and if we concede that E.H. Norman's major study resonated poorly with the new topical concerns in American scholarship, then I think it is easier to understand why Norman's work went into eclipse during the mid- to late 1950s. In that scholarly context, his work became a valuable straw man, and he became more an object of criticism than praise. For a path-breaking work, that fate was inevitable.

The line of analysis I have just set out needs to be qualified with at least two emendations, however. First, the writings of Hall, Craig, and Jansen were not the only force influencing reaction to Norman's writings. Professor Dower has offered one appraisal of the political atmosphere in American universities during the 1950s, which undoubtedly had some influence on the response to Norman's studies. Other appraisals of that atmosphere are possible. The concerns that shaped historical study in general during the 1950s and 1960s also influenced the treatment of Norman's work. Then, as now, mainstream historians in American institutions laid heavy emphasis on intellectual and political history. Under such circumstances, the kind of socio-economic history that *Japan's Emergence* represented was practised by relatively few American historians in any field, and those who did practise it found themselves a professionally weak minority.

Secondly, I do not wish to imply that Professor Hall's decision became an unchallenged orthodoxy overnight. I do think his essay was timely. In combination with the writings of Craig and Jansen, Hall's views had significant influence on the large numbers of graduate students who began entering Japanese history in the 1960s because, more often than not, those students encountered in what they read the views defended in Professor Hall's essay. I do not wish to imply, however, that the design Professor Hall laid out in 1957 adequately represents his methodological position. In later studies, he has dealt with a variety of historical topics, and his own approach has broadened in step with the changing concerns of the historical profession itself.[15] Nor do I wish to contend that the political history method he outlined in 1957 ever became the sole paradigm for American research in Japan. Despite their strong affinities with Hall's approach, Craig and Jansen in their own monographs occasionally moved beyond a narrow concern with individual motivation and small groups – often, incidentally, in order to challenge Norman's views. Other historians writing at that time adopted even more divergent approaches.

The writings of Thomas C. Smith in particular offered a counterpoise to the kind of work Professors Hall, Craig, and Jansen published in the late 1950s and early 1960s. Smith's studies of that period exemplified what I have referred to as products of a different cast of historical mind or methodological preference. While he never made explicit his debt to Norman, and while he dealt in depth with topics that Norman was able to treat only lightly, Smith did carry on, in my estimation, a mode of historical writing and research reminiscent of Norman's work. This claim is best substantiated by a brief examination of his article on 'Japan's Aristocratic Revolution.'

Smith takes as his point of departure an observation by de Tocqueville that 'an aristocracy seldom yields [its privileges] without a protracted struggle.' He then goes on to demonstrate that, contrary to expectations, Japan's aristocracy not only yielded its privileges, it actually conducted a revolution against itself. Japan's aristocratic revolution occurred because (1) the merchant class acquiesced to the aristocracy's political rule, (2) divisions within the aristocracy facilitated the rise of 'radical innovators,' and (3) the aristocracy's claim to power were not based on possession of land. These conditions also made it possible for the new government, once established, to conduct a series of sweeping reforms that sped Japan's transition from an agrarian society to an industrial nation-state. Smith closes his essay by noting six ways in which this particular set of circumstances has made Japan different from other modern societies.

Once again, undue brevity fails to do justice to a subtle, provocative argument. But my purpose is not to detail the argument itself. Rather, I want to tease out the methodological and philosophical premises that inform this example of Professor Smith's work. In so doing, we shall highlight the features of an alternative to the political history method, and I think we shall find some evidence of the Norman legacy at work.

The most immediate and striking distinction between Professor Smith's essay and Professor Hall's is the former's dramatic emphasis on cross-cultural comparison. The questions posed are ones that arise by examining Japan in the light of European history. Are all aristocracies really conservative? If they are not, what consequences ensue? By recognizing that the Japanese aristocracy during the Meiji transformation was innovative, and by examining the implications of this departure from form, Smith was able to offer intriguing explanations for many of the comparatively distinctive features of the modern Japanese state. Dismissing the parochial tendency to view Japan as a unique embodiment of the human experience, Smith sought to understand it as merely one variant in a spectrum of experiences, using controlled comparison as the best technique to illuminate what was indeed distinctive. E.H. Norman had used similar comparative observations to highlight the insights of his work. Although Norman was not the principal influence shaping Smith's style of history, Smith's work did perpetuate a tradition that Norman had initiated.

Another fundamental difference between the two approaches concerns the role of the individual in history. While the individual is for Professor Hall the occupant of centre stage, for Professor Smith he is essentially a member of large social groupings on whom the forces of history work their will. Indeed, only two post-Meiji individuals are mentioned by name in the essay, and in both cases the purpose is to illustrate concretely how members of a particular status or generational group responded to the opportunities history presented them. One figure mentioned was a provincial banker, the other an Ōsaka businessman. Neither was a major political actor. We find here, I think, a vision of the role individuals are offered by the grand sweep of history and, unconsciously perhaps, modest celebration of the anonymous figures in history who appealed to E.H. Norman.

The particular techniques Smith employs to achieve his vision of the Restoration are not made explicit in the essay, nor do they become clear by reading it. If I may use other evidence as documentation, however, I think it is possible to illustrate another fundamental departure from the political history method. Shortly before publishing his *Yale Review* essay, Professor Smith had completed a study entitled *The Agrarian Origins of Modern Japan*.[16] Relying not on 'information concerning specific events and incidents but on the documents that record the basic routines of human life,' such as family registers, diaries, account books, letters, and so on, Professor Smith was able to offer a vivid portrait of social conditions among the Japanese peasantry over a two-century period. In his most recent work he has used temple registers and other quantifiable, serial data surviving from the Tokugawa period to illustrate in comparable detail changes in wealth, family structure, and landholding patterns, again over a period of nearly two centuries.[17]

Two points warrant comment. First, Professor Smith's work demonstrated for Japan historians that they can deal with far more than political incidents and events. A very broad spectrum of human history is open to inquiry, including everything from aristocratic revolts against moribund generals to peasant resistance against usurious gentry. Smith's work also showed Japan historians that a broad range of material is open to them, awaiting merely ingenuity in its discovery and exploitation. Even a peasant ledger offers valuable evidence. Thus, an openness to new data and new techniques is actually fostered by a kind of philosophical disposition that is itself reflected in the broader scope of historical writing – and understanding.

Finally, and perhaps it goes without saying by this point, Professor Smith holds a view of the proper concern of historical inquiry that is at marked variance with the one articulated by Professor Hall in 1957. For Hall, the motivations of individuals shape history. They act out their parts against a backdrop of socio-economic conditions whose delineation the historian regards as a subordinate task. For Smith, delineating that backdrop is itself the historian's primary task. Whether Smith believes that by delineating that backdrop we also offer sufficient explanation of historical change is a question that I feel his written work leaves ambiguous. But there is no ambiguity on one point. It is a legitimate, significant historical pursuit to illuminate the broad sweep of historical change by depicting its appearance among and consequence for groups, classes, and institutions, broadly defined.

Some of the confusion and a bit of the antagonism that have arisen among historians of Japan are a product of mutual scepticism focused on these issues. Socio-economic historians, doubtful that the study of ideas offers a sufficient explanation for human behaviour under complex circumstances, find their scepticism reciprocated by political historians, who doubt that socio-economic explanations – especially when couched in class terms – offer explanations any more sufficient. Some intolerance thus operates in both camps. But by giving reign to their scepticism, political historians have sometimes closed themselves off from an understanding of the social theory, or sociological thinking, that informs much of the work their counterparts write. An aversion to sociology is perfectly understandable, especially given its present pathetic condition. But I think the failure to appreciate rudimentary sociology has occasionally muddled disclosure in our field, and it has certainly helped shape the reaction to Norman's writings.

Although Professor Smith's studies from the late 1950s and early 1960s won acclaim from some quarters of the historical profession, they did not exercise the dominant influence on Japanese history in America. There were two practical reasons. First, very few students entered Stanford to complete PHD degrees in Japanese history before the early 1960s.[18] Most Japan historians trained before about 1962 for Harvard, Columbia, or Michigan, where older programs were more comprehensive and probably better financed. Secondly, broad studies of socio-economic change still represented a minor rivulet in the history field at large through the mid-1960s. The young historian eager to rise in the profession was better advised, therefore, to write an intellectual biography or an in-depth political study, and most of them did.

The diminishing level of interest shown in E.H. Norman and his major work during the 1960s was thus attributable to several causes. Most important perhaps was simply the force of one mode of inquiry within the history profession at large. Many historians remained preoccupied with questions of individual motivation and political behaviour during critical events, and they paid little attention to broad issues in the fields of social and economic history. This general tendency also influenced several of the leading American historians of Japan during that period. As a result, both senior scholars and the younger historians working under them directed their attention towards political history and away from socio-economic history. As they did, they also diverted their attention from many of the issues and problems that E.H. Norman treated in *Japan's Emergence*.

When the revival of interest in Norman occurred during the early 1970s, I would venture to suggest that it derived from two sources. One source was the Vietnam War. The war exercised its effects in many ways, but from a purely intellectual, or academic, point of view, I think its influences are easily described. The kinds of professionally cautious, geographically and chronologically circumscribed studies that dominated East Asian history in the 1960s offered meager fare with which to understand the intrusive changes the war caused in Vietnam, China, and the United States. Fed by a sense of moral outrage, many younger people were able to cast off the intellectual timidity that had become the mantle of scholarly respectability. While studies did not always become more venturesome in scope, some students did begin asking radically different questions, directing their attention to aspects of Japanese history that had long been ignored. To what extent E.H. Norman's work guided or inspired their study, it is probably impossible to measure, but it does seem that some found inspiration in his writings.

A second tendency that may have stimulated renewed interest in Norman's writings, once Professor Dower brought them to mind again, has been the transformation of historical study in America since the late 1960s. The most telling changes have arisen because more historians have found helpful in their research the methods, concepts, and premises of the social sciences, in particular those of anthropology and sociology. The once small minority engaged in writing social history has grown in number and influence. Although they remain a minority in the profession at large, and even more so in the Japan field, historians influenced by the social sciences have won respect for their work. New publications such as the *Journal of Interdisciplinary History* and the *Social Science History Journal* have given them a voice. And the American Historical Association has given them the stamp of approval by publishing articles that use novel data, techniques, and approaches. In this atmosphere, I think it is only natural that some students, reacquainted with Norman, have found his work appealing, while recognizing at the same time, of course, how far beyond his work the field itself has gone in the past forty years.[19]

In the four decades that have passed since the publication of *Japan's Emergence*, many studies have appeared that obviously supersede it. We have seen earlier in this essay how much research during the 1950s and 1960s was directed towards illuminating the causes and background of the Meiji Restoration, the topics Norman treated in the first two substantive chapters of *Japan's Emergence*. In the early 1970s, a study appeared that is an authoritative capstone to that body of research, William Beasley's *The Meiji Restoration*.[20] Combining with remarkable skill and insight both the broad social approach and the detailed political approach, Beasley has produced a work that will long stand as a landmark in Western analyses of the Restoration, its background, and its early years.

Norman's necessarily superficial treatments of 'Early Industriali-zation' and 'Parties and Politics' have also been superseded by sub-sequent studies. In the field of economic history, Henry Rosovsky, Thomas C. Smith, and Kozo Yamamura have markedly advanced our understanding of subjects Norman dealt with sketchily. In the field of political history, many scholars have examined the problem of estab-lishing a constitution, the evolution of the early political parties, and the inception of parliamentary politics. While more obviously could, and will, be done on these topics, they offer less promising grounds for fresh inquiry than other aspects of Norman's work.

The two aspects of *Japan's Emergence* that warrant the greatest atten-tion, for purposes of revision or fresh interpretation, are bureaucracy and the 'agrarian settlement.' These are two realms of human behav-iour that have as yet been only lightly explored. None the less, they are topics whose understanding is essential if we are to illuminate the evolution of Japan's modern history. And, for the purpose, we can do no better than to start precisely where Norman did, in the last three decades of the nineteenth century.

Norman's own examination of the bureaucracy was brief and un-systematic. He portrayed it as a kind of overlord which exercised power when the state controlled the economy. (See pp. 240–1 and 313.) Such treatment is obviously unsatisfactory, because the minis-ters of the central government and their bureaucracies have also exer-cised power over many other aspects of Japanese society from the early 1870s onward. Although he may not have had time or space to examine this subject in detail, Norman understood perfectly well its importance, for he noted on page 313 that 'it might not be an exag-geration to say that the key to understanding Japanese political life is given to whoever appreciates fully the historical role and actual posi-tion of the bureaucracy.'

Since he wrote that line in 1940, a number of scholars have followed his cue. Bernard Silberman has illuminated some of the structural fea-tures of the Meiji bureaucracy, while Robert Spaulding has depicted its organizational evolution. Other scholars have cast light on limited aspects of the bureaucracy in shorter pieces that deal with particular individuals or with groups such as the elder statesmen (*genrō*). But we have yet to reach the point where studies shed light on the central questions: How did the bureaucracy arrive at its decisions? How did its decisions influence political and economic developments? How did its power compare with that of other groups in the central government?

Norman ventured one tantalizingly brief observation concerning the role of the bureaucrats. He saw them as 'mediators who reconcile the conflicts between the military and financial or industrial groups' (313). This is an interesting and plausible claim, but I doubt that it offers an adequate analysis of the role of the Meiji bureaucracy. His perspective does suggest, however, one important observation. The bureaucracy cannot be studied in isolation; its political role must be examined within the broad and constantly shifting context of national political power.

While intensive case studies of single ministries, their recruitment patterns and decision-making processes, will be necessary, they will not be sufficient. They will help to shed light on the way the bureaucracy arrived at its decisions, and on the influences such decisions had.[21] But we should venture boldly beyond case studies in at least two ways. First, we must illuminate how incumbent ministers, officials, and staff used their authority to influence developments and contend for power among other agencies in the central government.[22] In short, we need to examine the bureaucracy as simply one element in an equation of power that included such formal agencies as the legislature, the Privy Council, and the cabinet, and such informal agencies as the elder statesmen. Secondly, we should also venture to understand the political role of non-incumbent or retired bureaucrats, those omnipresent figures who seem always to be stalking the corridors of power in Japan. Some may disagree that they are a manifestation of bureaucratic power at all, but I think we must leave this question open. Obviously the ex-bureaucrat, who was also a party member, a business consultant, senior statesman, and even a cabinet minister, was not merely a bureaucrat. Just as obviously, he was not merely a party member either. By appreciating his links to the bureaucracy, however, we recognize an important form of ancillary bureaucratic power in action. And attuned to the complexities of the roles played by individuals and organizations, we may finally develop a more incisive understanding of the bureaucracy's position in prewar Japan.

Study of the 'agrarian settlement' poses an equally demanding task. In what I find to be a quite unsatisfactory thirty pages on this subject, Norman none the less highlights six crucial topics and suggests briefly their interrelationships. His topics include the land tax, peasant dis-possession, surplus agricultural labour, the evolution of a domestic market, the origins of foreign trade, and the relationships between landlords and industrialists, on the one hand, and a poor peasantry on the other. While his explanations are very provocative, they are not always compelling; they sometimes seem wrong. But perhaps for these reasons, they now offer what is perhaps the most promising line of inquiry yet to be stimulated by *Japan's Emergence*.

Owing largely, I think, to the authoritative attributes of Henry Rosovsky's writings, American students of nineteenth-century Japanese history have not paid very much attention to the rural economy in the period from 1868 to 1900 or so.[23] Sydney Crawcour has attempted to rectify this oversight in an essay that traces the links between the studies of Thomas C. Smith, which come to an end with the Restoration, and those of Rosovsky, which begin around 1885.[24] But Crawcour's is an exercise in logic and methodology; it does not offer very much empirical evidence to illuminate what really happened in rural Japan.

Our understanding of rural economic change in that period has implications that reach well beyond the narrow field of Japanese history. During those years Japan faced a problem that has recurred frequently in modern history, and will continue to arise in some countries: How does a society manage the transition from an agrarian economy to industrialism without severe social and political disruption? The last three decades of the nineteenth century witnessed Japan's initial attempt to deal with this problem. While we know a great deal about the ultimate outcome, I believe we are still remarkably ignorant about the processes that produced the outcome and their consequences for people in all walks of life.

One of the key issues bearing on the process of transition is the use of surplus agricultural capital. Although Norman treated this subject with some ambiguity, he implied that rural landlords did not use their capital very effectively. Other students, in particular James Nakamura and Thomas Smith, have suggested just the opposite. They have offered a good deal of indirect, and some direct, evidence to assert that entrepreneurial landlords employed surplus agricultural capital quite effectively to build a flourishing industrial and commercial economy in late nineteenth-century Japan. But we still have woefully little empirical evidence that provides a tangible picture of that economy and its evolution. We need such studies, not the least because such evidence could produce an entirely different understanding of that evolution.

If undertaken in the framework of holistic local history, research on this topic would shed light on a range of other critical problems as well. For example, knowing how resources were allocated in rural communities would help us to understand who exercised power in villages and regions, and who, in turn, influenced the policies of the central government. Such studies offer an even more important perspective on the socio-economic condition of the peasantry. Was the adjustment to new patterns of economic organization and behaviour as smooth as it appears? How did the transition from handicraft to factory-based spinning in the 1880s, and from cottage to factory-based weaving in the 1900s and 1910s, affect rural households, villages, and regions? Did the adjustment result in improved living standards for all? Or did it lead to wider differences in the economic status of farm households? If so, how did political relations among landlords and tenants change as a result? Finally, there is a close relationship between rural change and the process of city development in nineteenth-century Japan. Norman, for instance, claimed that most urban migration then was short-term. His claim may be correct. But until we have more empirical studies that demonstrate how rural economic change contributed to the growth of cities, and vice versa, we will suffer poor understanding of Japan's urbanization.

The questions I have just posed are prompted in large measure by attention to new types of historical inquiry. And to answer such questions, I think we are best advised to use – thoughtfully, of course – some of the methods the new history offers. For example, we could illuminate the texture of agrarian society by employing some of the techniques that historians practising the *annales* tradition have used to such good effect. We could also employ the methods of those who study *mentalités* as a means of appreciating the subjective features of social relations in rural Japan, a topic of ascending importance given recent studies.[25] The methods of demographic history, heretofore confined mainly to the Tokugawa period, could also be fruitfully applied to the Meiji era (availability of sources permitting), where population patterns differed and thus presumably had different implications for economic development. Family history methods could also be adopted in order to depict social and psychological consequences of change in the Meiji era. And, at least after 1890, some of the new political history techniques could be used to shed light on the political alterations that took place in rural Japan.

In some measure, it will be new business for historians of Japan to address questions like these, for they are provoked by contemporary concerns in the profession and are best pursued by using its current methods. But in some measure, also, these questions represent old business. After all, E.H. Norman brought them to our attention forty years ago. From this perspective they are unfinished business, as Norman implied when he wrote: 'I do not set my own ambitions in this field higher than ... to refuse to believe that the full and final answer to any important historical problem has been given' (105). We may not offer a final answer by pursuing these questions either, but the search itself holds promise of significant findings, and I think it offers a constructive alternative to the present debate.

NOTES

1 New York 1940, originally. I rely in this essay on the edition that appears in John W. Dower, ed., *Origins of the Modern Japanese State: Selected Writings of E.H. Norman* (New York: Pantheon 1975).

2 *American Historical Review* 45 (1940), 296

3 *Pacific Affairs* 20, no. 3 (September 1947), 328

4 *The Far Eastern Quarterly* 2, no. 4 (August 1943), 396

5 The essays appeared later in *Pacific Affairs*, as follows: Harry D. Harootunian, 'E.H. Norman and the Task for Japanese History,' *PA* 41, no. 4 (Winter 1968–69), 545–52; Bernard S. Silberman, 'E.H. Norman: Structure and Function in the Meiji State, a Reappraisal,' *PA* 41, no. 4 (Winter 1968–69), 553–9; Kozo Yamamura, 'E.H. Norman as an Economic Historian,' *PA* 42, no. 1 (Spring 1969), 17–24; and David Abosch, 'Political Consciousness in Japan: A Retrospect on E.H. Norman,' *PA* 42, no. 1 (Spring 1969), 25–31. Hereafter, for the sake of convenience, I have placed page references to a particular essay in parentheses immediately following the quotation.

6 Gary D. Allinson, 'E.H. Norman, Modern Japan, and the Historian's Agenda,' *The Japan Interpreter* 10, nos. 3 and 4 (Winter 1976), 393–402

7 George Akita, 'An Examination of E.H. Norman's Scholarship,' *Journal of Japanese Studies* 3, no. 2 (1977), 375–419

8 To underscore his assertion that scholars claim Norman often used primary sources, Professor Akita quotes a statement made on page 10 of Professor Dower's essay. However, Dower refers in that context to the whole of Norman's work and to his studies of Andō Shōeki in particular, not to *Japan's Emergence*, which is the object of Akita's attack.

9 Herbert P. Bix, 'The Pitfalls of Scholastic Criticism: A Reply to Norman's Critics,' *Journal of Japanese Studies* 4, no. 2 (Summer 1978), 391–411

10 Yoshio Sakata and John Whitney Hall, 'The Motivation of Political Leadership in the Meiji Restoration,' *Journal of Asian Studies* 16 (1956–57) 31–50

11 Thomas C. Smith, 'Japan's Aristocratic Revolution,' *Yale Review* 50 (1960–61), 370–83

12 Albert M. Craig, *Chōshū in the Meiji Restoration* (Cambridge: Harvard University Press 1961)

13 Marius B. Jansen, *Sakamoto Ryōma and the Meiji Restoration* (Princeton, NJ: Princeton University Press 1961)

14 One recent study of *fudai daimyō* in the late Tokugawa period does not even bother to cite Norman in the bibliography, a gesture that most scholars were still making through the 1960s.

15 Even as his own views have modified, however, Professor Hall has continued to emphasize the particularistic features of Japan. For example, in an essay delivered in 1975 he spoke of the fundamental importance of 'contexts of plausibility,' a conception that inherently emphasizes indepth understanding of Japan in preference to the pursuit of comparative analogies. John W. Hall, 'Japanese History in World Perspective,' in Charles F. Delzell, ed., *The Future of History: Essays in the Vanderbilt University Centennial Symposium* (Nashville, Tenn.: Vanderbilt University Press 1977), 173–88. Quotation appears on p. 180.

16 Stanord, Calif.: Stanford University Press 1959

17 Thomas C. Smith, *Nakahara, Family Farming and Population in a Japanese Village, 1717–1830* (Stanford: Stanford University Press 1977)

18 To the best of my knowledge, only three persons won PHD degrees in Japanese history at Stanford in the 1950s.

19 With these remarks I do not wish to imply that historians are the only ones who are interested in Norman's work, or the only ones who might use it. Professor Roger Bowen's recent studies demonstrate this is certainly not the case. I have confined my remarks to historians because, under present academic conditions, they more than other specialists will be dealing with issues that Norman raised.

20 Stanford: Stanford University Press 1972
21 None the less, a recent thesis demonstrates how detailed study of one institution can offer provocative explanations for much broader problems. See David C. Evans, 'The Satsuma Faction and Professionalism in the Japanese Naval Officer Corps of the Meiji Period, 1868–1912,' PHD dissertation, Stanford University, 1978.
22 It appears that Kenneth Pyle is engaged in just such a study, but for the early twentieth century. See his 'The Technology of Japanese Nationalism: The Local Improvement Movement, 1900–1918,' *Journal of Asian Studies* 33, no. 1 (November 1973), 51–66.
23 See, especially, Henry Rosovsky, 'Japan's Transition to Modern Economic Growth, 1868–1885,' in Henry Rosovsky, ed., *Industrialization in Two Systems* (New York: Wiley 1966), 91–139.
24 E.S. Crawcour, 'The Tokugawa Period and Japan's Preparation for Modern Economic Growth,' *Journal of Japanese Studies* 1 (1974), 113–26
25 See Ann L. Waswo, *Japanese Landlords: The Decline of a Rural Elite* (Berkeley, Calif.: University of California Press 1977), and reviews by Richard J. Smethurst in *Journal of Japanese Studies* 5, no. 2 (1979), 473–83, and by Stephen G. Vlastos in *Journal of Asian Studies* 38, no. 3 (May 1979), 580–3.

Tōyama Shigeki

THE APPRECIATION OF
NORMAN'S HISTORIOGRAPHY[1]

Twenty years have passed since the tragic death of E. Herbert Norman, and evaluations of his historical writings have changed considerably in that time. New appraisals of his work not only influence contemporary historiography, but could even have implications for modern politics.

Norman's work on Japan's modern history influenced studies of Asian and Japanese history in Europe and America during the 1940s. In the fifties, McCarthyism dictated that his scholarship and thought be censured as 'red.' Then, a decade later, when modernization theory had taken over the mainstream of Japan studies in the United States, Norman's work was criticized as dated. 'Beginning in the 1950s, Norman's work was courteously shelved by his American successors. By the 1960s even *Japan's Emergence* was largely ignored in the classroom, relegated to libraries and a bibliographic cliché. Thus the current basic textbook in the field – *East Asia: The Modern Transformation*, by John K. Fairbank, Edwin O. Reischauer, and Albert M. Craig – published in 1964, does not even include Norman in its suggested bibliography.'[2] In Japan until the mid-1950s, many doing research in the field began by reading Norman. Japanese translations – *Japan's Emergence As a Modern State* (Jiji Tsūshinsha 1947), *Soldier and Peasant in Japan: The Origins of Conscription* (Hakujitsu Shoin 1947), *A Forgotten Thinker: Andō Shōeki* (Iwanami Shoten 1950) and *Kurio no kao* [The Face of Clio] (Iwanami Shoten 1956)[3] – appeared in succession and gained an audience not limited to professional historians. None the less, the time came when learning from Norman ceased to be 'fashionable,' which I cannot help but feel was influenced by the trend in American academic circles. And just as Norman was ignored in America, no comprehensive, serious critiques of his historiography appeared in Japan, either.

The American 'Conference on Modern Japan,' where Edwin O. Reischauer and his students were the central participants, met six times between 1962 and 1968 and on each occasion issued voluminous reports in which a few references to Norman's work appear, but the references are all critical. In the final report, J.W. Morley defined Norman's studies as a Marxist interpretation of Japanese history and stated that 'Norman borrowed from both schools of Marxist-Leninist interpretation, but relied particularly strongly on the Lectures [Kōza-ha] faction.[4]

But Norman was *not* a Marxist. Anyone who reads his works without prejudice will understand that fact and in the discussion that follows I am going to prove it. In any case, it contributes nothing to our understanding of Norman's historiography once again to make an issue out of his alleged Marxism. The McCarthy era 'witch hunt' was a frenzied, irrational attack on freedom and reason. It is clear today that 'very little if any Communism, espionage, or treachery was uncovered but everyone was intimidated. Fearfulness has handicapped our officials ever since.'[5] [One might well substitute 'scholars' for 'officials.' TS] Admittedly, the American modernization scholars did indeed point out the weak and vulnerable aspects in their criticism of historical materialism, but they exaggerated them and only revealed how ridiculously shallow is their own understanding of historical materialism. The caustic remark of E.H. Carr in *What is History?*, which first appeared in 1969, just as modernization theory was coming into vogue, seems right to the point. In connection with Karl Popper's and Isaiah Berlin's criticism of the materialist view of history, Carr observed: 'During the past five or six years, almost everyone in this country or in the United States who has written an article about history, or even a serious review of a historical work, has cocked a knowing snook at Hegel and Marx and determination, and pointed out the absurdity of failing to recognize the role of accident in history.'[6]

That Norman drew on the fruits of Japanese Marxist historiography was natural and proper. Any sensible scholar recognizes the great contribution Marxist historiography made in pioneering the scientific inquiry into modern Japanese history. Norman was not the sort of scholar who would delete a work from the bibliographies and ignore it because it belonged to a particular school or reflected a particular view of history. 'The corollary to this is that no political party, no religious creed, no social class can claim a monopoly in the service of freedom' (*The Face of Clio*, 29; cited hereafter as *Clio*) And much less can scholarship. 'We can never hope to find out the absolute truth about remote events, but out of the continual confrontation of different views will come a deeper awareness of the main issues' (*Clio*, 105).

It is clear from the works cited in elaborate footnotes that *Japan's Emergence As a Modern State* (hereafter, *Emergence*)[7] draws freely and impartially on the research results of various schools: the so-called positivist school, the socio-economic history school, and historical materialism. Quantitatively, non-Marxists comprise the overwhelming majority of authors cited. However, Norman's theoretical frame for interpreting the structure of Japan's modern history, its logic, and development seems to be derived largely from the achievements of materialist historiography. Even so, in the documentation to *Emergence*, with the exception of references to historical materials from Hirano Yoshitarō's *Nihon shihonshugi shakai no kikō* [The Structure of Japan's Capitalist Society], the appearance of Hattori Shisō's name in connection with the controversy over the landlord class, and citations from a work by Kobayashi Yoshimasa, there is no mention of either the title *Nihon shihonshugi hattatsushi kōza* [Lectures on the History of the Development of Japanese Capitalism] or the works of Hani Gorō and Yamada Moritarō. The achievements of the Rōnō (Labor-Farmer) school, starting with Tsuchiya Takao, are frequently cited. By contrast, *Nihon shihonshugi hattasushi kōza* and Hani Gorō's works appear in the footnotes to *Soldier and Peasant in Japan* (hereafter *Soldier*).[8] It is difficult to understand why *Emergence*, published in 1940 and based on Norman's 1939 PH D thesis, failed to list the central books and essays of the Kōza school, despite the fact that he came to Japan in 1938 to gather historical materials. References to Hani's writings and *Nihon shihonshugi hattatsushi kōza* appear for the first time in the footnotes to *Soldier*, published in 1943 and researched while he was working at the Canadian embassy in Tokyo between 1940 and 1941. Clearly, Norman had some conscious reason for keeping references to the Kōza school to a minimum.

Consider the well-known debate over whether and to what extent the peasant uprisings of the late Tokugawa–early Meiji period were revolutionary. Its protagonists were Kokushō Iwao and Ono Takeo, later Kokushō and Hani. In *Emergence* Norman cites Kokushō's study [*Hyakushō ikki no kenkyū*, 1928] but he makes Fujii Jintarō and Ono the main participants in the controversy and fails to mention Hani. Let me cite another instance. *Emergence* (173) presents the thesis that 'the impelling force of the liberal movement [Freedom and People's Rights Movement, TS] came from the great mass of small peasants, tenants, and city poor who rallied to it urging the reduction of taxes, and the establishment of representative institutions, even demanding representation in the liberal movement.' This thesis corresponds with Hirano Yoshitarō's point in *Nihon shihonshugi shakai no kikō* (163) that 'it was precisely such small peasants and city poor, together with the former semi-feudal tenants (and tenants caught up in semi-feudal production relations who were being driven off the land in increasing numbers) who became the propulsive force of the bourgeois "Freedom and People's Rights Movement."'[9] Norman, in his footnote on this issue, refers to a book by Ono Takeo and the account of Osatake Takeshi and Hayashi Shigeru in *Gendai Nihonshi kenkyū* [A Study of Contemporary Japanese History]. Hirano's book is cited chiefly to introduce historical facts and materials; it seems as though Norman deliberately tried to avoid specifying it as the basis for an important historical judgment.

Given Norman's character and the great importance he attached to friendship, it is quite possible that, at a time when Japan-U.S. relations had reached a low ebb, he worried over the effect that the publication of *Emergence* would have on Japanese materialist historians. The work was, after all, a historical critique of Japanese militarism. He may also have been concerned with the reaction of American public opinion because of his relationship with Harvard University, his place of study up to that time, and with the Institute of Pacific Relations (IPR), his publisher. There is no denying the caution which led him to request, just prior to his death, postponement of publication in Japanese of a new edition of *Soldier*.[10] This was the demonstration of an astute political sense and the importance he attached to 'public affairs,' or to the duties of a citizen in a society of 'self-government' (*Clio*, 96, 31).

I am not competent to discuss the role and nature of the IPR; but according to Warren Cohen (professor at Michigan State University), at the time of the Manchurian Incident the IPR, which included an American Council, as well as Japanese and Chinese councils, was still politically neutral. However, beginning with the outbreak of the

Japan-China War in 1937, private organizations concerned with America's Asian policy proliferated and the American Council of the IPR 'secretly' supported the most famous of them, the 'American Committee on Non-Participation in Japanese Aggression' (established 1938).[11] When Norman wrote his 'Author's Preface' to *Emergence* (dated 1 January 1940), Japanese-American relations were deteriorating rapidly, but they still had not reached a deadlock. Japan-U.S. talks started in November 1939 between Foreign Minister Nomura Kichisaburō and Ambassador Joseph Grew. The international situation was complex and touchy. The conclusion of the German-Soviet Non-Aggression Pact in August 1939 strengthened anti-Soviet, anti-communist feeling among the American people and complicated the Japan-U.S. negotiations, while isolationist and pro-German sentiments appeared for a while to dominate American opinion.[12] Although the American council of the IPR was turning gradually in an antifascist, anti-Japanese direction, *Emergence* was published as a volume in the Far Eastern Relations Inquiry Series of its International Secretariat. It was thus understandable that its author would take pains to avoid quoting from materialist historians, particularly works of the Kozā school, which reflected the theoretical position of the Japan Communist party. He probably expected that his analyses and conclusions would be more effective if based on the works of the socio-economic history school and the positivist school, the mainstream of Japanese historiography.

The next work, *Soldier*, has a preface dated April 1943. Approximately two years earlier, in June 1941, the German-Soviet war had begun; in December the Pacific War erupted; the United States, Britain, and the Soviet Union established their antifascist alliance, and their peoples became united in the struggle against fascism. In both scholarship and the arts, American friendship with the Soviet people blossomed and exchanges with Marxists briefly flourished. Thus at the time he wrote *Soldier*, Norman did not need to take public opinion into account, as he did at the time of *Emergence*.

Such is my understanding of the circumstances surrounding the publication of *Emergence* and *Soldier*. I do not say there is proof that these circumstances affected Norman's citations, but it is likely because works of history, like historians themselves, are products of their age. Yet, along with the influences of such external circumstances there was, I think, a subjective reason, stemming from his scholarship, that Norman avoided citing Kōza-ha works: the spirit in which Norman approached historical research was different from that which supported the theoretical views of the Kōza school. I will elaborate on this statement later. Let me say now, to avoid misunderstanding, that my conjecture that Norman learned more from the works of dialectical materialist historians, including members of the Kōza school, than his footnotes indicate, does not mean that I believe he adopted the methodology of dialectical materialism or that I think he relied heavily on the Kōza school. However, starting with his maiden work and continuing throughout his scholarly life, Norman's historical research reflected a critical evaluation of contemporary politics. Any outstanding historiography is a product of the tense interaction between critical concern for the present and the demands of objectivity imposed by the discipline of history. Norman's critical concern for contemporary politics is apparent in his repeated emphasis, in lectures and essays, on the value of freedom of speech and thought.

Norman's view of history is amply discussed, particularly in his study of Andō Shōeki and in *Kurio no kao*. The tenor of his thought is revealed in the following statements: 'But even in Japanese feudalism, the historian must beware of such simple formulae as "the people" versus despotic power.'[13] 'How dangerous it is to distinguish great political struggles by painting them black and white' (*Clio*, 75). 'I hope I have learned to beware of some of the more stereotyped views of the [French] Revolution as to both its causes and effects' (*Clio*, 108). 'History has never been a straight line nor a simple equation of cause and effect nor the victory of right over wrong nor an inevitable progress from darkness to light' (*Clio*, 12). Such were the things he warned against. What he wanted to emphasize was that 'history being by its nature a subtle and complex discipline, when abused, is bound to lead us into pitfalls' (*Clio*, 97), and that 'increasing our sense of the complexity of history [should] save us from becoming dogmatic or fanatical in our historical judgment' (*Clio*, 105).

I strongly believe that there is common ground between Norman's view of history and G.B. Sansom's. Sansom also said: 'I think that our Western studies of Japanese history would advance more rapidly and more usefully if we could – for a time at least – abandon our preconceived notions as to what is good and what is wise.' On another occasion he added, in connection with foreign pressure during the

Bakumatsu period, that since the lasting effect of international exchange is something which appears over a long period of time, 'it is impossible to make deterministic conclusions.' 'All we can do is examine the constantly unfolding situation and from there try to draw out some moderate interpretations.'[14] These words, like Norman's, describe the modest approach of the historian to the subtlety and complexity of history. The two men had in common a background as diplomats and outstanding scholars of Japanese history. Sansom, as the senior historian, wrote the preface to *Soldier*, and in the text of his *The Western World and Japan* he gave Norman the highest commendation: 'For a penetrating analysis of early industrialization, with its political and social concommitants, the reader is referred to the excellent work of Herbert Norman, *Japan's Emergence As a Modern State*, which is full of good historical data and valuable commentary.'[15]

Sansom speaks of 'a long tradition of the liberal humanities in the West';[16] Norman, too, states, 'It is not too strong to say that no person can be cultivated who has not a feeling for history.' Certainly the historical works of both men are permeated with the richness of a humanistic education grounded in the Greek and Roman classics. In his essays Norman sometimes abruptly inserts pointed barbs about the present, to the reader's delight. That can be called a characteristic of narrative in the tradition of European humanistic historiography, but not of Marxism or of Japanese historiography. One might add, however, that this habit does not enhance the methodological rigor of the discipline of history. Never the less, Norman could not avoid injecting a touch of humour. Let me give one example. In *Soldier*, after having cited the episode in which Ōmura Masujirō, leader of Chōshū han's *kiheitai* [shock troops], criticized a comrade 'who offended him by wearing his long samurai sword during a conference,' Norman immediately added: 'Ōmura might well be startled were he alive today to see the fashion now current in the Japanese army where it is a common sight to see an officer trundling about with a long cumbersome samurai sword at his side' (*Soldier*, 35). One might criticize this as an unhistorical comparison, but one can also admire it as a clever historical criticism which epitomized accurately the historically regressive character of the Imperial army at that time.

The kind of historical writing that is steeped in the humanistic tradition flourishes better in random essays than in scholarly treatises that follow rigid logic and systematic organization. It is perhaps at its best in treatments of personalities. The account of John Aubrey's collection of biographies, which appears in *Clio*, is a good example; Norman's comparative studies show the same strength. In *Andō Shōeki*, he explained that 'since we have so few biographical and literary details concerning Shōeki, a comparative approach, if not pursued too systematically when it would become both tiresome and misleading, might bring into relief different aspects of his many-sided thought, suggesting also how it was conditioned by his intellectual and social environment' (298). Norman's use of a comparative historical approach, well documented and drawing on ancient and modern, Eastern and Western sources, makes the reader feel that he is glimpsing an accurate image of Andō Shōeki.

The comparative element also explains why Sansom's historiography is so enjoyable. He says at the beginning of *Japan in World History*:

There is a kind of history – so some historians allege – which deals with great events and from which we can draw useful inferences; which furnishes us not only with understanding of the past but with material for predicting the future. This is history on a grand scale. It deals with trends and forces and the lives of great men. But it is not the kind of history I have in mind. I am thinking of what the French call 'la petite histoire'; of everyday life as it is lived not by prime ministers and secretaries of state and other historical figures who are or ought to be exceptional, but by ordinary human beings who in their communities and societies make the raw material from which history is shaped.[17]

Sansom sought 'la petite histoire' in cultural history and also in biographical studies of personalities; one can see that the strong point of Norman's historiography also lay in the smaller histories of communities of ordinary human beings. He wrote, 'I like to see [Andō] as the uncompromising enemy of tyranny and oppression, who spurned the conventional defence of feudal rule peddled by the obsequious scholar-official, and on the other hand as the vehement spokesman of the voiceless millions of his countrymen' (*Andō Shōeki* 319–20). And again: 'Brave deeds, the marching and counter-marching of armies, the declarations of politicians somehow leave Clio unmoved. She seems to be impressed rather by the laborious efforts of a people who, unaware of their individual importance, contribute their anonymous might in creating the treasures of some culture or by those who have vigilantly guarded a humane precedent or revived some forgotten liberty' (*Clio*, 80). Maruyama Masao titled his eulogy of Norman 'An Affection for the Lesser Names' – how aptly it captures the distinctive feature of Norman's historiography.[18]

Norman says, 'While for many the study of history can be a relaxation, a delight and a pleasure, it is, I am convinced, in the last analysis a habit of the most civilizing nature.' Norman's character as a historian is shaped by the interaction of two sometimes antithetical convictions: that history is to be enjoyed, even reveled in, and that history has the duty and function to 'help to make us live peacefully and co-operatively with all mankind' (*Clio*, 111).

Norman must have enjoyed displaying his personal feelings in *la petite histoire*. But as Sansom says, it is the duty of the historian at the same time to write 'history on a grand scale' which 'furnishes us ... with material for predicting the future.' *Emergence* was regarded, perhaps by Norman himself, as his representative work; a judgment in which I concur. The view of history which lies at the heart of *Emergence* is basically identical with that discussed in *Clio*, although in the former the influence of materialist historiography is more pronounced.

The distinctive approach to history revealed in *Emergence* leads to two apparently self-contradictory assessments. For example, in that work Norman clearly describes the Meiji government as 'autocratic' and 'absolutist,' but says 'it is a cause for amazement that its leaders accomplished so much rather than a cause for blame because they had to leave so much undone in the way of democratic and liberal reform' (47). Moreover, while he states that farmers, *rōnin*, and lower-class samurai constituted a direct threat to Tokugawa rule, he maintains that peasant revolts were stimulated by opposing impulses, one anti-feudal and one reactionary.

Norman once more offers a dualistic assessment in his comments about the remnants of feudal relations in the Meiji Restoration: 'The anomalous, the accidental and the outmoded have been turned to good purpose; a weakness, if you like to call it that, has been transformed into an advantage' (*Emergence*, 9). What he calls a 'good purpose' and an 'advantage' is the comparatively rapid and smooth achievement of national integration and industrialization. Depending on the perspective, 'weakness' can appear to be an advantage or, simultaneously, a liability. The evaluation of historical figures and phenomena is dynamic, not immutable. For example, Norman states that the Meiji leaders, intent on maintaining Japan's independence, prudently avoided relying too heavily on foreign capital. Nevertheless, he notes, that policy only pushed 'the predominant position of state enterprise supported by the financial oligarchy, the retardation of the tempo of industrialization, and the heavier tax burdens on the population, particularly on the agricultural community' (117). Norman's assessment of both motivation and result serves to highlight the problem of how much choice the political leaders had under the specific historical conditions of the Meiji period. From an examination of domestic and international conditions he concluded that the options for Japan in the transition from feudalism to capitalism were fewer than in the cases of some advanced modern countries. Conditions, says Norman, dictated the rapid achievement of modernization and of integration of the state, and those goals required autocratic power, which in turn made independence without insurrection possible. 'It was only through an absolutist state that the tremendous task of modernization could be accomplished without the risk of social upheaval which might attend the attempts to extend the democratic method in a nation which had emerged so suddenly and so tardily from feudal isolation' (102). Needless to say, this evaluation does not mean that *Emergence* attempted a whitewash of absolutism. The theme of the entire narrative is the way the power of the people influenced the course of history, and the process of the growth and collapse of liberal opposition groups.

Norman's evaluation of history can be criticized as being syncretic or relativist. But while he cautioned against determinism and dogmatism, he did not go to the opposite extreme of trivial relativism. In his words, the 'central problem of history is to discover and explain the nature of change whether in nations or states ... The crucial problem is to distinguish between deceptive surface changes and those that are deep and therefore harder to detect but in the long run of the most decisive character' (*Clio*, 8). To fix one's attention on changes that are 'deep' and 'of the most decisive character' is to probe deeply into the laws of historical development, regardless of whether one's understanding diverges from historical materialism. He attacked uncritical admiration of Japan's modernization in the context of the laws of history: 'This often condescending admiration whose object is worthy of a more understanding if less effusive appreciation, becomes at times quite fatuous in its talk about the "miracle" of Japan, as if, somehow, Japanese development had transcended all the laws of history and nature' (*Emergence*, 207).

In making historical evaluations, he used a variety of yardsticks and sought to express the 'delicacy and complexity' of history; yet he took pains to focus on what is most essential. In determining the role and position of different political groups he observed: 'To ascribe to each group its own proper position, its relation to other parties of society, to judge between any of these groups and say this one is master and that one servant, this would be something of a Sisyphean task, but one which none the less ought to be shouldered' (*Emergence*, 209). To determine what is basic is neither determinism nor dogmatism. To search for the essentials is a task, he tells himself, which the historian must shoulder, no matter how Sisyphean it may seem. This is precisely Norman's attitude in conducting historical research.

What, then, is Norman's basic frame of reference? It is the general process of the formation and development of capitalism. *Emergence* points out the link between the overthrow of Tokugawa feudalism 'from above' and the curbing of the antifeudal struggles by the peasantry and city poor 'from below.' At the same time, he says it is difficult to accept Freda Utley's interpretation that the Restoration reforms were 'not a revolution for emancipation from feudalism, but rather a counter-revolution to re-establish the power of the feudal military aristocracy to which they [lower-class samurai and *ronin*, TS] belonged.' Instead, Norman places the basic significance of the Restoration on the following very explicit point: '[T]he Meiji Restoration ... represents an anti-feudal movement inasmuch as it broke through feudal particularism and opened the way for a new State and all that it implied, the creation of a national market, a revolution in property relations – in short a modern capitalist society' (*Emergence*, 43). He also says that the 'garish luster' of contemporary Japan, where the development of large-scale industry took place while feudal relations remained in the villages, was historically determined, the product of a modernization that had only two generations behind it. 'For good or ill, as the industrial civilization of New Japan grows, it will scarcely leave any space for the patriarchal and often genial traditions of its medieval past' (*Emergence*, 9). Although the process of Japan's capitalist transformation differs from that of England and France, Norman's investigations convinced him that in the long run Japanese capitalism had to develop according to the same laws that governed capitalism everywhere.

Norman's interpretations of Japan's modern history differ from those of the Kōza school, for example, in his views of the Restoration, the role played by Meiji leaders, and the feudal legacy. His views are rather closer to the positions of the Rōnō school or the socio-economic history school. The Kōza school, as it is generally understood, emphasizes the basic factors and structural characteristics of historical developments; it disregards secondary elements. It concentrates on structural analysis rather than the explanation of change. A content analysis of *Emergence* seems to corroborate my original supposition that the essential nature of Norman's scholarship was incompatible with the propensities of the Kōza school.

To counter the charge that historiography centred on evaluating the development of capitalism is historical materialism, let me borrow an idea from Carr – that the historian advances his work through the 'dual and apparently contradictory process' of the simplifying and multiplying of causes. Speaking of the conflict between determinism and free will in history, Carr remarked that 'all human actions are both free and determined, according to the point of view from which one considers them.'[19] Historical materialism tries to demonstrate that class struggle and socialist revolution are the inevitable results of the economic factor in history. However, by making his frame of reference the development of capitalism and modernization, Norman tried to indicate his confidence in the advance of freedom and progress towards democracy. As he explained in a special introduction to the Hakujitsu Shoin version of *Soldier and Peasant* (translated by Kugai Saburō), 'In the conclusion to this book I ventured to point out that at the time of the Meiji Restoration and in the most important subsequent periods, the Japanese people, for many complex reasons, were unable to achieve with their own strength the overthrow of the forces of despotism and feudalism, which was absolutely necessary for the creation of a democratic, peaceful nation' [translated from the Japanese]. But that only shows that 'the cause of liberty can best be served ... by the conviction that further progress can come only by pursuing long and often circuitous routes' (*Clio*, 83); and it is not an expression of disbelief in the law of progress in history. The proof is to be seen in the preface to *Soldier and Peasant*, where Sansom states that 'the record does not show the Japanese people as traditionally subservient. They have displayed the virtues of patience and loyalty, but in their national character there can also be detected a certain turbulence, a disposition to resist authority too flagrantly abused' (xi). These may be seen as words spoken in behalf of, and in sympathy with, Norman's attempt to clarify the record of resistance of the Japanese people. Norman probably saw in Sansom a friend who understood him. Despite the many differences in their historical views, I see evidence of common ground.

As an attempt at 'relating to the present some of the generalizations drawn from an earlier age,' *Emergence* was written with the hope that the reader would be 'constantly keeping the present in mind' (3). Similarly, the significance of *Soldier* was summed up by Sansom as follows: 'This essay on the origins of conscription in Japan is not, as the casual reader of its title might suppose, a little excursus for the pleasure of historians, of no interest to students of the present. To my mind it constitutes an admirable lesson to the generals and the privates of the great army of writers on contemporary Far Eastern Affairs' (ix). Thus the two books dealt with the Meiji period, but Norman and Sansom both insisted that they were really works of contemporary history. When, during World War II, the forces of antifascism and antimilitarism pushed European historiography towards contemporary 'relevance,' Norman stood in the vanguard. It is not only Marxist historians who based the critique of the present on historical studies, or whose keen awareness of contemporary issues inspired historical analysis. In what might be called his last testament, *A Vindication of History*, the French historian Marc Bloch, who perished in the anti-German resistance movement, quoted these words of his teacher, Henri Pirenne: 'If I were an antiquarian I would only have eyes for the old. But I am an historian and that is why I love life ... This ability to understand living things is surely the outstanding characteristic of the historian.'[20] To become such a historian, 'there is no way but to be in constant contact with the present' [translation from the Japanese]. This 'constant contact' with the present caused Bloch to join the resistance in 1940. The same concerns imparted to Norman's scholarship an underlying element of criticism of contemporary political trends. Calmly and indomitably he resisted the slanders of McCarthyism in order to defend to the last his position.

The American modernization theorists are mistaken in asserting that, because Norman's work incorporated the fruits of Marxist historiography, he was warmly welcomed by historians in post-war Japan where the materialist view of history has been a powerful influence. On the contrary, what drew Japanese historians to Norman's writings was the discovery in them of the expression par excellence of a European historiographical tradition that was open to Marxist scholarship, and a productive ground for mutual criticism and dialogue between Marxist and non-Marxist historians. Japanese Marxist historians did not find in the work of their non-Marxist colleagues the same 'ground' that they found in Norman, although controversy over the works of Ōtsuka Hisao and Maruyama Masao did spark the beginning of a short-lived dialogue between Marxism and non-Marxism. As a result, they placed too much emphasis on Norman, a fact that shows the weakness of Japanese historiography in the 1950s. Their basic intent, however, comes out clearly in reviews at the time of Norman's works, in the record of a roundtable discussion with Norman, and in his eulogies.

Today once again Norman's work needs to be reread and restudied, by Japanese as well as American and European historians. First, because increasing specialization and fragmentation of historial studies has deprived history of 'much of the human quality that should be inherent in it' (*Clio*, 7). It is necessary to reconstruct a historiography which reflects 'the broad sweep of history written in the grand manner' or, somewhat more accurately, which reflects the consciousness that 'what is important in history is the grand outline and the significant detail' (*Clio*, 93). Secondly, the effort is needed to develop a perspective completely different from modernization theory – or from John W. Hall's notion that the historian must 'detach himself from the actual flow of history around him' if he is to create value-free criteria for comparative study.[21] Although I do not think the nearly decade-long effort of the 'Conference on Modern Japan' was entirely useless, the results of that discussion proved for me that a unified, comprehensive grasp of history obliges one to make value judgments. The historian cannot possibly 'detach himself from the actual flow of history.' To maintain the autonomy of the discipline of history, he must grapple with the flood of facts, but the way in which he does so will differ according to his view of history.

To develop creativity in contemporary historical studies it is important to establish a common ground of mutual understanding and mutual criticism. We ought to find suggestions and encouragement in Norman's work in our attempts to resolve these problems. Maruyama Masao, who was in the United States from 1975 to 1976 wrote that 'it was a great joy for me to discover that, in contrast to the early 1960s when I visited Harvard, American scholars are beginning to appreciate my friend [Norman] whom I loved and respected.'[22] This appraisal of Norman is a turning point for American scholars.

NOTES

1 From *The Japan Interpreter* 13 (Summer 1980): 1–14, translated from the Japanese by Herbert P. Bix and appearing originally in *Shisō* 634 (April 1977): 26–36 under the title 'Nōman shigaku no hyōka no mondai.' Reprinted with the permission of *The Japan Interpreter*. [Translator's note: Norman's continuing significance in Japan is attested by the recent appearance of his collected works in four beautifully translated volumes by Ōkubo Genji, who also wrote detailed biographical notes and explanations to accompany each volume. His exemplary notes constitute the basis for a future biography of Norman's life and work. HB]
2 John W. Dower, 'E.H. Norman, Japan and the Uses of History,' in J.W. Dower, ed., *Origins of the Modern Japanese State* (New York: Pantheon Books 1975), 31–2. This essay relates the political circumstances in wartime and post-war Japan and America to trends in historical scholarship in both countries, gives a detailed examination of Norman's writings, and argues for their reinstatement.
3 [Citations in this article from *Kurio no kao* refer to the Japanese edition used by Tōyama, though quotations from Norman's work were all checked with the original English manuscript (unpublished).]
4 James W. Morley, ed., *Dilemmas of Growth in Prewar Japan* (Princeton: Princeton University Press 1972), 25
5 John K. Fairbank, *The United States and China*. Revised edition (New York: The Viking Press 1958), 274
6 E.H. Carr, *What Is History?* (New York: Alfred P. Knopf 1962), 120–1
7 New York: Institute of Pacific Relations 1940. All citations refer to this edition.

8 Reprint by Institute of Pacific Relations, 1943. All citations refer to this edition.

9 Iwanami Shōten 1977, p. 163.

10 Norman's last letter, written to Okubo Genji two days before his death, is introduced by Okubo in the 'Afterword' of his translation of *Soldier and Peasant* in the Iwanami Shōten edition.

11 Warren I. Cohen, 'The Role of Private Groups in the United States,' in Dorothy Borg and Shumpei Okamoto, eds, *Pearl Harbor as History: Japanese-American Relations 1931–41* (New York: Columbia University Press 1973), 428–58

12 Robert E. Sherwood, *Roosevelt and Hopkins: An Intimate History* (New York: Harper and Brothers 1948), 127

13 *Andō Shōeki and the Anatomy of Japanese Feudalism,* in *Transactions of the Asiatic Society*. 3rd ser., vol. 2, December 1949. Subsequent references in the text abbreviated as *Andō Shōeki*.

14 George Sansom, *Japan in World History* (New York: IPR 1951), 26–7

15 London: The Cresset Press 1950, 499

16 Sansom, *Japan in World History*, 3

17 Ibid., 44

18 Maruyama Masao, *Senchū to sengo no aida* (Between Wartime and Postwar) (Tokyo: Misuzu Shobō 1976), 620. Maruyama's eulogy appears in the present volume, pp. 81–6.

19 Carr, *What is History?*, 118, 124

20 Marc Bloch, *Apologie pour l'histoire ou métier d'historien* (Paris: Armand Colin 1952), 13

21 John W. Hall, 'Changing Conceptions of the Modernization of Japan,' in Marius B. Jansen, ed., *Changing Japanese Attitudes Toward Modernization* (Princeton: Princeton University Press 1965), 14

22 Maruyama, *Senchū*, 63

Part Three

Norman on Freedom

Much of what has been written in the preceding pages has concerned Norman's political beliefs, his ideological commitments, his scholarly debt to this or that school of Japanese historiography, and so on. This is all well and proper and totally befitting a Festschrift of this sort, but in the end it remains inadequate to the task of explaining Norman. To fully understand this writer, scholar, diplomat, and political victim, Norman's words themselves must be read. This final section of the book provides this opportunity.

Of the four chapters which follow, one ('People under Feudalism') has previously appeared in print in English. The others have been heretofore inaccessible to English-reading audiences. Each of the readings in its own way is important in providing valuable insight into Norman's views on, respectively, the impact of Japan's feudal past on its post-war politics, the meaning of democracy in the context of the occupation and the emerging Cold War, the importance of understanding history in interpreting the present, and the value of East Asian studies to a liberal education.

*The one continuous thread that ties these ostensibly different topics together is the concept of freedom. Though the problem of establishing a condition of freedom is present, of course, in all Norman's earlier writings (*Japan's Emergence 1940; Soldier and Peasant 1943; *and* Feudal Background 1945*), nowhere is it of greater concern nor more systematically treated by Norman than in the following articles written between 1947 and 1954. The reason for this difference is obvious. Whereas his earlier writings were academic, objective, and aimed at a scholarly audience, these later essays are non-academic, openly subjective as 'reflections' of this sort always are, and were addressed to different sorts of publics whom Norman sought to convince as well as to inform. A coarse contrast, not altogether unfair, might suggest that the earlier writings were written in his head, the later ones in his heart.*

The first of these essays, 'People under Feudalism' (1947), is probably the most academic of the four. Yet his objective is not so much to inform his Japanese audience as to make it understand that the legacy of feudal rule in Japan made extremely difficult the establishment of a condition of freedom in modern Japan. Norman identifies 'induced social indifference' and political passivity of the Japanese people as an effect of centuries of oppressive feudal rule and as causes of later Japanese aggression abroad. He argues that despite the 'inherent humanity and decency of the common people,' years of subjection to government practices of censorship, legalized torture, and secrecy conditioned Japan's common people to accept oppression at home and imperialism abroad as the normal state of affairs. Just how a people of a feudal temper prone to political passivity escaped from this sorry legacy Norman brilliantly suggests in the closing portion of his 1947 speech. In an analysis that some today might call 'neo-Marxist,' Norman argues that the capitalist mode of agricultural production, pioneered by the farmers of Nagano, induced a 'progressive spirit' of politically enlightened self-interest that caused rural folk to be 'less docile to unbridled authority' and then, during the occupation, more 'receptive to the [democratic] reforms that have been carried out.' Whether one agrees with the economic basis of this analysis or not, it must be acknowledged that it was strikingly original and suggestive thirty-five years ago.

It can reasonably be guessed that Norman believed the rise of capitalism was a precondition of a popular democratic drive for the kind of self-government he describes in his 1948 address 'Persuasion or Force.' In this essay, however, there is no hint of anything like a Marxist analysis suggesting that base determines superstructure. Rather Norman writes as a social contractarian who sees government as 'a representative committee into whose hands' a freedom-loving people has 'temporarily granted executive authority to act on behalf of the whole community for a limited period of time.' This state of affairs, necessary to a condition of political freedom, he makes clear, was by no means predetermined by ironclad economic laws of history, Marxist or otherwise, but instead freedom developed along an unknown course, 'tortuous, [and] leading sometimes into a cul-de-sac from which painful detours [had] to be made.' Once arrived at, freedom of expression in all its varied forms helped maintain a condition of freedom which, Norman says, was promoted and defended by aristocrats and common people alike.

If these first two speeches of Norman's are marked by a tone that would seem to quite naturally resonate from a reformist and democratic occupier in the immediate post-war period, then his 1953 article 'On the Modesty of Clio' reveals the sober and reflective musings of a scholar qua diplomat who had been suddenly removed from the centre ring of the circus of political activity. Though no less concerned here with the problem of freedom than before, by 1953 Norman had been victimized by the bastardized McCarthyite version of free expression – slander – and thus could painfully reflect on the demagogue who 'defiles the sacred words of liberty and freedom,' as well as on 'the strong men of history' who, like Alexander the Great in Gordos, 'cut through complex social and political problems by some swift act of military movement or dictatorial decree.' Clearly, the McCarthyites in the first instance and Douglas MacArthur in the second served as his models of men who lack an appreciation of the complexity of history (and its muse Clio), and therefore a proper appreciation of the meaning of freedom. Given the time and the political climate in which he wrote this article, and the targets of his ire, it should come as no surprise to learn that Norman chose to have this piece published in Japanese only.

A year later, now safely ensconced in the more civil atmosphere of New Zealand, Norman returned to a topic of discussion for which he was particularly well suited – 'The Place of East Asian Studies in the Modern University (1954).' This address in the most concrete of terms is really a plea for institutionalizing liberal values in the university. These, he made clear, are the product of a broad, cosmopolitan education that encompasses the humanities and the sciences. In such an educational setting, Asian studies have a place; their 'scope wide enough to appeal to the philosopher or man of public affairs, to humanist, philologist, historian or artist.' Truly learned people, he was saying, if some freedom in interpretation might be permitted, will most likely understand the vital importance of free expression to the maintenance of an open society. This lesson, timeless in its import, is one that all his writings sought to communicate. May it never be forgotten.

People under Feudalism[1]

I would like to express my deep sense of appreciation to the sponsors of this meeting and to the citizens of Nagano for the very kind reception they have extended to me in connection with the memorial service for my father. When I lived here in Nagano as a boy I never imagined that I would return after twenty years to give a speech here. Although I am not fond of public speaking, I feel most honoured by the occasion and I am therefore very happy to stand here before you.

I have chosen the subject of my address for today partly because, when requested to make this speech, I was told to choose some historical topic in which I was interested, and the study of the late Tokugawa and the early Meiji periods has been my special interest; and partly because from a topic of this rather wide nature I hope to be able to draw some wide generalizations. These generalizations, I fear, may be only too commonplace to you, and some of them may also be wide of the mark. However, I can only ask for your sympathetic understanding, especially for a foreigner rash enough to address you in your own language on a subject from your history; but more particularly, on this occasion perhaps I can expect the tolerance and generous partiality of the citizens of a city who on this occasion are extending their hospitality to a returned son of the city.

It has been for many years, and particularly during the war years, a favourite pastime of foreign observers of Japan to generalize about the nature of the Japanese people. As these observations are often drawn from a rather limited first-hand observation, or even in more cases from a second- or third-hand knowledge, a commentator can prove that almost any set of qualities is inherent in the Japanese. For instance, one can draw up a list of complete contrasts from the remarks of such observers; for instance, that the Japanese are rigid and highly conventional in their behaviour and, on the other hand, that they are adaptable and quick to change their views; that they are docile and submissive, and again that they are turbulent and easily excitable; that they are painstakingly polite and, on the other hand, insensitive and thoughtless; that they are frugal and thrifty on the one hand and pleasure-loving and lavish on the other; that they are brave and fearless of death, yet are timid, especially in matters of civic life; that they are highly disciplined, and yet their army has revealed many instances of insubordinate behaviour. This sort of contrast could be extended, and no one would be the wiser for it.

I venture to suggest that these sets of contradictions in the Japanese character might be resolved if we approached the subject historically. This may be a pet idea of mine since I am more addicted to history than any other study, but I do feel that foreign observers should guard against viewing the Japanese as a mysterious and inscrutable people whose behaviour and institutions are immune to rational analysis and understanding. It has become fashionable to say that foreigners can only come to understand them intuitively by long years of experience. Yet I believe they can be described as culturally predictable and as following patterns of behaviour which can be understood to the extent that people will take the trouble to study their history and institutions.

Following the historical approach, I think that if one knew enough about the early epochs of Japanese history (for instance, Heian, Kamakura, Tokugawa) and took into account the effects of borrowing Chinese institutions which proved durable in Japan, one could, I believe, understand the social behaviour of the people of those ages. What I shall attempt to do in a very limited fashion this afternoon is to depict something of the people's life under late feudalism and to draw from that two or three political deductions.

Feudalism in general, and more particularly Tokugawa feudalism, was characterized by the following features: the strict separation of classes, or rather the freezing of classes; the binding of peasants to the soil through the prohibition of the right of free movement; the prohibition of free trade and manufacture; the enforcement of hereditary professions through the elaborate systems of guilds; the enforced disarming of the common people and, especially since the days of Hideyoshi, the right to bear arms restricted to the privileged class, the samurai; the strict and minute control by superiors of the private affairs, such as marriage, of their inferiors, or of lords over their vassals and of heads of families over the members of their families; the enforcement of the idea of collective responsibility, particularly for the collection of taxes and the control of crime; and, in the field of ideas, the strict prohibition of heterodox philosophy and the suppression of Christianity.

If we approach the subject from the philosophy of the privileged class, we might summarize the feudal government in the following way. The Tokugawa rulers, although acknowledging continually their debt to the orthodox school of Confucianism, acted on the principle of the Chinese political school of Legalists, notably Han Fei Tzu and Kuan Tzu. In their own day, the Legalists in China were regarded as iconoclasts because they rejected the appeals to tradition and the reliance on supernatural guidance, and based government on the principle of 'actual facts of the world as it now exists.' They might be described as pragmatists, or better, amoralists. To what extent their philosophy was consciously adopted by the Tokugawa Bakufu, I am unable to say, but the guiding principles of the Bakufu were amazingly close to the principles of these Legalists. These are the dominant principles: (1) The only good is that which benefits the state. (2) There is no such thing as private morality, but only public morality. In this connection, we have the remarkably revealing views of a contemporary, Ogyū Sōrai: 'Morality is nothing but the necessary means for controlling the subjects of the empire. It did not originate with nature, nor with the impulses of man's heart, but it was devised by the superior intelligence of certain sages (seijin), and authority was given to it by the State. Morality may be regarded as a device for governing the people.' To continue the summary of these principles: men are evil by nature and can only be influenced by fear of drastic punishment, on the one hand, and by the temptation of lavish rewards on the other; because human nature is depraved, harsh law is necessary; the ruler of the state is concerned with strengthening its military power; people have no rights but only public duties.

Let us examine in more detail the principles of government on which the Tokugawa rulers acted. The guiding philosophy of the Tokugawa bureaucracy may be summed up in the well-known phrase, kanson mimpi (revere officials, despise the people). Flowing from this idea, which reflects a basic fear of the people, came the following typical Tokugawa regulations: the people were not allowed to hold public meetings and their right to petition to their lords was strictly controlled, as exemplified in the case of Sakura Sōgorō. People were not permitted to have access to codes of law since, by studying precedence, they might discover means to evade the law. The philosophy of *kanson mimpi* can well be seen in a Chinese maxim which was the favourite of the bureaucrats of the Tokugawa age: 'Make the people obey but do not make them understand.' Despite certain lip service paid to the idea of a benevolent ruler looking after his people, the above principles of government were carried out with remarkable consistency; for example, at the end of the Tokugawa regime in a memorial of Tokugawa Nariaki (Mito) which is very revealing in this connection. He began by stating that the people were the foundation of the state and therefore it was the duty of the administrators of responsibility to take care of them. However, this was only in theory, because he went on to say that if out of solicitude for the welfare of the people the heavy revenues were relaxed, this would only hurt the samurai who lived on rice revenue, and the samurai as the rulers of the state could not be sacrificed, thus there could be no relaxation of the heavy taxation. Furthermore, if once peasants who, he stated, are stupid, experience a relaxation on the part of the government authorities, they would become habituated to concessions and thus would be more difficult to control. Here we have revealed in the memorial of a very astute Tokugawa bureaucrat the idea of the basic opposition of interests in feudal society between rulers and ruled. He was particularly alarmed because of the serious peasant uprisings which had taken place shortly before.

The corollary to this concept of despising the people was the elevating of the samurai to the status of the dominant class; thus we have the maxim governing the Tokugawa legal and social practice: 'Courtesy should not be extended to the commoner and punishment should not be administered to the gentleman.' In fact, one way the samurai could incur official rebuke was to be convicted of leniency to a plebeian. Supporting this whole concept was the authority coming from the legacy of Ieyasu setting up the samurai as the superior of the four classes and enjoining the samurai to cut down a plebeian who did not behave to him in a proper manner. Social status was emphasized by sumptuary edicts which minutely laid down what quality of apparel and what type of clothes different classes and subdivisions of classes were permitted to wear. Most onerous was the system of the *gōnin-gumi* (five-man group) by which individuals were held collectively responsible for the behaviour, debts, and taxes of their group. By this system also mutual espionage was encouraged, particularly with reference to the control and the suppression of Christianity. Nor were even the members of the privileged class immune from the prying into their affairs by the agents of the *ōmetsuke* (chief censors or inspectors) who, together with their other functions, gathered secret information on the activities of feudal lords and reported in confidence to the Shogun on the behaviour of his ministers. Secret agents were similarly active among all classes of people with a view to nipping in the bud even mild opposition to the feudal authorities.

Perhaps the most hateful feature of the administration of justice was the practice of torture. As in most feudal societies, torture was legally recognized as part of the normal judicial procedure, and was never stinted in the cross-examination of suspects and, even worse, of witnesses. These tortures were as grisly as could be imagined, and were designed to break the will of the most resolute spirit. Public executions were a regular feature of punishment for comparatively trivial offences with the purpose of striking terror into the minds of the populace. Nothing was left undone to impress the imagination of the people with the irresistible power, the myriad-eyed vigilance, and the despotism of authority. It was so natural in such a stifling atmosphere that it was said, 'Justice is dark among the upper class and clear among the lower.'

In the world of ideas and of intellect, feudal authorities maintained the strictest control over the importation of foreign ideas, and prohibited the reading and studying of Confucian unorthodox books. An index (*kinsho*) of prohibited books was kept in Nagasaki where the office of the inspector of imported books (*shomotsu-aratameyaku*) banned any books which referred even slightly to Christianity or heterodox Confucian teaching. In 1790 there was a further stringent measure known as the 'prohibition of heresies,' by which unorthodox teaching was more firmly repressed than ever before. In the preamble to this measure, an indication of the intellectual attitude of the feudal authorities can be appreciated when one reads, 'It is enough to follow the books of old, there is no need to write new ones.' Knowledge itself was considered dangerous and likely to disturb the mind of the commonalty; it was to be jealously hoarded by the elite, its transmission to unauthorized persons closely controlled. The mastering of the written language (though Japanese in its syntax, it requires thousands of Chinese characters) was a laborious and time-consuming process; this very difficulty was not unwelcome to the official class since it buttressed the esoteric, exclusive nature of culture and learning. Secrecy became a fetish with the bureaucracy; to keep the people in the dark concerning state affairs became an end in itself. This secrecy was justified on the grounds that the people would be more docile if kept in ignorance of political affairs, as the lord of Echizen wrote to Nariaki of Mito in a private letter: 'What one calls secrecy is meant to prevent commotion in the people's mind.' As a result of this, people had to depend for news upon rumour, and it may be because of these artificial obstacles in the way of getting accurate information that the Japanese community was so prolific in rumours. Even scholars favoured by the feudal authorities were warned not to discuss state matters. For instance, in one official document we read, 'Do not discuss national policy,' while one of the most statesmanlike men of his age, Matsudaira Sadanobu, wrote, 'It is well for a scholar-gentleman to think seriously on the state, it is not well for him to discuss his thoughts on the nation.'

It is no wonder that men with searching minds, who were parched by the dry sands of orthodox learning, who yearned to slake their thirst in the stream of fresh learning and knowledge, eagerly studied Western works, especially Dutch, even at the risk of their lives. Thus the greatest and finest intellectual leaders of that day almost without exception, such as Takashima Shūhan, Sakuma Zōzan (a son of this province), Watanabe Kazan, Takano Chōei, and Hashimoto Sanai, when their intellectual pursuits became known to the authorities, were subjected to persecution, assassinated, executed, or forced to commit suicide. As an anonymous chronicler of that day wrote, 'Among the fifty or sixty executed are the most famous scholars of our country.' One of the great original minds of the middle of the eighteenth century, Andō Shōeki, was scarcely known to his contemporaries, and his work has been lost to the public until modern times.

Finally, as a means of confounding the people's native good sense, corrupting their humanity, and distracting their minds from domestic ills, the authorities deliberately sowed the seeds of hatred for foreign people. With astonishing frankness, one of the Tokugawa edicts began as follows, 'We must make the people hate the foreigner, and the foreigner hate us.'

This whole system of intellectual repression bred the well-known vicious circle, so that by encouraging in the people ignorance, mental sloth, and chauvinism, the rulers themselves became mentally torpid and dull. Except for two or three of the great feudal lords of the late Tokugawa period, it is notorious that most of them became so degenerate, either morally or intellectually, that they were incapable of efficiently managing their clan affairs, so that more and more the management of public affairs came into the hands of the lower-class samurai who, as you know, were to be the leaders of the Meiji Restoration. The general intellectual atmosphere of that age is well summarized by Okuma Shigenobu in his memoirs: 'The binding of the people's freedom was exactly like being entangled in a spider's web. In general, the people had to live under the order "be stupid, be stupid."'

I have tried to give you in a very superficial and, I fear, rather haphazard manner, the general picture of the political philosophy of the feudal authorities, the crushing regulations which they forced upon the people, and finally the obscurantist policy in the field of ideas and intellect, all of which finally left Japan at the end of the Tokugawa period spiritually and intellectually exhausted to such an extent that the effect was felt long into the succeeding era. I wish now to turn to some evidence of the people's reactions to their feudal environment.

Life under the onerous despotism of Tokugawa feudalism left deep imprints on the minds and spirits of the Japanese. And yet, in spite of centuries of isolation and regimentation, I believe it is a remarkable tribute to the inherent humanity and decency of the common people in general that there is considerable evidence that the feudal authorities did not succeed in brutalizing the people or in converting them into fanatical chauvinists. I would like to give two or three examples to illustrate this point. First, there is the very interesting account given by Japanese sailors in the late Tokugawa period describing their humane treatment when they were saved at sea by American mariners. At the end of the description they plaintively asked why their government regarded all foreigners as enemies. 'Foreign sealers treat Japanese mariners well and without meanness. They most kindly received us who had suffered from wind and rain on the high seas or who had endured cruel cold and excessive heat or were ill and without medicine so that both strength and spirit were failing. These foreign sailors in no way hurt our fishing as they are only interested in fishing [seals]. For what reason does our government treat foreigners as enemies?'

More significantly, however, we have the first-hand evidence of the few foreigners who either visited Japan or were shipwrecked and have recorded almost unanimously the kind treatment they were accorded by the common people and, in contrast, the frequent harsh treatment of the officials. Although one might cite several examples, one or two will suffice.

Perhaps the most dramatic was the case of Captain Goloin who, in 1811, was closely bound and sent as a prisoner from Kunishiri to Matsumae. I quote from his memoirs:

In every village, on our arrival and departure, we were surrounded with crowds of both sexes, young and old, whom curiosity to see us drew together; and yet on these occasions we never experienced the slightest insult or offence. All, particularly the women, contemplated us with an air of pity and compassion. If we asked for drink, they were emulous to supply us; many asked permission of our guards to entertain us, and on their request being granted, brought us sake, comfits, fruits, or other delicacies. We were fed cakes secretly when detained in the guard house in Hakodate; I thanked him as well as I was able; and was greatly astonished that a man, who from his dress apparently belonged to the very lowest class, should be actuated by so powerful a feeling of benevolence, as to hazard his own safety for the sake of conveying comforts to an unfortunate stranger.

Secondly, one of the earliest British diplomats in Japan, Sir Ernest Satow, records that in his visit to Chōshu the common people were friendly to his party except when there were samurai or officials present.

Finally, I would like to draw upon that extremely interesting anonymous record, written about 1811, the *Seiji kemmon roku*. After describing the miserable life of the peasants, their poor diet, the exacting tribute they paid and harsh treatment they endured from the local officials, the writer says,

Some people say that there is a difference in the affection and sensibilities of the upper and lower classes, as between parents and children or man and wife, but I do not believe this is so. The poor always endure their hardships helping each other in such ways as they can, even living in each other's houses. On cold winter nights they cover each other with rags or even give them up to others and as they devour their scanty meal they gaze at the bottom of the rice bowl. Their affections are warm so that if a man and wife are absent for a whole day they think it is as long as three years, but in spite of these feelings they have to send their small children to distant provinces to work as apprentices under contract or they may send away the young man who is the chief support of the family.

Thus, in spite of the harshness of life, compassion was still to be found often in lowly and humble quarters, and it is a matter of much encouragement that the core of human decency was not crushed out of the people who lived in such circumstances.

However, it would be expecting too much of the innate goodness of human nature to believe that centuries of feudal rule could not but leave their mark on the social habits and political practices of the Japanese people. A very striking example of the persistence of feudal habits of thought, even in a person who was an outstanding spokesman of liberalism in the early Meiji period, is to be found in the memoirs of Kōno Hironaka. 'As I read it [Mill's *On Liberty*] on horseback their occurred a great revolution in my former thought which had been nourished on classic learning, i.e., Chinese, and which had been strongly influenced by anti-foreign feeling (*Jo-i Ron*). *Except for the moral teaching of loyalty and filial piety* (*chūkō*), my former thought was utterly destroyed and then I understood that we ought to esteem freedom of man and the rights of man.' Even so advanced a thinker as Kōno believed he had achieved a revolution in his thinking, but he excepted from the scope of that revolution the most typical expression of feudal thought, namely *chūkō* (feudal loyalty and filial piety).

I believe that one of the most common features in any oppressive society, not only in the case of Japan, is the tendency for people who are themselves repressed by their superiors to vent their vexation and spleen on someone beneath them. This means, instead of standing up for one's own rights, to accept injustice silently and to get release for resentment by abusing another innocent person. Applying this historically, I think it is no accident that in the early Meiji era, the lower-class samurai, feeling vexed by the government policy of commutation of rice pensions and the loss of special samurai privileges, expressed their resentment by pressing for a campaign against Korea and, failing in that, succeeded later in a punitive campaign against Formosa. Similarly, in more recent times, I believe that many Japanese found a release from the social pressures at home in the harsh treatment of some of their neighbours on the Asiatic mainland.

Another result of the feudal policy of collective responsibility is the comparatively weakly developed sense of individuality. Putting it another way, the individual is sensitive to environment, and except in the case of a very strong character, the social atmosphere is decisive in determining the behaviour of the individual. This may explain why in modern Japan a man behaves differently with his family, in his office, among his friends, or in the army, acting politely and considerately in one place, roughly and harshly in another, yet without feeling any inconsistency in his behaviour. Perhaps the pressure of various social environments on a Japanese makes him act more in conformity with them than with his own individuality; this has given rise to the contradictory description of Japanese qualities which I listed at the beginning of my speech. So strong is the sense of environment that it takes extraordinary moral courage for an individual to act according to his own conscience.

Because in the past the Japanese authorities have discouraged or prevented the people from taking part directly in public affairs, the Japanese have acquired a habit of passivity. This means looking on with folded arms while an injustice is being committed. The need for vigilance in protecting human rights was eloquently expressed by an early English democrat of the seventeenth century in the following words: 'For what is done to any one, may be done to every one: besides, being all members of one body, one man should not suffer wrongfully, but all should be sensible, and endeavour his preservation; otherwise they give way to an inlet of the sea of will and power, upon their laws and liberties; which are the boundaries to keep out tyranny and oppression; and who assists not in such cases, betrays his own rights; and is overrun, and of a free man made a slave when he thinks not of it, or regards it not, and so shunning the censure of turbulency, incurs the guilt of treachery to the present and future generations.'

In former times in Japan only too rarely did one witness that righteous indignation which, when displayed in an effectual and mature fashion, has so often stopped the hand of the tyrant, the bureaucrat, the chauvinist, and the obscurantist. It is perhaps because of this induced social indifference that there has been rather lacking in Japanese culture, especially literature, the quality of compassion (by this I do not mean sentimentality) for the weak and unfortunate.

In conclusion I would like to focus a few remarks on the history of this province. It may have been a blessing in disguise, but Nagano prefecture in feudal times was not one of the prominent rice-producing fiefs. Despite its strategic importance in the balance of clan forces, particularly as seen in the early wars between Takeda Shingen and Uesugi Kenshin, by the late Tokugawa times its position in the feudal economy was such that exactions did not fall so heavily on the people as elsewhere. Following the Meiji Restoration, Nagano forged ahead as one of the most important areas in sericulture and mixed farming. Thus the farmers of Nagano, by producing silk, escaped some of the social and economic implications of the pre-eminently rice-producing areas where there were more marked feudal survivals. The Nagano farmer, by his comparatively early experience with the commercial market, developed a more businesslike and modern psychology, aware of his dependence not only on the Japanese, but on the world market for silk. Thus, many of the Nagano village folk did not remain with their eyes fixed stonily on the ground before them as is often the case in other agricultural areas, but looked beyond the village to a wider horizon. This made for greater initiative in developing agricultural techniques, greater ambition for the education of their families and, in short, a much more progressive spirit than could be found in many other parts of the country. It was the comparatively weaker hold which feudal habits had upon the people of this prefecture, and the corresponding degree of their sturdiness of spirit and independence of mind, which may well have been one of the reasons why my father felt so much at home among the people of this area. It may also be why Nagano people have acquired a reputation which I consider to be highly complimentary to their character, that is, their reputation with old-fashioned bureaucrats of being susceptible to new ideas and less docile to unbridled authority.

I do not think it is any accident that some of the pioneers in the democratic movement in Japan deliberately chose Nagano as one of the chief political bases for their activities. For instance, Nakamura Tahachiro conducted his first compaign for general suffrage in Nagano prefecture. That warm, human-spirited figure, Kinoshita Naoe, as a journalist on the *Shinano mainichi* found this province a congenial milieu for his talents. In more recent times, Nagano prefecture has been justly famous for its comparatively high standard of education and for the high level of literacy which is to be found even in the more remote areas; a tribute both to the zeal for learning on the part of the parents and the children, and to the devotion of the teachers in those villages.

Thanks to the democratic reforms following the war, this prefecture's opportunities for development and progress will be further enhanced, particularly with the new trend towards decentralization. This move towards a greater local autonomy will relieve to a great extent the burden of that heavy-handed bureaucracy in Tokyo, which in former times impeded and depressed the physical and spiritual life of the people of this and other outlying provinces. Just as the people of Nagano emerged eighty years ago from feudalism with a comparatively free, enterprising, and independent spirit to make of their province one of the most advanced areas in Japan, so today Nagano has emerged from the black years of war and oppression with its towns destroyed and the spirit of her people brisk and receptive to the reforms that have been carried out. Therefore I have every confidence and hope that it will hold a high position both in material and cultural progress among all sections of Japan.

NOTE

1 An address delivered by Norman to the citizens of Nagano, Japan, on 21 June 1947. Printed, with an introduction by John W. Dower, in the *Bulletin of Concerned Asian Scholars* 9, no. 2 (April–June 1977): 56–61. Reprinted here with the permission of the *Bulletin*.

Persuasion or Force: The Problem of Free Speech in Modern Society[1]

To speak here in Keio University under the shadow of so fertile and powerful a thinker as Fukuzawa Yukichi demands that one contribute something original, pertinent to current problems, and above all composed in a lucid style. Fully aware of these requirements, I naturally hesitated at first to accept the invitation since I felt unable to guarantee that any talk I could give would meet the demands of such an occasion. When I finally agreed I was none the less keenly sensible both of the honour of speaking on the thirtieth anniversary of the founding of this institute and of the responsibility I have undertaken in appearing here under such auspices.

In endeavouring to meet this responsibility I chose a subject in which I believe Fukazawa himself had shown a deep and sympathetic interest. Accordingly, while I do not flatter myself that Fukuzawa, were he alive, would necessarily agree with all I say, at least I shall try to present the subject in the same spirit of frank inquiry and objectivity with which all his works are informed.

It would not be appropriate or even necessary in this lecture to attempt a review of the history of the struggle for freedom, especially the freedom of speech. But by way of introduction at least I wish to make some generalizations with the purpose of clearing the ground for my central argument.

The twin concepts of freedom and liberty have been the battle cry of oppressed groups since the beginning of recorded history. The nature of that freedom which was demanded has often proved illusory to idealists who expect perfection in this world; it has deceived historians and philosophers who, seeing in later history the frequent betrayals of liberty, have impugned the motives of those early advocates.

Many groups suffering from disabilities or oppression, once they themselves have succeeded in gaining political power, have proved as oppressive as the dominant force which was overthrown or compelled to grant concessions. This has proved particularly true in the history of the religious wars in Europe in the sixteenth and seventeenth centuries. The course of the history of freedom is never along a direct and straight path. Rather is its course tortuous, leading sometimes into a cul-de-sac from which painful detours have to be made. Nevertheless to assume, because the original intentions of reformers and crusaders were not always sufficient in themselves to prevent their ideals from being betrayed, that therefore all future struggle is vain and illusory would be a cowardly surrender profiting only the enemies of freedom. On the contrary, it is precisely from the lessons of past betrayals or frustrations that later leaders in the cause of freedom have profited, laying surer foundations for their own attempts.

If one thing is clear in the history of the modern world, it is that freedom is not something constant and assured like the air around us. It has to be consciously won and jealously guarded. It can be lost through negligence or apathy in countries where it has reigned for many years. Thus, the struggle for freedom is continual, although it need not always assume dramatic or violent form. It is often a prosaic, but none the less important, struggle against apathy, indifference, and cynicism.

Just as the history of liberty is full of ups and downs, of advances and retreats, so it has drawn as its champions men of varied types and abilities. Some leaders have been men of saintly character, unselfish, disinterested, patient, not even shrinking from the certainty of martyrdom – such men as John Huss, Giordano Bruno, Sir John Eliot, and Sir Thomas More. More often they have been persistent, obstinate characters, so single-minded in the pursuit of their chosen goal that they could be termed fanatics. They have often been turbulent, angry, and impatient men, intolerant of all but their own opinion, prickly, irascible, and sometimes as exasperating to their associates as to their enemies. Of this category one might mention the seventeenth-century Leveller John Lilburne and later lovers of liberty such as Tom Paine and William Cobbett. Others again have been more resolute in action than persuasive in speech, leaders completely convinced of the righteousness of their cause even if it led to personal disaster. Such figures were John Brown, Toussaint Louverture, Garibaldi, and Oshio Heihachiro. Others again have been men extraordinarily gifted in eloquence who launched bitter shafts of satire against the thick hide of prejudice, cant, and obscurantism. These men were often vain, jealous of their fellows in the same cause, and greedy of acclaim. One thinks at once of Voltaire. Others again have been men of the world – witty, dissolute, but high-spirited. One could instance John Wilkes and Charles James Fox in eighteenth-century England and Danton in France. Again, there have been indefatigable publicists, superb propagandists in the cause of freedom, men with a gift for popularizing difficult subjects in the interest of public enlightenment. In this field one thinks of the great Diderot, Alexander Herzen, Thomas Jefferson, and pre-eminent in Japan, Fukuzawa Yukichi.

There were also equally courageous and effective leaders of freedom's army such as the burghers and townspeople who endeavoured to make their city an oasis of freedom and culture in the surrounding wilderness of tyranny and violence. While many of their names are unknown to history, one recalls such champions of municipal freedom as Cola di Rienzi in Rome, Etienne Marcel in Paris, James and Philip van Artevelde of Ghent, all men of the fourteenth century; and a most striking example closer to you, the city fathers of Sakai who made of their city, in the words of a contemporary Jesuit missionary, 'the Venice of Japan – free and republican.'

Perhaps more decisive in the campaigns fought on behalf of freedom has been the army of anonymous and less-known humble folk who have provided the rank and file in the battalions of freedom. One thinks of editors of ephemeral journals who were imprisoned for articles that offended tyranny. In passing, I would like to mention the almost forgotten name of Richard Carlisle, the journeyman turned editor, who in nineteenth-century England by his suffering and writing helped perhaps more than any other in winning freedom of the press.

In short, both aristocrats and plebeians, men of wealth and members of the working class, persons of all creeds and character from the saint to the debauchee, people of varied and conflicting motives ranging from the most disinterested and selfless to the vain and egocentric have been enrolled under the banner of liberty. All that Liberty asks of her devotees is that they expend generously and unconditionally in her service what talents and abilities they possess.

The corollary follows that no political party, no religious creed, no social class can claim a monopoly in the service of freedom. It is thus the duty of every citizen to view the struggle for liberty as a vast complex process, keeping clear a broad perspective and realizing that the interests of liberty may be served by many different groups and varied personalities. Many people again have come to look upon the freedom of expression as something of a luxury in politics, such as a motor car or an expensive painting is in private life. That is to say, they look upon freedom as desirable but not essential to normal life. So far from being a luxury or something with which society can dispense as it can some budgetary item, I believe freedom to be the very essence and life-blood of any self-governing society.

I must now digress for a few minutes from my central theme to the closely related question of self-government which I have just raised. I do not wish to be dogmatic in describing what have been and are today self-governing communities. In a modern, complex society no nation can be as completely self-governing as were the ancient city states of Athens or early Rome, where the small number of citizens, the comparative homogeneity of classes, and an intense civic spirit made it possible for any adult male to take direct part in some phase of government. For this reason, Aristotle could not conceive of a state larger than that of 30 000 citizens. Yet insofar as men today strive for a decent and rational way of life, they will endeavour to discover and practise the difficult but only proven means to that end, namely the way of self-government.

Self-government is a word which I prefer to use to describe that way of life which is often summed up by the overworked and even abused catchword – democracy. Now by self-government I do not mean to imply something mystical, abstract, or academic. It is a most reasonable, common-sense, and civilized way of life for any modern society, whether it calls itself republican, a constitutional monarchy, socialist or capitalist, or a mixture of these last two as most societies are today. Self-government is an art which takes time and patience to practise successfully; there must be room for trial and error, and above all it demands of the citizens a high degree of control and understanding. Further, it requires that the people of a community regard their government not as an exterior force to which they look for commands, but as a representative committee into whose hands they have temporarily granted executive authority to act on behalf of the whole community for a limited period of time. Self-government by its nature means that the people look upon government officials as their servants or as their deputies and not as their masters. It is the very opposite of that old concept, *kanson mimpi*.[2] There must therefore be adequate machinery to discipline, direct and, if necessary, dismiss unsatisfactory public servants. Further, it demands of the citizens that they respect each other's rights as jealously as they would their own. Only in this way can the individual have that self-esteem which Fukuzawa so often preached. Such a society will then not only be free in the fullest sense of the word, but genuinely cultured. I think it could be best described in the words of Fukuzawa: 'Cultured liberty is not obtained at the cost of others' freedom; it consists in approving of masses' rights, allowing them to enjoy various advantages, accepting their views, and assisting them to develop themselves to the fullest extent, so that a general equality may be established.'

Now self-government does not meen freedom from control. On the contrary, laws passed by the government are morally binding upon all members precisely because they are presumed to be laws passed with the active approval of the majority of the citizens. This does not mean that a minority cannot criticize existing laws. On the contrary, no matter how important or vital a law may appear to the majority, there should be no restraint on anyone who wishes to discuss or criticize existing or contemplated legislation. But to keep within the bounds of a self-governing society one may use only persuasion and not force. And by force I mean not necessarily riotous behaviour, but even the passive refusal to comply with such laws as conscription, taxation, and so on. In a self-governing community a man who evades taxation is as unpatriotic as a man who wilfully destroys public property. To take an example of a most serious step in any self-governing state, let us consider for a moment a law enabling conscription. No member of this community can justifiably refuse to obey the law if it has been properly enacted. But he should not be inhibited from opposing this act if he so wishes, in speech or in writing or by pressing his representative to oppose it. For anyone to resist the law of a self-governing community does not make him a democrat but an anarchist. Such a person is not objecting to tyranny, but is rejecting the concept of self-government.

Let me give the most simple example I can of what I mean by freedom of thought in a self-governing community and, at the same time, the moral obligation of the members of that community to obey its laws. In the conduct of a normal meeting there is first the election of a chairman, in whom is vested the collective responsibility of conducting the discussion and of recognizing the claims of individual members of the audience to express their views so that the meeting will not become a chaotic hubbub of voices clamouring to be heard. Having agreed to this extent of self-government, the meeting will demand of the chairman that everyone who wishes to air his views be given a hearing. If, however, someone interrupts another speaker and tries to drown out his voice or otherwise silence him, the chairman, with the full consent of the majority, will call the recalcitrant individual to order. If this individual persists in arrogating to himself the opportunity of speech allotted to another, he will eventually be asked to leave the hall because he is interfering with the common wish of the majority. As a last resort he will even be ejected from the hall. On the other hand, no matter how unpopular the opinion of an individual, he must be allowed the chance to express his views fully when he is given the floor by the chairman. This is the simplest example one can give of self-government, but at least it illustrates the principle I am attempting to define.

The problems involved in freedom and self-government have been sharply posed by Plato in his two dialogues 'The Apology of Socrates' and the 'Crito.' In the first, Socrates is warned by his judges to desist from his teaching which is regarded as subversive. If he agrees to desist, he is told, he will be released unpunished. To this demand Socrates cannot agree, although the judges warn him that it will mean his death if he does not. His argument is that Athens is a free city and no judge or official is properly empowered to decide what he, Socrates, shall or shall not teach. He fully admits the legal right of the state to punish him if they see fit, but he cannot see its right to curtail the freedom of expression.

In the other dialogue, the 'Crito,' Socrates has been condemned to death and is awaiting execution of sentence. His friends are calling upon him in prison to console him and one of them, Crito, urges him to escape – which is not at all impossible. On this occasion Socrates refuses, saying that he has no right to disobey the decision of the government. Even though the judgment passed against him may be mistaken or unjust, it is the duty of a citizen to conform with the decisions of the state. Thus Socrates was as determined to obey the law which is about to deprive him of his life as he was to disobey the instructions of his judges to surrender his right to express his beliefs. In a passage of great beauty, in which he reveals the tremendous emotional appeal which in its heyday Athens must have had for all its citizens, he tells Crito that he has knowingly consented to the laws of Athens for seventy years, during which time he has also enjoyed the rights and privileges of a citizen. Now that his own life is in the balance, should he suddenly withdraw his consent to the state of Athens to enforce its own laws? To do so, he replies to his own question, would be unworthy of a citizen of a self-governing state such as Athens. In passing let me remind you here that Socrates is speaking of the civic obligation of obedience in a society of which he felt himself to be an intimate and integral part. We cannot assume from this what his attitude might be had he been living in an oppressive society repugnant to him.

In the first dialogue, the rights and duties of disobedience are preached. In the second, it is stated that a free citizen must bow to the laws of a self-governing state. Plato himself does not attempt to answer this paradox, perhaps because he wished simply to stimulate the enquiring attitude on the part of his readers. I do not wish to concern myself at the moment with attempting to resolve this paradox. I have referred to Socrates, however, to illustrate two points: first, how delicate and intricate a problem is involved in the relation between freedom and self-government, and secondly, by abridging free speech a self-governing society will no longer find itself self-governing in the true sense of that word.

It seems to me that without freedom of expression no community can properly be self-governing. In fact, even though it might preserve the framework of democratic practice through rule of majority, if there is no opportunity for the mass of the populace to hear debated the central questions of the day, it is impossible for a majority to be well-informed and thus in a position to vote intelligently. Hence comes the paradox that in modern politics a majority of the people, if not given guarantees of freedom of expression, can be so deceived and rendered so ignorant that they actually vote against their own interests. Majority rule is generally regarded as the keystone of democratic government. It should not be regarded as a mystic or magic formula. In itself it is meaningless unless there are certain conditions present. It arose originally as the practical working method in the experience of various chambers of government, even while the mass of the people was still unrepresented. As a practical concept it owed much to mediaeval commentators on canon and ancient laws, particularly to Marsilius of Padua. Building on this foundation, the kings of fifteenth-century England taught their parliaments to defeat the will of the privileged and refractory minorities. The same was contemporaneously done by the French kings and their Estates General. Nations and rulers that did not utilize the majority principle were often faced with continual stalemates and embittered factionalism, and this in turn opened the way to dismemberment or political retrogression. Thus in Spain, for example, the intransigents of the Cortes who jealously clung to their right of *disentimiento* were responsible for fixing upon the country a regime of naked absolutism. A chaotic, undisciplined Diet was largely responsible for Hungary's loss of freedom, and in Poland the same situation invited dismemberment.

When in modern times most states gave the franchise to all adults in the community, majority rule was of course the most practical working method for self-government of the people. That the franchise is in most countries restricted to citizens over twenty-one indicates that the very young are not considered mature enough to exercise a responsible vote. If this restriction applies to those still of school age, should it not also be true of those people who have been subjected to the rigours of oppression, to continual exposure for a period of years to false and demoralizing propaganda, while at the same time they have been kept ignorant of what is happening in the rest of the world through distortion and suppression? In such a community – and I think the best example might be Nazi Germany – if, for instance, in the year 1938 or 1939 a plebiscite had been called as to whether or not the people supported Hitler, and they were given convincing assurance that their vote was really secret, I think anyone must admit that an overwhelming majority would have voted in support of Hitler. Would that prove that either Germany was a democratic country or a self-governing community? To ask the question is to invite the answer. Is the majority always right no matter what the issue? To admit that, I believe, is to make a farce of the whole idea of democracy. When the German people had been so worked upon by the whole diabolical symphony of cajolery, terror, race hate, lust of plunder, flattery, and deception, with no opportunity for calm and fair debate of the burning questions of the day, in such an atmosphere of hysteria and deceit, no matter how a vote was conducted the outcome could not reasonably be called a reflection of the general will of a genuinely self-governing community.

Both foreign and native observers on the future of defeated fascist nations are vaguely aware of this problem when they say it would take at least a generation for these nations to become effectively democratic. What this really means is that since the majority have had their minds poisoned and their mental vision blurred, it would take at least a generation for old minds to be purged and new minds to be formed under the influences of a free press and freedom of thought, so that the normal machinery of a democracy could function in a meaningful way. I do not mean to imply by this that a politically backward or socially confused country such as post-war Germany should not be permitted to vote. I am simply warning against the assumption that in such an unhealthy or politically immature society a majority vote will necessarily be an accurate reflection of the true interests of the people.

Freedom of expression and thought are the only avenues by which a community can inform itself of what are its own interests and then express its desire by voting. Even enlightened despots realized the importance of a public opinion unshackled from fear. Thus we read of a French king in the age before the decline of French feudalism who thanked the Estates General for the boldness of their remonstrances and said, 'We prefer to speak to free men rather than to serfs.' In Japan, as you know, even under the heavy-handed rule of the Tokugawa, the comparatively enlightened shogun Yoshimune in 1721 instituted a complaint box (*meyasu-bako*) by which he could hear even in restrained tone and accent the voice of public opinion. Francis Bacon, writing in the age of Tudor absolutism, advised rulers to listen even to unpalatable counsel. If benevolent despots were vaguely aware of the necessity for the health of the community of some expression of uninhibited opinion, how much truer would that be for a self-governing community. In our modern age, it seems to me we have come to a time where there can be no excuse for tolerating any barrier upon qualified freedom of the press and of expression.

I am not one of those who regard the people in the mass, when they are not put under the stress and strains of oppressive rule, as prone to behave stupidly or capriciously. When given access to the relevant facts in a situation the people make the sensible and decent choice; I believe the record of history upholds this view of mine. Especially is this true of people in their natural desire to have friendly and peaceful relations with neighbouring peoples. I can recall no instance of a people who, without first being subjected to an intense and protracted war propaganda, have spontaneously demanded to make aggressive war on another people. It is precisely those rulers who are determined to exploit their people's blood for aggressive wars who are most concerned first to clamp down controls upon the people and to inflame them with jingoism so that their minds are filled with hate and fear, so much as to make impossible a clear and untrammelled expression of the popular desire for peace. I am sure, in the light of the tragic history of Japan in the years before the war, you would bear me out in this assertion.

No one can deny that there are dangers and risks involved in a state where the people enjoy comparatively unstinted freedom. Undoubtedly taking advantage of this situation there will be views expressed that will be highly obnoxious to many people; some views will be propagated that directly attack the concept of self-government and freedom. Yet must that society be steadfast and patient to permit these views, confident that the good sense of the majority will be a bulwark against domination by such retrogressive ideas as will be circulated. Yet to curtail freedom because of the ever-present likelihood that evil views will be circulated is to set in motion an even more dangerous policy. This policy of partial repression cannot be guaranteed from inhibiting what may prove to be healthy and sound views; it cannot even be guaranteed to repress entirely undesirable opinions, because ideas have an elusive way of escaping the net of the law.

This dilemma of liberty in a modern society has been brilliantly posed and effectively answered by one of the most penetrating theorists in Japanese history and at the same time a devoted advocate of freedom, namely Ueki Emori. Writing in the early Meiji period, actually in 1880, in his treatise *Genron Jiyū Ron*, to combat the government policy of repression of publication and speech, Ueki assessed the whole problem as follows:

Freedom of speech is a matter of the utmost urgency to the nation ... When there is freedom of speech the government is well acquainted with the people's intentions. Once aware of them it can genuinely effect the unity of people and government ... When there is no freedom of speech the administrators of the government can trespass upon the people's rights. This can happen very easily if there is no freedom of speech.

Some people object that when there is freedom of speech, then bad theories and evil prejudices will get abroad and lead the people astray and this cannot but cause injury to the people of the nation. This is, however, a very stupid objection and one which runs counter to reason. When there is no freedom of speech there is notwithstanding no guarantee that wrong views will not get abroad which will do harm ... It is therefore necessary that such views be refuted, but without freedom of speech there is no opportunity to correct error; evil views and prejudices will be given free rein spreading rampant among the people, then monstrous chimeras and the demons born of ignorance and prejudice come forth into the light of day. But even if wicked ideas and prejudices are trumpeted abroad, if there is freedom of speech contrary views can refute them; false arguments can be clearly exposed and in this way evil views will be effectively controlled.

Freedom of expression then is the very citadel of a self-governing society. If one wing or rampart of the citadel is surrendered, the whole fortress is in danger. Thus, if qualifications to freedom of expression are permitted, then the first inroads have been made for a later assault upon the very arcanum of liberty. It is for this reason that the early legislators of the United States adopted what is the first amendment to their Constitution: 'Congress shall make no law abridging the freedom of speech.' It is important to note that this statement is unqualified and admits of no exceptions. There is not even an exception made in favour of times of danger or war. It is here perhaps where Socrates, of whom I have just been speaking, joins hands across the centuries with the makers of the United States Constitution. According to one eminent American scholar, the men who adopted the Bill of Rights were not ignorant of the necessities of war or of national danger. It would in fact be nearer to the truth to say that it was exactly those necessities which they had in mind as they planned to defend freedom of discussion against them. Out of their own bitter experience they well knew how fear and hate, war and strife, drive men into acts of blind, unreasoning suppression. They planned accordingly both for the peace which they desired and for the wars which they feared. In both cases they established unqualified prohibition of the abridgment of freedom of speech. I believe the political faith and creed of men such as Jefferson are needed more today even than in their age. With the tremendous mechanical development in the media of expression through papers of mass circulation and radio, the issue at stake is even more momentous than in preceding ages. It is a matter of life and death that citizens of modern communities be given all the relevant facts of a situation in which they must make some decision.

To those who object that there must be some qualifications to freedom of thought I would ask in return, what ruler or governing committee such as cabinet or even parliament is wise enough to decide what is expedient for the people to hear and what is not expedient. If it is argued that by curtailing liberty at a time of crisis the policy of the lesser evil only is being followed, I would then ask, could anyone give assurance that by so choking the avenues of freedom greater evils are not being stored up ahead. Rulers who adopt repressive measures justify their acts by saying the people are too stupid or immature to know the facts of life. Once of course repression is firmly fixed upon the people, they become incapable of rational and useful decisions. But rulers who are always itching to put obstacles in the way of freedom of thought and expression and who give the excuse that the people are too excitable and irrational to be exposed to the truth are actually fearful of the native good sense and the basically peace-loving character of the people. There is an interesting vindication of this concept from a contemporary account of that crucial period in English history known as the Long Parliament in the early seventeenth century. Of that period it is written, 'Astonishing as it might be, it was seen that the common people were sensible of public interest and religion when lords and gentlemen seemed not to be.'

How steadfast and decent are the people in their desires and hopes, I would again wish to illustrate by calling to witness a figure who is perhaps not commonly regarded as predisposed in favour of democratic government, namely Machiavelli. In a work of his which is unfortunately less known than *The Prince*, namely the *Discourses on the First Ten Books of Titus Livius*, Machiavelli gives his dispassionate and considered interpretation of history. There is in it a remarkable chapter entitled 'Leagues and Alliances with Republics are More to be Trusted than Those with Princes' (as the context of the chapter shows, Machiavelli meant by republics a self-governing state like Athens in its prime). Although the passage is somewhat lengthy I would like to quote it because of the moral which Machiavelli draws from the historical account advanced.

Alliances are broken from considerations of interest; and in this respect republics are much more careful in the observance of treaties than princes. It would be easy to cite instances where princes for the smallest advantage have broken their faith, and where the greatest advantages have failed to induce republics to disregard theirs; as in the case of the proposal of Themistocles to the Athenians, when in a general assembly he told them that he had something to suggest that would be of greatest advantage to their country; but that it was of such a nature that he could not disclose it publicly without depriving them of the opportunity of availing of it. The people of Athens therefore appointed Aristides to whom Themistocles might communicate his suggestion, upon which they would decide according to the judgment of Aristides. Themistocles thereupon showed him that the fleet of united Greece, relying upon the treaty still in force, was in such position that they could easily make themselves masters of it or destroy it, which would make the Athenians arbiters of all Greece. Whereupon Aristides reported to the people that the proposed plan of Themistocles was highly advantageous but most dishonest, and therefore the people absolutely rejected it; which would not have been done by Philip of Macedon, nor many other princes, who would only have looked to the advantages, and who have gained more by their perfidy than by any other means.

I do not speak of the breaking of treaties because of an occasional nonobservance, that being an ordinary matter; but I speak of the breaking of treaties from some extraordinary cause; and here I believe, from what has been said, that the people are less frequently guilty of this than princes, and are therefore more to be trusted.

If in this lecture I have raised more questions than I have answered I will not be dissatisfied, provided you will help to seek the answers. In matters of politics one is rarely able to give final answers to any question. But of this I am convinced, that in spite of the comparative freedom and the reforms effected in Japan, you will have to be assiduous in extending liberty and vigilant in guarding it. This holds true not only of Japan but of all countries. Despite the hardships facing the people of Japan, there is hope of seeing it become a bulwark of peace and freedom. Though the problems you face are unique and trying, I am sure they would not daunt a Fukuzawa who met and surmounted what were in his day unique and baffling problems. It is easy, I know, for someone like myself to speak words of encouragement, but let me assure you that no one today, of any nationality, can speak to others on a subject like this with an air of condescension. So I am speaking this afternoon with the greatest sincerity and frankness of which I am capable. Every nation has its own peculiar problems, some more desperate than others. Even the great powers are wrestling with problems of hitherto unimagined difficulty. In this present world all of us, regardless of nationality, to a remarkable extent share each other's problems; we rejoice in the victories of freedom in any quarter, are solicitous for its advancement everywhere, and mourn its eclipse even in distant lands. Thus I beg you to do all in your power to cherish the freedom that you have, and make good use of it or it will atrophy like some organ which is left unused. Once liberty is dead, people must lose their self-respect; despair, envy, deceit, and malice will grow apace like weeds in a deserted garden. We have seen in the past generation how a nation can lose its freedom and yet wage a terrible war; but no people who have lost their freedom can bequeath any lasting benefit to succeeding ages. They will leave behind no inspiration or generous work to which their descendants can look with pride and gratitude. This was well expressed by J.S. Mill a century ago when he wrote, 'A state which dwarfs its men in order that they may be more docile instruments in its hands even for beneficial purposes, will find that with small men no great thing can really be accomplished.'

I urge you to be brisk and vigilant in defence of liberty; by making Japan a citadel of freedom and free culture you can prove yourself to be the truest patriot. Thus you will not only contribute to making Japan a healthy, free, and self-governing community, but you will at the same time make it a country of hope and encouragement to others who have not yet achieved that degree of freedom.

The world is tired of war and of force. Not only as between different classes in a nation but as between nations themselves, force must give way to persuasion and reason if the world is not to retrogress fatally. Force is terribly easy to use, especially against some unpopular minority in the community. It is possible in this way to silence the voice of those whom an impatient government is irked to hear. But by so doing the community carries within it an embittered and disaffected member. The same is true today of relations between great and small nations.

Persuasion is not only the way of reason and humanity, it is now the sole path of self-preservation. Thus we are, all of us, whatever our nation or status, faced with the stern alternative: PERSUADE OR PERISH.

NOTES

1 An address delivered by Norman at Keio University, 26 November 1948, on the occasion of the thirtieth anniversary of the founding of the Fukuzawa Research Society.
2 The Chinese characters literally signify 'respect officials, despise people.' [EHN's note]

On the Modesty
of Clio

Some historians such as Carlyle have been fascinated by the strong men of history; men who cut through complex social and political problems by some swift act of military movement or dictatorial decree. To take one of the earliest examples, we have Alexander the Great who was of course much more than a conqueror or successful general, but one story of his career illustrates the point I shall try to make.

Someone of the town of Gordos, whose name is unrecorded, had contrived to tie such an elaborate knot that no one could unravel it. An oracle had prophesied a spectacular career for anyone who could untie it. Arriving in Gordos, Alexander at once examined the knot, drew his sword and cut through it while his soldiers cheered his stroke. Now Alexander was a man of great parts, but of violent and impatient nature. Perhaps he inherited his high spirit from his mother, Olympias, who was a formidable figure, suggesting a priestess of a primitive cult or an Amazonian queen. Plutarch records that her husband, Philip, never felt quite the same towards her after finding a huge serpent curled up beside her on the couch. Olympias came from the wild and rugged country of Epirus, where woman's position had remained more independent than in most parts of Greece; she has been described by the Hellenistic scholar Bevan as one of the 'tigress princesses' of the House of Macedonia. With such heredity one can appreciate better something of Alexander's bold character and keen imagination. I have always felt, however, that his act in the town of Gordos was not quite as brilliant a stroke as later writers have judged. In fact, when I first read the story as a boy I was disappointed at this exploit. Somehow it seemed to be an anticlimax. It was like solving a difficult problem in algebra by looking up the answer at the back of the book; since the process of solution is the essence of algebra, merely to learn the answer beforehand is distinctly dull, nor does it make for any educative advance.

The danger of concentrating excessive power in the hands of one man lies in the overpowering temptation he will have to solve problems by some simple, violent act which gives the illusion of settling the problem. But as the sequel often shows, his seemingly bold stroke may have entirely evaded the issue or, even worse, have exacerbated it. Thus, to some ambitious autocrat it has seemed easier to be rid of the irritations arising from a troublesome neighbour by invading his territory rather than to enter into protracted and tiresome negotiations with him. Yet even if he overruns that country and despoils its people, their descendants will still remain to present even graver problems than those originally at stake. At the beginning of a great war even the wisest rulers have rarely been able to foresee the shape of things which will emerge at the end. When I recall the lines of Basho, written as he reviewed the battleground fought over by the Minamoto and the Fujiwara, I cannot venture to say what the poet's inner meaning might have been; to me, however, the haunting and melancholy lines suggest the utter futility of trying to 'make history' simply by violence.

To the schoolboy reading his history, Elizabeth is painted as the great sovereign who defeated the Spanish Armada. Yet I cannot but feel that her genius lay in exactly the opposite direction, namely in her extreme reluctance to resort to war unless it was forced upon her, as was the war with Spain. It is no detraction from her greatness to say that her hatred of war was chiefly because of its vast expense and economic waste rather than from humanitarian sentiment. We know how trying she was to her ministers by her endless procrastinations and vacillations. Yet she clearly understood that English interests and prosperity could best be served by maintaining peace and pursuing the arts of peace. Thus, by her masterly diplomacy she prevented an alliance of the Catholic great powers directed against England which, if formed, might have overwhelmed her. It was this sense of realism in Elizabeth and not the emotional and often fatal yearning for expansion that helped England to emerge from a small island off the northeast coast of Europe to become a great centre of world trade and intellectual activity.

Now I do not suggest that Providence or the most secular concept of the 'idea of progress' has, like some *deus ex machina*, stayed the hand of tyrants and war makers and, perhaps more dangerous, of fanatics driven by the illusion that they are instruments of Divine Grace, to prevent them from spreading havoc, impoverishing society, corrupting morals, and bringing general decline upon nations and people. The destruction of the brilliant Provençal culture in the twelfth century, in the campaign known as the Albigensian Crusade, succeeded not only in obliterating a joyous and rich community, but in postponing the prospects of the Renaissance north of Italy for many generations. Of this crusade carried out in the name of religion the historian H.C. Lea writes:

In the twelfth century the south of France had been the most civilized land in (Christian) Europe. There, commerce, industry, art, science had been far in advance of the age. The cities had won virtual self-government, were proud of their wealth and strength, jealous of their liberties and self-sacrificing in their patriotism. The nobles, for the most part, were cultivated men, poets themselves or patrons of poetry, who had learned that their prosperity depended upon the prosperity of their subjects, and that municipal liberties were a safeguard rather than a menace to the wise ruler. The Crusaders came, and their unfinished work was taken up and executed to the bitter end by the Inquisition. It left a ruined and impoverished country, with shattered industries and failing commerce. The native nobles were broken by confiscation and replaced by strangers ... A people of rare gifts had been tortured, decimated, humiliated, despoiled ... The precocious civilization which had promised to lead Europe in the path of culture was gone, and to Italy was transmitted the honour of the Renaissance.

Similarly, under the pretence of religion cloaking their lust for gold, the Conquistadores of Spain shattered the unique vessel that was Aztec and Incan civilization. Busbecq, the Flemish diplomat, letter-writer, and scholar, who lived during the years of the Spanish conquests, in an epigram of four words neatly epitomized this page of history: 'Pietas obtenditur, aurum quaeritur' (religion is the pretext, the object is gold).

Thus, as a tentative axiom one might say that while men can by violence destroy peaceful and prosperous civilizations, the corollary would seem to be that the slow and painful progress towards either a material prosperity or a higher culture is not achieved by any such bloody and dramatic acts. This is not to say that a cruelly oppressed nation or people may not on some occasions have found a forceful breaking of their bonds a necessary prerequisite for further progress. But such an act is usually nothing more than the climax of a long and arduous period of social and psychological development, as de Tocqueville so convincingly argued was the case with the French Revolution. A spontaneous act of mob violence can never achieve a basic change in the social and political structure of a great nation.

The old type of history textbook dwelt upon only such dramatic things as wars and alliances, conquests and annexations, the careers of great men and the lives of kings and queens. Not only is such history easier to write, but it was no doubt considered more arresting to the impressionable minds of the young. This type of textbook was effectively caricatured in a little book, *1066 and All That*, which summarized English history in a series of threadbare platitudes and half-truths. In more contemporary times, a few paragraphs might be casually thrown in at the end of each epoch covering 'the manners and customs of the period,' but this would be more as an afterthought or perhaps a careless concession to the growing importance in advanced education of political economy and related social sciences. But to the more mature historians, the real essence of a people's history can be distilled only out of what is at first glance the driest of material. Clio, the muse of history, perhaps the shyest of the nine sisters, does not readily show her face except to the most persistent and understanding votaries. One of these was Maitland who, out of the mediaeval yearbooks, from a mass of cold and crabbed documents, was able to present a subtle analysis of the society and institutions of feudal England. Similarly, by vastly enlarging the scope of the Latin inscriptions, Mommsen laid a wide and solid foundation for a history of Rome that goes beyond a critical study of the old annals.

In Japan, the late Mirua Shūkō from his studies of documents relating to the history of the city of Sakai and his study of Japanese law has thrown into bold relief many aspects of the social and institutional history of Japan. Mr Tsuda Sōkichi created a new epoch in Japanese historiography by his rational interpretation of the oldest chronicles setting forth an account of early Japanese history; also, out of his work *Bungaku ni arawaretaru waga kokumin shisō no kenkyū*[1] he brought to life the ideas and cultural modes of Japan from early times to the end of the Tokugawa epoch.

So strong, however, is the tradition of the great men in history, that even in the fields of law and politics we are continually inclined to look for some single apocalyptic act of legislation as the beginning of all liberty (or the end of it according to the period and nation studied). Thus, for example, Magna Carta is frequently cited as the foundation of British liberties, whereas even a cursory study of this document and its later history should punctuate such a concept. To list but a few of the popular misconceptions of Magna Carta: The Great Charter of 1215 was never the law of the land save for a few weeks, until King John felt strong enough to repudiate it. On the accession of Henry III a new charter was issued, which again was revised in 1217 and in 1225. The 1225 version of the charter, which was to remain its most important form, was confirmed by Edward I in 1297, but it was no longer the famous Charter of Runnymede Meadow but that of 'the time of King Henry, our father' and already quite a different charter, much more tolerant of the king's authority and omitting amongst other items the earlier attempt to reform abuses relating to villein tenements. Perhaps the greatest confusion comes from the thirteenth century use of the word 'liberty.' Its use in the Great Charter was not in any sense a grant of general liberty, but a confirmation of special baronial privileges. A liberty in those days was a definite, clear-cut monopoly of jurisdiction, usually a royal recognition of unchecked power of a lord over his tenants in the manorial courts, and as such it is hard to see how the enunciation of such feudal privileges in the Great Charter has much to do with the liberty of the English people as a whole. In short, it was an attempt that failed in the long run, of a jealous feudal ruling class to maintain against royal pressure their centrifugal powers.

Nor did Magna Carta assert in any form the principle of 'no taxation without representation.' Rather did it reflect the desire of the barons to evade payment of rent they owed the crown for their lands unless they chose to do so. Therefore, it represented a baronial revolt under the slogan 'no rent' rather than a struggle over the principle of taxation. Finally, as legal scholars have clearly shown, Magna Carta had no connection with the establishment of jury trial nor did it in any way anticipate habeas corpus. We might have been put on our guard against such misconceptions of Magna Carta if we had noticed that while there were baronial and ecclesiastical invocations of the charter, there were no *popular* appeals to it until the sixteenth and seventeenth centuries, when it was to a large extent refashioned by Sir Edward Coke as a weapon in his contest on behalf of the common law courts against the prerogative of the crown. Even stranger perhaps is the absence of any reference to it in Shakespeare's play *King John*; curiously enough, this thoroughly disreputable monarch was quite popular with Elizabethan audiences, who loved to hear abuse and defiance hurled at popes and prelates.

The question naturally arises, if Magna Carta played so little a part in mediaeval England in the steep and crooked path leading towards popular liberties, what instrument or institutions were available for this purpose? To this question I will not be so rash as to attempt an exhaustive and complete reply, but will merely single out one or two illustrative examples.

There is no doubt that following the Norman Conquest the common people, that is to say below the status of gentry, suffered a debasement of their status and it was many centuries before the concept of equality before the law was established. Those centuries witnessed some kings who ruled according to the best traditions of the realm and others who overstepped the limits permitted a ruler who was expected to obey the law of the church and of his own kingdom. Perhaps even more grievous for the common people was the heavy-handed rule of feudal magnates. There is no doubt, however, that on numerous occasions the weaker section of the community found some protection, though often imperfect, both against acts of royal absolutism and baronial rapacity in the common law courts which are justly the pride of the English legal historian.

The common law, in contrast to the Roman concept that the will of the monarch has the force of law, in the phrase attributed to the mediaeval jurist Bracton, laid it down that 'the king was under God and the law.' This law was, therefore, above and beyond the mere caprice of a ruler; it is further described as one that conforms to reason so that nothing basically irrational or impossible can be expected to be enforced in the court which administered it.

There are two cases in the fourteenth century in the reign of Edward III, the technicalities of which I need not detail here, which illustrate this point. In the first case, a collector of the king's taxes was compelled by the common law court to return cattle which he had distrained when it appeared that he had no warrant under seal, and this meant that no official of the crown could collect the king's taxes without the proper warrant. In the second instance, a sheriff bearing a letter from the king under his private seal said that a case before the court of the King's Bench should be dismissed because the defendant already had the king's pardon and could therefore not have damages inflicted upon him. This was rejected by the court and the sheriff was informed that it could not refuse to pass judgment merely by being shown a private letter from the king; the court then proceeded to impose a fine upon the sheriff and issued a writ which outlawed the defendants. This case really meant that Edward III as king of England could pardon offenders but he might not instruct a sheriff to disregard the law. In other words, when he acted as king his acts must conform to the law and when he chose to act by private letter as Edward Plantagenet he could not interfere with the course of the law which bound the whole realm, including himself.

The full details of how common law courts acted as a curb on the arbitrary whim of the feudal monarchy do not make dramatic reading, but out of such stuff is the sober texture of history woven rather than from the flashy and colourful epics of battles and the pageantry of the great. Later, the common law courts were to play an even more important part in the history of English liberty. The Tudor monarchy was as ruthless and autocratic as any in contemporary Europe, but it presented the curious spectacle of absolutism *by consent*. In those tumultuous decades when the feudal magnates were being destroyed and the Catholic monasteries expropriated, quite naturally a number of people suffered varying degrees of hardship, but the mass of the people, and particularly the dominant sections of the community – the new aristocracy, the trading classes, and the country gentry – were solidly in support of the Tudor monarchy to which they owed their rise in the world. Other peculiar features were that this monarchy lacked substantial sources of revenue; it had no standing army or regular police force and no huge bureaucracy such as battened upon the peoples of contemporary France and Spain. It is doubtful, even had the Tudor monarchy continued beyond Elizabeth's death, whether that remarkable equilibrium of crown and communities would have continued indefinitely, unchallenged at least, without some powerful organs of absolutism. The Stuarts, lacking the personal popularity of the Tudors, starting with James I relied more and more upon those courts derived from royal prerogative, such as the Star Chamber and High Commission, as instruments of absolutism. But the whole absolutist program of the Stuarts was frustrated because, in their desire to create an imperial bureaucracy and standing army to overawe the people they lacked sufficient revenues; in order to raise these they resorted to such arbitrary means that they united against them the most influential communities of the country. Before these issues came to a head, they ran into a stubborn obstacle in the common law as championed by Sir Edward Coke. Now Coke can scarcely be described as a tribune of the people; he was a pedantic, cantankerous old man, overflowing with conceit and a vast store of legal lore. His unquenchable veneration for the common law brought about his downfall, but also rendered his name illustrious in history. Thus, in spite of himself Coke served the cause of popular liberties.

When James attempted to overrule the courts and decide matters of jurisdiction as between conflicting tribunals, Coke ventured to argue with him. In front of the assembled judges of England, Coke told James that according to the law the king in person could not adjudge any cause. 'But,' said the king, 'I thought law was founded upon reason and I and others have reason as well as the judges.' 'True, it was,' Coke responded, 'that God had endowed his Majesty with excellent science and great endowments of nature; but his Majesty was not learned in the laws of his realm of England, and causes which concern the life or inheritance of goods or fortunes of his subjects are not to be decided by natural reason, but by the artificial reason and judgment of the law, which law is an art which requires long study and experience before that a man can attain to the cognizance of it.' Whereupon the king grew so uncontrollably angry that he appeared to menace Coke who, in trepidation, fell on all fours, from which position he continued to put up a learned argument, finally quoting the famous words attributed to Bracton that the king should not be under any man but under God and the law.

The sequel to this extraordinary scene was that James's efforts to intervene directly in judicial proceedings were defeated, but Coke was dismissed. I am not sure whether he would have been too happy to hear of his posthumous fame when his ponderous work, *The Institutes*, was quoted with such great effect by the Levellers – notably Lilburne, who used to defend himself in court with Coke's classic on the common law spread out before him.

As the Stuart monarchy steadfastly persisted in its efforts to establish absolutism on a permanent basis, it finally collided with what might be called the highest court in the land, namely Parliament. (The constitutional historian Professor McIlwain of Harvard has written a famous book on the origins of Parliament with the significant title

The High Court of Parliament, indicating that this institution from its inception carried both judicial and legislative authority, though in its early history these two functions were not clearly differentiated.) The parliaments of Charles I witnessed the emergence of independent leaders within the House of Commons of whom surely the greatest was Sir John Eliot. A resolute advocate of popular liberties, he was to be venerated in later generations as the stoutest defender of parliamentary privilege. He incurred the hatred of Charles for his leading part in drawing up the Petition of Rights in 1628. He was the hero of that remarkable scene of adjournment in March 1629, when the Speaker of the House had received a secret instruction from the king to adjourn the House as soon as he perceived that Eliot and his party would move resolutions that trenched upon the king's prerogative. Some of Eliot's supporters, suspicious of the Speaker's designs and anticipating his move to rise and adjourn the House, forcibly held him down so that he could not properly read a message from the king until Eliot's three resolutions on taxation and religion were passed. This open thwarting of Charles's will resulted in Eliot's fourth, and what proved to be his final, imprisonment. He was offered a chance of release provided he would make a fulsome apology to the king, but Eliot maintained that the words he had spoken in the House concerned only the House itself and no other authority and so he remained in the Tower. The king's hatred of him had grown so inveterate that it did not relent even after Eliot's death. A sick but unbroken man, he was to remain in prison for three years, until his death. When his son petitioned the king for his father's body that it might be buried in his own native parish in Cornwall, on the bottom of the petition the answer was written:'Let Sir John Eliot's body be buried in the church of that parish where he died,' which meant burial in an unmarked grave in the courtyard of the Tower. It is fitting, therefore, that this great defender of parliamentary privilege should have the honour of having his portrait given precedence in the gallery leading into the House of Commons.

Despite the brilliant and doughty leadership which these parliamentary figures gave the cause of liberty in that age, following the outbreak of the Civil War and the execution of the king it soon appeared to the masses of parliamentary soldiers and smaller people of the country that the absolutism of the king had been replaced by the arrogation of excessive power by Parliament. Accordingly, the radical wing of the parliamentary army, known as the Levellers, finally broke with Cromwell and launched a fierce struggle against the arbitrary rule of Parliament. As one of the Levellers' pamphlets pertinently asked: 'We were ruled before by King, Lords and Commons; now by a General, Court Martial and Commons; and we pray you, what is the difference?'

These pioneer democrats perceived that for the future there was as great a menace to individual liberties from powerful political parties and oligarchs turning popular institutions to their own exclusive interests, as from the somewhat old-fashioned autocrat. A study of the struggle between Cromwell and the Levellers is most instructive for understanding the complex course of the Puritan Revolution in the seventeenth century, but I cannot properly attempt that task here. Suffice it to say that the Levellers' program represents an extraordinarily precocious anticipation of advanced political democracy, including amongst other things universal male suffrage, regular parliaments, and adequate pay for members of Parliament. They were the first genuine political party in England that represented the masses of common people. The Levellers had their regular party organizations, elected committees, propagandists, and two weekly papers carrying both news of general interest and editorials on current problems. The more colourful of these two papers, with the rather disarming name of *The Moderate* presents an interesting chapter in the history of political journalism which is so little known that a few words on it might be justified here. It was started in June 1648 and suppressed in September 1649. Its editor was a self-educated man, Gilbert Mabbot, a cobbler's son. He was widely read in history, English, French, Greek, and Roman. His style was sharp, pungent, and direct; only rarely did he permit himself the luxury of rhetoric. His paper was an admirable organ for the startling doctrines preached by the Leveller leaders such as Lilburne, Walwyn, and Overton. This paper maintained such a sustained criticism of the tyranny of the army's 'grandees' – that is, the Cromwellian senior officers – that it was eventually suppressed. In its campaign on behalf of the rank and file of that army whose pay was long in arrears, there are the following moving lines from some infantry men of Colonel Pride's regiment: 'This regiment,' they wrote, 'hath had but one month's pay since May [it was then December 1648], having marched 1,300 miles this summer. Sir, we can die, but not endure to see our Mother England die before us.'

One more incident illustrates the unprecedented manner in which the Levellers succeeded in arousing the interest and winning the support of women. Ten thousand women signed a petition addressed to Parliament, known as the 'Petition of the Women' (a report on it appears in the issue of *The Moderate* for 2 April 1649), which supported the demands of the army Levellers and sought amongst other things the release from prison of the Leveller leader, John Lilburne. When some women appeared with the petition at Parliament, a member, with incorrigible male complacency, told them to stay at home and wash their dishes, to which one of the women gravely replied, 'Sir, we have scarce any dishes left us to wash and are hardly sure of keeping those we have.'

It was obvious that Cromwell, who drew his power from the wealthy merchants and gentry of the more prosperous counties, could not tolerate for long this opposition to his rule. He is reported to have cried out in anger: 'What is the purport of the Levelling principle but to make the tenant as liberal a fortune as the landlord. I was by birth a gentleman. You must cut these people in pieces or they will cut you in pieces.' Finally, the Leveller agitation culminated in a mutiny in the ranks of the parliamentary army at Burford; after some sharp encounters it was put down. Immediately afterwards, in June 1649, the great merchants of London, who had often cursed Cromwell for his efforts to levy taxes on them and who had kept their purses tight closed against contributions to pay the army which had fought on their behalf, celebrated the downfall of the Levellers by a magnificent banquet in Grocers' Hall in honour of Cromwell and his chief general, Fairfax.

There was another side to the picture which may serve as a typical warning of the dangers of painting any great political struggle in black and white. One of the chief ministers of Charles I's personal rule was Laud, Archbishop of Canterbury. He was a fanatical believer in the concept of the divine right of kings; stiff-necked and intolerant in religious policy. Yet there was a less well-known aspect of his political thought; from his rather old-fashioned mediaeval concept of society he strongly opposed the policy of enclosure, which was being carried out ruthlessly by large landowners in the interests of converting their lands from tillage to the more profitable pasture land. With profits to whet their appetites, landlords quickly forgot the unwritten but time-honoured obligations to their customary tenants. These tenants, many of them turned adrift as a result of enclosure, knew not where to look

for redress. If to the local justice of the peace, he was usually the largest land-owner in the district, or if to Parliament, he found that there
the land-owners enjoyed overwhelming political influence. Their last
hope was to appeal directly to the Privy Council and the king's ministers, and curiously enough here they found a sympathetic ear in the
person of Archbishop Laud. With all his faults, Laud did not lack
principle or courage and no matter how powerful the landlord, he
would allow no man (if it was in his power) to violate the 'common
law of Christ' as he called it, that is, to evict tenants from ancient
holdings for the sake of profit. Inspiring the lesser clergy with his
crusading zeal, Laud succeeded often to a considerable extent in
thwarting the will of the landlords so that, in the words of Clarendon,
'many nobles and worthy gentlemen are curbed and tyrannized over
by some base clergy of mean parentage. The shame which they call the
insolent triumph over their degree and quality and levelling them
with the common people was never forgotten and they watched for
revenge.' Their revenge was close at hand when Parliament had Laud
tried and executed by a bill of attainder in 1645.

The defeat of the royalists in the Civil War did not alleviate the
plight of the tenants and small holders, rather was it worsened under
the rule of Parliament. Now Clarendon, the conservative historian of
the Civil War, writing only a few years after these events, admits that
there was great prosperity in the countryside during the Cromwellian
era. This statement has been accepted as true by later historians but
has required interpretation. Thus the social and economic historian
Thorold Rogers in his massive study, *History of Agriculture and Prices
in England, 1259–1793* (Oxford 1866–1902), has further qualified this
prosperity as flowing mostly into the hands of the great landlords. 'It
was a period,' wrote Rogers, 'of excessive misery among the mass of
the people and the tenants, a time in which a few might have become
rich, while the many were crushed down into hopeless and almost
permanent indigence.'

Such then was the complexity of the period that the classes which
profited least during the Interregnum, the victims of enclosure and of
sharp practices of the wealthy merchants, were not as dispirited as
one would otherwise have thought to see the end of the Protectorate
and the restoration of the monarchy under Charles II.

Cromwell, one of the greatest heroes of Carlyle, like Alexander the
Great, was certainly more than a successful military leader. I for one
do not see how a historian can morally blame him for resisting the

radical demands of the Levellers which, admirable though they were in principle, were in that age not practical politically in England. Yet by cutting his Gordian knot, that is by his military victories, by the execution of the king and the forceful suppression of the Levellers, Cromwell left untouched perhaps the most pressing problems of that age, namely those relating to land, enclosures, and a satisfactory constitution – a problem with which he vainly wrestled in his later years. Perhaps his greatest merit lay in his effective struggle on behalf of freedom of conscience, that is, of the right of the Puritan minority to retain their own form of religion against the pressure of the orthodox majority. I would certainly not wish to suggest that Cromwell's career was meaningless nor would I argue that his policy did not leave a mark on the course of English history. Yet it was the stout resistance of the parliamentary leaders and, most outstanding, of Eliot, even more than Cromwell's military dictatorship, which effectively proved for later generations both the ineffectiveness and the danger to the crown itself of any attempt by the king to rule arbitrarily without the consent of Parliament. In the field of political theory, the brilliant pamphlets and arguments of the Levellers, and particularly of Gerrard Winstanley, on the agrarian question, on the secularization of the state, and on the need for a popular education and state-supported scientific institutions, rather than the literary remains of Cromwell, adumbrated the future course of social and political democracy.

History is notoriously elusive and, paradoxical as it seems, perhaps most difficult is the interpretation of modern history. So close is the chronicler of contemporary events to the scene that in later days his alarm at some bogey of his own imagination appears ridiculous, while his blindness to some portentous event looming before his very eyes casts doubt on his capacity to observe and understand. In his preface to his incompleted 'History of the World,' Sir Walter Raleigh shrewdly saw the pitfalls lying in wait for the historian of contemporary events when he wrote: 'Whosoever in writing a modern history shall follow truth too near the heels, it may happily strike out his teeth. There is no mistress or guide that hath led her servants into greater miseries.' Raleigh was perhaps even wiser than he knew, for his account of Henry VIII dangerously irritated James I, who scolded the author for being 'too saucy in censuring princes.'

Brave deeds, the marching and counter-marching of armies, the declamations of politicians somehow leave Clio unmoved. She seems to be impressed rather by the laborious efforts of a people who, unaware of their individual importance, contribute their anonymous mite in creating the treasures of some culture or by those who have vigilantly guarded a humane precedent or revived some forgotten liberty. Perhaps the gravest offence one can offer Clio is to turn history into a series of mechanical clichés, for instance to label some tradition or institution as 'feudal' and then dismiss it as worthless. This does not mean to worship the past with a dull and uncritical eye but rather to examine from every possible approach the nature of some institution, to see how it has changed with other changes in society, how despite an unpropitious past, its potentialities in the light of new developments may render it of the greatest advantage to those desperately in need of a weapon against tyranny. From the most unlikely material surprising advantages may be taken by men of discernment and moral courage. Thus in the seventeenth century the old common law of England, reeking of dim court houses, somnolent clerks, and dusty parchments, became in the hands of public-spirited lawyers and devoted popular leaders a most effective bulwark against despotism. In that age Parliament too was converted by a brilliant galaxy of tribunes, first and foremost Sir John Eliot and his associates Coke, Hampden, Pym, Seldon, and Digges, into the chief instrument to repel the Stuart grasping after despotism. Yet within a few years this same institution under Cromwell became an obstacle to the further untrammelled growth of popular liberties. In later ages too it required extensive reform before it could be said to represent to any extent the will of the people. Similarly, in the nineteenth century the law had acquired so many cumbersome and obsolete features, the penalties for a number of petty offences were so harsh that no jury would care to convict a man charged with such minor offences, that a general overhauling was necessary and was to a large extent carried out. No human institution can be guaranteed to remain indefinitely as a bulwark of liberty; in new circumstances it can turn into the very opposite. Thus we see the spectacle of many people who invoke what they believe to be the most advanced or democratic principles when that institution or tradition to which they appeal has long since changed its original nature and become either an obstacle to further growth or just meaningless.

Clio loves to have her little jokes; she delights to make use of the most modest human material and to refute and confound the pretentious and proud out of their own words. Many a demagogue who by his ranting defiles the sacred words of liberty and freedom can be seen for what he really is by his false interpretation of some events or precedents which he recklessly invokes for his support.

A thing is not bad simply because it is old, or good because it is new; conversely, everything old is not necessarily good nor everything new, bad. It is always useful to examine the use to which some institution has been put in the past and what purpose it might serve in the present before simply condemning it because it is either old or new. To use a crude but often effective test, one may esteem some old custom or tradition when these are made the object of attack by notorious demagogues and would-be dictators. Thus it may be that the cause of liberty can best be served by the patient and unrelenting defence of bulwarks long since won but endangered by neglect and, secondly, by the conviction that further progress can come only by pursuing long and often circuitous routes. Many a short cut in history has in fact turned out to be a cul-de-sac. Such undramatic and prosaic aspects of civil life as municipal reform and the building up of a tradition of pride in local independence and achievement may be the surest foundation for future generations to build on. Similarly, the way to reform does not necessarily lie through the continual enacting of legislation which, by becoming complex and intricate, may only confuse the people. Most issues that appear to be new can often be equitably settled by existing constitutional practice in any reasonable, well-ordered state. To keep multiplying government decrees and regulations on the theory that in this way new issues can be solved usually results in legislative confusion and popular apathy. Above all, the interests of liberty and justice can best be served by a people who have learned to examine political developments not by clichés and labels but by an attempt to assess their effect in a society which is continually changing. A people with this character will inevitably compel their legislators and representatives to speak words that will have to conform, in some degree at least, to the realities and needs of the situation, rather than indulging in those empty platitudes and careless promises which so frequently debase the prestige of popular institutions.

Clio is a very shy and modest maiden and the most exacting of mistresses to serve; yet she is no snob. She will reveal her sweet and pensive face both to the most humble citizen whose understanding is not corrupted by the clichés and labels which form the debased currency of the sensational press and demagogues, and also to the student who has learned to view all human institutions not as immutable but as relative to society and other institutions, subtly undergoing changes and transformations as part of the massive and ceaseless movement of history itself.

NOTE

1 A Study of National Thought through Literature

The Place of
East Asian Studies
in a Modern University

I am very sensible of the distinction which the chairman of the Victoria University Council and principal have conferred upon me by asking me to address the graduating class of 1954. There is a certain nostalgia which this occasion brings to me as I recall my own graduation day in Toronto and also because my college in the University of Toronto bears the same name as yours.

We live in troubled times when it may seem as if science has progressed at too great a speed, relative, at least, to man's ability to organize his life rationally. Yet it is useless to decry the progress of science. To try to put the clock back would be the height of perversity. It may be that, by concentrating on the war potential of science, mankind is getting into unknown and dangerous depths. Yet we know that without science there would be famine, plagues, and many forms of avoidable suffering. We see the paradox that as the world gets richer in the results of sciences, there is a growth of irrationalism and, on a lower level, of Philistinism. We see more fanaticism in the world of the past two decades than in any time since the French Revolution. This cannot be laid at the feet of science, but perhaps it is the fault of society at large and particularly of the educational system that turns out citizens who are not mature in their thinking. The scientific method itself is one to honour and respect. It calls for intellectual honesty, tolerance, a refusal to silence anyone who advances new or unpopular theories. It means a willingness to listen to everyone; scientific research to reach its fullest development requires an atmosphere of freedom and independence. The real essence of a higher education, it seems to me, is to inculcate the habits of intellectual honesty, the enquiring mind, and a respect for the cultural accomplishments of other ages and civilizations. The threat to human values comes from a contempt for the proper scientific method; it comes from intolerance and dogmatism, from the fear of where free inquiry may lead. These are very real dangers, as can be seen from the history of contemporary peoples, where political and intellectual freedom has been choked.

I am aware that the attraction to the young student of some branch of science is very great, and I do not wish to give any impression that this appeal is somehow unhealthy or undesirable. Quite the contrary. What I believe could be unfortunate, however, is that in an age of increasing specialization the student, whether he is training to be a scientist or to follow one of the professions, in his intense application to his narrow field may fail to acquire a deep-rooted love for the humanities. The student may become impatient or contemptuous of the contributions to culture of other civilizations; he or she may take dangerous short cuts to any thinking about international affairs through mental laziness which refuses to trace the complex problem back in history to a rich variety of factors and forces. Perhaps it is the lack of cultural balance arising from so much specialized learning today that leaves the field open to charlatanism in politics and to vulgarity in the arts. I have an uneasy feeling that in some quarters the word 'culture' is suspect and is only mentioned apologetically. As long as we jealously guard our British traditions, we will be free from the threat to free inquiry that comes from a totalitarian society, but we are not, however, immune from that subtle erosion of good taste and critical standards which comes from the power and ubiquity of mass media in entertainment, from the greater specializations in study, and from the jarring tempo of modern life. In the age of the common man there is a marked tendency for mediocrity in the arts and letters to flood the whole field, leaving little room for the best.

An age devoted to science need not necessarily be divorced from the civilizing influences of the humanities. On the contrary, there is even a greater need in such an age for this influence if we are not to suffer from spiritual anaemia. The Greeks ranked Pythagoras with Homer and, while it is natural to give greater publicity to the scientist who makes new discoveries, we must encourage the teaching of the classics, of modern languages, of the arts, of history, not because they provide some ornament to a personality or a sort of luxury that can be dispensed with, but because a community that is not leavened by a love of the humanities will surely become barren and sterile. I may be told that in this age of specialization no student can afford to study more than one branch of learning unless he be prepared to take two or more degrees in succession, which very few have either the time or the money to do. It would be presumptuous of me, even if I were able, to discuss how a university could be organized or administered in a fashion to give, for example, the scientific faculties some opportunity to keep up an interest in arts and letters. Suffice it to say, however, that such attempts have been made in some universities, and I believe successfully. Also I am aware that Victoria University College provides in an admirable fashion for those already gainfully employed to continue to seek a well-rounded education. The well-balanced education was aptly described by Milton: 'I call therefore a complete and generous education, that which fits a man to perform justly, skillfully, and magnanimously all the offices, both private and public, of peace and war.'

Against the background of these general remarks on the relevance to a healthy society of a continuing concern for the humanities, I wish to direct my remaining words to the possible contribution that can be made to a university by a department of East Asian studies or, somewhat more loosely, oriental studies. I have no specific information except what has been made public as to the plans for the establishment of such a department here in Wellington, but I will say this much: the idea of my saying something of the value of oriental studies is not unknown nor, I hope, even unwelcome to the chairman of the Victoria University College Council and to your principal.

It is a commonplace that the revival of learning in fifteenth- and sixteenth-century Europe, which meant a new and lively devotion to the classics of Greece and Rome, had an incalculable influence on the whole range of the intellectual life of Western Europe in those centuries. Even in this age of science and specialization, the classics can give a sense of proportion, wisdom, and intellectual solace of which modern man stands so much in need. I am not suggesting for a moment that a study of Oriental cultures would play today a role similar to that of the classics during the Renaissance. But I am certain that they would give a stimulating and varied experience to the student of history, or of art, or of international affairs, and, above all, they could assist our Western peoples to see beneath the surface of the thought patterns of two Oriental nations which are at once ancient and modern, past and contemporary, and the future development of which will have profound implications not only for Pacific nations but for the whole globe.

An oriental or East Asian department would normally be equipped to teach the Chinese and Japanese languages, literature, arts, and history, though few universities can afford the full range implied in this and have to sacrifice some aspect of the program. For a convenient, though not too accurate parallel, I might compare the function of an oriental to a classical department which teaches both Greek and Latin, together with the philosophy, history, and literature of these two ancient cultures. In other words, it is designed to be a well-rounded study of a whole civilization, using language primarily as a key to enter the treasure house of these civilizations. Carrying through with the comparison, Japanese might be regarded as analogous to Latin and Chinese to Greek, not in any linguistic sense, but simply in the relations of the one culture to the other. The Chinese, like the Greeks, founded a unique civilization in antique times, but unlike them maintained it throughout periods of upheaval and conflict down to our modern day. Like the Greeks too, the Chinese in their relations with the outside world were prone to regard themselves as the centre of all culture and to refer disparagingly to a foreigner as a barbarian.

I must repeat that this comparison of the two oriental cultures with the two Mediterranean civilizations cannot really be pressed far, but I simply mention it to show the interrelationships of the two segments which comprise the Mediterranean, on the one hand, and the oriental civilization on the other. It is certainly feasible to study either language and literature independent of the other, but, as with our classics, the more you know of the one, that is, Greek or Latin, the more it will help you with the other, regardless of which may be your special field. Merely because the Japanese borrowed the Chinese script, it is sometimes assumed that the languages are closely related, but actually in structure they are as diverse as any two languages can be. But the enormous influence of Chinese culture upon Japan in the field of philosophy, literature, art, medicine, and so forth – and I am now speaking of the pre-modern age – would indicate that the study of Japanese civilization without some knowledge of the Chinese will give a distorted or incomplete picture. Alternatively, to study Chinese without Japanese would not be quite as crippling, since, until recent times, the Chinese debt to Japan has been light. On the other hand, in the last few generations, Japanese studies of Chinese history, literature, and archaeology have been valuable and in some cases are pre-eminent. Thus the sinologist without a knowledge of Japanese would be like the modern classical scholar who cannot read French or German, in which languages so many basic studies of the classics have been published.

In the briefest possible fashion I would like to suggest the scope of these studies. Let me take China first and I will speak of only one aspect of China – and not the China of contemporary politics, nor the China of trade and diplomacy, but rather the China of scholarship.

It is probably true to say without fear of exaggeration that up to the beginning of this century, nowhere in the world has scholarship been more diligently pursued and generally respected that in China. On the authority of an American sinologist, Professor Dubs, one may say that until about 1750, when large-scale printing and publishing tilted the scales in favour of Europe, China had more books than the rest of the world combined. Chinese printing began a full five hundred years before European. Quantity is not the only consideration, impressive as this is. As an example of quality let me describe briefly a Chinese history of imposing greatness.

In the first century before Christ there lived a Chinese official Ssu-ma Chi'ien, who wrote the first of the great Chinese histories from the remotest times to his own day. It is divided into chronicles for each emperor's reign, followed by a set of tables of important families, properties, and lists of various officials and their duties. There then comes a series of treatises on weights and measures, the calendar, ceremonies and music, laws and punishments, economic policies, astronomy, portents, and geography of the Empire with details on irrigation and water control. The remainder of the work is a set of biographies and memoirs describing the important people of the age, not only scholars and men of consequence, but also notorious rascals, eccentrics, and famous beauties. It concludes with the author's autobiography and views of history. This history, known as the 'Historical Memoirs' (shih-chi) has been partially translated into French by Chavannes and a few scattered chapters into English. Its full Chinese text, if translated into English, would represent about a million and a quarter words. There has been a vast literature of annotation, emendation, and commentary which combined would be several times as long as the history itself. If a student could systematically study and explore this one work, he would have a remarkable knowledge of

ancient Chinese society and government. It set the pattern for the succeeding twenty-four standard histories which bring Chinese history
down till the end of the dynastic period about fifty years ago. Of these
standard histories the greatest is still probably the first, and scholars
generally acclaim its author, Ssu-ma Chi'ien, as the equal of Thucy-
dides for reliability while, of course, his scope is more encyclopaedic
than any Greek or Roman historian.

While the quality of scholarship has usually been maintained at a
very high level in China, literacy has been restricted to a narrow
circle. This has tended to emphasize the importance of the scholar in
Chinese traditional society and also to cut across the growth of a hereditary aristocracy. It is for this reason that Chinese families have in the
past sacrificed so much to provide a promising son with the best available education – the only sure path to worldly success. Much of this, I
am sure, is known to all of you, but it is worth emphasizing in order
to indicate what an enormous and rich field is presented by Chinese
studies. The first Westerners to study Chinese scientifically were the
Jesuit missionaries of the sixteenth and seventeenth centuries, and on
the foundation of their work a small group of professional scholars,
mainly French, were pre-eminent for a period of a century in this
field. The outstanding names are those of Edouard Chavannes, who
died just after the First World War, H. Maspero, and P. Pelliot, who
died just after the Second World War. In England the late Professor
Herbert Giles for his lexicographical labour and Dr Arthur Waley for
his translations are outstanding names. There are still some very great
scholars in Europe, notably Karlgren in Sweden and Duyvendak in
Holland, but the main centre of Western sinology is the United States,
where a generation or two of intense training, constant interest and,
above all, financial means have endowed the leading universities with
impressive oriental institutes.

Japanese studies, in which my bearings are a little more accurate
than in the greater ocean of Chinese studies, are of more recent origin
as far as Western scholars are concerned. China was known earlier
and more intimately to Europe chiefly because of the isolation of
Japan until the middle of the last century. The great continuous sweep
of Chinese history, its immense forest of historical works, only the
fringes of which have yet been penetrated by Western scholars, present perhaps a greater challenge to the student. Like its own landscape
gardening, Japanese studies seem somehow neater and trimmer, the

eye can more easily encompass the whole prospect, and it is much more conveniently organized. While China has been torn asunder through the centuries by destructive civil wars and foreign invasions, Japanese treasures of art, history, and literature suffered comparatively little through damage even from World War II. Thus, even aside from the new difficulties presented by the rise of a Communist China, standard collections of Japanese literature and classics have always been easier of access and purchase than is the case with Chinese.

Japanese studies, as far as the Western scholar is concerned, seem to appeal less to the philologist and more to the historian of cultural history, pre-eminent among whom is Sir George Sansom. In modern history, Japan offers an excellent subject both because of the richness of the basic source materials and, what is important for the student of sociology and economics, because of a greater range and reliability of statistics than has ever been possible in modern China. Japanese history, while perhaps more compact than Chinese, like it has been very little explored by Western scholars. One must examine the material on any subject with great assiduity even to draw level with the work of Japanese scholars in the field who have, of course, an obvious headstart over any Westerner. As for my own personal interest, I find the study of modern Japan fascinating for its combination of the traditional mixed with the modern, for its example of the first Asian state to make a successful transition from a feudal to a modern society. Japanese politics with its cliques and family influences, the role of personalities who often exercise power from behind the scenes, the factors behind the ascendancy of the militarists in prewar Japan, the extent to which democracy may have taken root since, all these are, I believe, rewarding not only for the student of political history but for the student of our contemporary world, since Japan, even out of defeat, is reappearing as an important power and, I trust, a force for peace and security.

I may be asked, in view of the time-consuming and exhaustive effort needed to acquire even a slow reading knowledge of either Chinese or Japanese, why should not the student interested in the Far East content himself with such translations of literature, history, and so on, as are to be found in Western languages? I would reply that for the student who wishes to gain merely a casual acquaintance of oriental affairs, to read material in translation is certainly better than having nothing at all. On the other hand, translations of standard works from these two languages are an infinitesimal fraction of even the most important authors and historical masterpieces. Some of these translations are almost unreadable because they are written in a particularly execrable style, which characterizes inferior translations from any language. Translations from a language as elusive as Chinese and as complex as Japanese are notoriously unreliable. 'Everything,' Lord Chesterfield wrote, 'suffers by translation except a bishop.' While remaining grateful for the efforts of the scholar-translator, such as Arthur Waley, anyone who takes even a cursory look will discover that he cannot hope to have a real understanding of the history and culture of these two nations or, indeed, of their present position in the world, unless he takes the trouble to learn something of their language and, through the language, of their life and letters. I believe that a conscientious student who learns the language of these countries, although living thousands of miles away, may derive, in some ways, as accurate and reliable a picture of its society and life as the casual Westerner residing in those parts who does not take the trouble to read or even in many cases to speak the language.

One may be asked what is the intrinsic reward from a study of oriental languages and culture. It is much the same as with the study of our own classics – the opportunity to associate with great minds and spirits of the past and to acquire a discipline that comes from application to a field such as, for example, Chinese history where even in ancient times scholarship of the highest order was exhibited. Aside from any intellectual or purely aesthetic pleasure, there is the practical prospect that only through grappling directly with the language and history of these two nations can a student expect to gain some insight, however limited, into the psychology, traditional behaviour, and political developments of these two peoples. There has been something of a fetish made of the mysterious and inscrutable Orient; whether you wish to call it a mystery, I can assure you the Orient will respond not to speculations over a crystal ball, but only to concentrated and well-directed study. Even so, there will be plenty of room for error and disagreement, but at least we should try to reduce the guess work.

Can a student in this field expect to be suitably employed later? I do not think that this is the proper occasion to go into this important practical problem other than to say that all over the English-speaking world there has been a small but steady demand for well-trained students of Japanese and Chinese both in universities and public life. My own feeling is that anyone who has put in arduous years of intensive study and has measured up to high standards will not be allowed to have his special knowledge grow rusty. I think also it should be quite feasible to arrange a course of study so that those with a specialist's ambition could secure a more intensive training, whereas those with broader and more general curiosity could find satisfaction for interest without being required to pass through the whole curriculum of languages and special training.

A study of Chinese and Japanese is eminently suited to a great university with a tradition of scholarship such as the University of New Zealand. In the modern world a university without an oriental institute is to some extent incomplete; the scope of oriental studies is wide enough to appeal to the philosopher or man of public affairs, to humanist, philologist, historian, or artist. In short, its appeal is truly catholic.

In concluding I wish to take this opportunity of wishing you, the graduates of Victoria University College, every success in the years ahead. I trust also, Mr Chairman, that you will not regard it as a presumption on my part but rather as evidence of enthusiasm and interest, if I express the very sincere hope that in the foreseeable future we will see established at Victoria University College a department devoted to East Asian studies.

Roger W. Bowen

IRONY OR TRAGEDY?

Change is a remarkably difficult concept to grasp in the abstract, but no less difficult in its reality, particularly as it is manifested by an individual human being. This is no less true in the case of a brief life. Norman lived to see but forty-seven summers, twenty-five or so as a politically conscious adult. In that short time, he changed from a classics student into a published Japanologist, from a graduate researcher into a provocative scholar, from a language officer into a skilled ambassador, from a doctrinaire Marxist into a Jeffersonian liberal, from an ideologue into a philosopher, from a hopeful lover of life into a suicide whose last words were, 'I must kill myself for I live without hope.' Devotees of History's Muse, Clio, will understand that these changes came about gradually and altogether naturally as Norman's life situation changed, but those who eschew the lessons of Clio will deny that such changes are possible.

It is from the failure to discern change and human complexity in an individual over time that ironies are perceived. It is all too easy, for instance, to detect historical irony in the fact that at the very time Norman was accused of being a communist he was expounding on the virtues of liberal persuasion, free speech, and human reason. To see irony in this situation is to see human character in dichotomous terms that are frozen in time: a person is either a liberal or a communist, was in the past either a liberal or a communist, and will in the future be either a liberal or a communist.

Hardened cynics will adopt a different but related position. They will argue that 'Norman's past caught up with him.' Facile paranoids, by contrast, will argue that his Jeffersonian democracy was simply a clever, duplicitous ruse consciously designed to fool potential critics.

But neither can be correct because all such views are grounded in ahistorical stereotyping. Nor can either understand as well that change in an individual does not mean negating one's past, but rather means incorporating it while transcending it.

In 1947, according to fellow occupationaire Eleanor Hadley, Norman was frequently and quite openly attending night-time Marxist study group meetings in Tokyo.[1] The ahistorical, the cynics, and the paranoids would see this act as evidence of an ongoing loyalty to communism; Hadley, however, who often accompanied Norman, describes Norman's attendance in terms of his desire to escape the administrative drudgery of his daytime liaison mission work and enjoy intellectual stimulation in the company of educated Japanese. Similarly, the same sorts of critics would question Norman's loyalty over his decision to attend in 1947 the Institute of Pacific Relations conference in England because they regarded the IPR as a communist front organization. But for Norman, who was still very much involved in scholarly pursuits, attending academic meetings or conferences was an altogether *private* affair which in no way interfered with such *public* duties as, say, helping Canadian capitalists penetrate the Japanese market. Norman certainly saw no contradiction in his behaviour; he was, after all, both a public and a private person. Only his anti-intellectual enemies, for whom the autonomy of the individual's private life had to give way to the public exigencies of combatting the communist menace, believed that Norman's private affairs constituted evidence to be used in publicly persecuting him.

During this period it was Army Intelligence that worked hardest in compiling evidence against Norman and his private acquaintances. One of the reports they wrote listed twenty-seven different people who 'are somehow connected with either Norman or Tsuru [Shigeto] or both, all of them have come close to our official attention before, some of them have been the subjects of extensive "loyalty investigations."'[2] Among the names named are Edward C. Carter, John Stewart Service, T.A. Bisson, Eleanor Hadley, Cyrus Peake, Owen Lattimore, John K. Emmerson, and certain Japanese 'Class "A" Communists' so identified by 'wartime Japanese police.' All were people whom Norman met in connection with the Japan Council of the IPR which, in the view of Army Intelligence, was 'heavily weighted with known "leftists" in control positions.'[3] All these names are also persons whom Norman mentions fondly in his private correspondence to his wife and brother, speaking of them as fellow Japanologists whose company and good conversation helped to break the tedium of official duties and with whom he was working for the purpose of re-establishing academic relationships between North America and Japan. But for Army Intelligence and then the FBI, with whom this evidence was shared, Norman's associations simply confirmed their suspicions that he was a communist.

Interestingly, it was his private associations rather than his public speeches, such as the ones in this volume, that most concerned his accusers. Had more careful attention been given to his public pronouncements, his enemies would have better understood Norman's passion for freedom and democracy. They would have also seen that he no longer believed that the attainment of these two human goals was only possible through a paradigmatic Marxian revolution.

'Politically Norman is a moderate liberal,' read a secret 1948 State Department biographical profile of Norman. The report noted that Norman 'has expressed his warm endorsement of the policies of General MacArthur'; that 'his leisurely manner belies his reserve of energy and his capacity for hard work'; that 'he was a pleasant and agreeable personality'; that he is 'quiet by nature and cautious rather than spontaneous'; that he is 'an American – as opposed to a British – Canadian.'[4]

This character portrait was of course modified a few years later once J. Edgar Hoover, FBI chief, provided State with new information about Norman's communist connections. The Hoover report itself followed an August 1950 Occupation counter-intelligence request to the FBI to determine whether General Willoughby's 'long held suspicions' of Norman's communism were correct.[5] By October 1950 J. Edgar could report that Willoughby's assumption was correct. The 'moderate liberal' of 1948, it turned out, had in fact been a communist at least since 1942. On 1 November 1950 the FBI sent copies of its 'Special Report' to the CIA, the State Department, the Department of Navy, and secretly by way of General Willoughby to the chief counsel of the Senate Internal Security Subcommittee, Robert Morris.[6] It was Morris who in 1951 and again in 1957 acted upon the Hoover report with the mindless confidence of a Moses in receipt of the Ten Commandments and persecuted Norman publicly for the apostasy of having believed in a false god.

History as well as Norman had been transmogrified with ahistorical illogic: after the autumn of 1950 the 'moderate liberal' of 1948 was again the suspected communist of the early forties. Norman had become, according to *all* of the major U.S. intelligence agencies, young again. *They*, not Norman, could not transcend the past. *They* remade Norman into a communist. And in America that was a crime.

This is not irony, but tragedy. Especially tragic is the fact that Norman was powerless, and the Canadian government only slightly less so, to protest the ahistorical assaults on his mind and reputation. The Norman who wrote in the late thirties that 'the real standard-bearer for humanity, for liberty, and man's right to develop freely is communism' was not the same man who in 1948 asserted that 'no political party, no religious creed, no social class can claim a monopoly in the service of freedom.'

To point out the *change* in Norman's views in a mere decade, however, is not to make a sharp distinction between a 'young Norman' and a 'mature Norman,' for throughout his life he remained a passionate advocate for freedom and humanity. Rather it is to suggest that the aging Norman could simply acknowledge that Clio's grand plan for making men free could involve standard-bearers other than an energized proletariat class.

Norman, the lifelong student of historical change, could see and articulate the meaning of change. His accusers, however, their vision obstructed by a blind fear of a newer, socialist form of freedom, could not. If there is irony in this, it is because the insightful fell victim to the sightless.

NOTES

1 Conversation with author in Tokyo, Japan, 14 May 1982
2 Letter from the General Headquarters, Far East Command, Military Intelligence Section, general staff to assistant chief of staff, G-2, Washington, DC, 30 November 1950, referring to contents of 26 September 1950 letter from same to same
3 Ibid.
4 U.S. Department of State, 'Summary of Information,' 11 April 1951, quoting 29 June 1948 U.S. Department of State, Division of Biographic Information report; released to author by U.S. Army Intelligence and Security Command, Fort Meade, Maryland.
5 Referred to in letter cited in note 2 above.

6 Report by Lt Colonel John W. Downie, Chief, Special Operations Section, Army Intelligence, 20 June 1957; and 'Memo for Record,' Army Intelligence, 30 April 1957; and G-2, GHQ inter-office memorandum, from Lt Colonel Roundtree to General Willoughby, 30 November 1950. Reference to receipt of 1 November FBI report in letter from Brigadier-General John Weckerling, Chief, Intelligence Division, G-2, to commander-in-chief, Far East Command, 22 November 1950. (At the time of this writing, the author had just received over 650 pages of documents from the FBI under the Freedom of Information Act. While much of this material has been censored, much that has escaped the censor's brush shows that the close cooperation between Army Intelligence and the FBI began about two months before Norman was recalled from Japan.)

Selected Writings of E.H. Norman

BOOKS

1940 *Japan's Emergence as a Modern State – Political and Economic Problems of the Meiji Period*. IPR Inquiry Series. New York: Institute of Pacific Relations

1943 *Soldier and Peasant in Japan: The Origins of Conscription*. New York: Institute of Pacific Relations

1945 *Feudal Background of Japanese Politics*. Secretariat paper no. 9, Ninth Conference of the Institute of Pacific Relations, Hot Springs, Virginia, January 1945. New York: Institute of Pacific Relations; reprinted in *Origins of the Modern Japanese State: Selected Writings of E.H. Norman*, edited by John W. Dower. New York: Pantheon Books 1974

1949 *Andō Shōeki and the Anatomy of Japanese Feudalism*. Transactions of the Asiatic Society of Japan, 3rd Ser., vol. 2. Tokyo

ARTICLES

1937 'Highlights on Recent Books.' *Amerasia* 1, no. 2, 84–90 (survey of eighteen books on China and Japan)

1938 'Some Recent Books on China.' *Amerasia* 1, no. 12, 571–7, 584 (review of nine books)

1943 'Soldier and Peasant in Japan: The Origins of Conscription.' *Pacific Affairs* 16 no. 1, 47–63; no. 2, 149–65

1943 Review of John F. Embree, *The Japanese* (War Background Studies, no. 7. Washington: Smithsonian Institution), in *Pacific Affairs* 16, no. 3, 363–4

1944 'The Genyōsha: A Study in the Origins of Japanese Imperialism.'
     Pacific Affairs 17, no. 3, 261–84
1945 'Mass Hysteria in Japan.' *Far Eastern Survey* 14, no. 6, 65–70
1947 Review of Edwin O. Reischauer, *Japan Past and Present*, in *Pacific Affairs* 20, no. 3, 358–9
1949 'Observations on the Trial of War Criminals in Japan.' *External Affairs* (Monthly Bulletin of the Department of External Affairs, Ottawa, Canada) 1, no. 2, 12–23 (anonymous)
1949 'Democratic Traditions in Japan.' *External Affairs* 1, no. 11, 12–13
1977 'People under Feudalism.' *Bulletin of Concerned Asian Scholars* 9, no. 2, 57–61

Contributors

Gary Allinson is professor of history at the University of Virginia. In addition to publishing numerous articles, he is the author of two books, *Japanese Urbanism* (1976) and *Suburban Tokyo* (1979), both published by the University of California Press.

Roger Bowen is author of *Rebellion and Democracy in Meiji Japan* (University of California Press 1980) and is presently working on a full-length biography of E.H. Norman. He is associate professor of government at Colby College, Waterville, Maine.

Victor Kiernan is emeritus professor of modern history, University of Edinburgh. Among his better-known publications are: *British Diplomacy ion China 1808–1884* (Cambridge University Press 1939); *The Lords of Human Kind* (Penguin 1972); and *Marxism and Imperialism* (Edward Arnold 1974). Since 1973 he has served as a member of the editorial board of *Past and Present*.

Arthur Kilgour did his undergraduate and graduate work at the University of Toronto. In 1947 he joined the Department of External Affairs. Before being appointed at Cairo in 1957, he completed a tour of duty in Southeast Asia. He left External Affairs in 1960.

Maruyama Masao is a professor of political science at the University of Tokyo. He has also taught at Harvard and Oxford universities. Among his better-known books that have been translated into English are *Thought and Behaviour in Modern Japanese Politics* (Oxford University Press 1963) and *Studies in the Intellectual History of Tokugawa Japan* (Princeton 1974).

Cyril Powles teaches religion and East Asian history at Victoria College, University of Toronto. He recently reviewed Okubo Genji's four-volume *Habāto Nōman Zenshu* (The Complete Works of Herbert Norman) for *Pacific Affairs*.

Kenneth Pyle is author of *The New Generation in Meiji Japan* (Stanford University Press 1969) and is editor of the *Journal of Japanese Studies*. He teaches Japanese history at the University of Washington.

Edwin O. Reischauer is university professor, emeritus, at Harvard University. His better-known publications include *The Japanese* (Belknap 1977) and *Japan, The Story of a Nation* (3rd ed, Knopf 1981). He was appointed by President John F. Kennedy to serve as ambassador to Japan.

Richard Storry was, until his death in early 1982, senior lecturer at the Far East Centre, St Anthony's College, Oxford University. His *A History of Modern Japan* (Penguin 1968) is a widely used textbook in university courses on Japan.

Tōyama Shigeki, professor of history at Yokohama University, is best known for his monumental interpretation of the Meiji Restoration entitled *Meiji Ishin*.

Index

Akita, George 12n, 103–5
Alexander the Great 141,170
Andō Shōeki x, 6, 16, 61, 82, 83
  (cited), 84, 127, 129 (cited)

Bentley, Elizabeth 49
Bisson, T.A. 56, 62, 196
Blunt, Anthony 50, 52
Bryce, Robert 49, 52, 55, 67
Burgess, Guy 50, 52

Cairo 47, 72–8 passim; *see also*
  Egypt, Nasser, Suez Crisis
Cambridge University: Norman's
  student days at ix, 5, 6, 25, 46,
  88, 89; Socialist Society of 52
Canadian missionaries: in Japan 4,
  16–19 passim
Clio (Muse of History): and Norman 83, 84; quoting Norman's
  description of 99, 124, 141, 173,
  182–5, 195, 198
Communist party: British 25; Japanese 7, 66; reasons for joining
  33–7; Norman's work for 40–1
Cornford, John 25, 33, 37, 38–9, 52

Diefenbaker, John 47–8
Dower, John W. 12n, 49, 92, 102–3,
  114

Egypt xi, 48, 65, 72–8 passim
Emmerson, John K. 7, 8, 56, 58, 62,
  65–6, 196

Federal Bureau of Investigation
  (FBI) 54, 55, 62, 63, 197
Fukuzawa Yukichi 155, 157, 167

Gouzenko, Igor 62

Hadley, Eleanor 196
Halperin, Israel 62
Harvard University ix, 6, 7, 52, 53,
  125, 136

Institute of Pacific Relations (IPR) x,
  52, 53, 56, 62, 125, 126, 196

*Japan's Emergence as a Modern
  State* 6, 9–11, 52, 79, 84, 87, 90,
  93, 94, 95, 97 (cited), 100–5,
  114–19 passim, 122, 124, 125,

126, 133; cited: 130, 131, 132, 134

Jefferson, Thomas 157

Kades, Charles 59
Keenleyside, Hugh 57

Lattimore, Owen 53, 55, 62, 196

MacArthur, General Douglas 6, 10, 56, 57, 58, 59, 60, 61, 64, 197
McCarthyism 53, 56, 85, 93, 122; and *Japan's Emergence* 122–3, 134, 141
Marxism 10, 11, 30–43 passim; Norman's attraction to 51–2; and Norman's scholarship 123–36
Mill, John Stuart 82, 151, 168

Nasser, Gamal Abdul (President) xi, 49, 65, 66, 74, 75
New Zealand xi, 64–5, 81; University of 194
Norman, Daniel ix, 17–19, 21
Norman, Katherine Heal ix, 18–19, 21

Okubo, Genji 15, 17, 81

Pearson, Lester B. (Mike) x, xi, 47–8, 57, 58, 61, 64, 67, 74, 75

Robertson, Norman 55

Royal Canadian Mounted Police (RCMP) x, 62, 63, 66

Sansom, Sir George 53, 87, 88, 90, 127 (cited), 128 (cited), 129 (cited), 192
self-government 158–60; and freedom of expression 161, 164–5; and franchise 162–3, and Machiavelli 166–7
Spanish Civil War 33, 35, 36, 77, 89
Suez Crisis xi, 49, 65, 72–8 passim; *see also* Egypt, Nasser

Thorpe, General Eliot 53, 55, 57
Tokugawa: Norman's interpretation of 124–5, 143; feudalism of 143–54
Trinity College, *see* Cambridge University
Tsuru, Shigeto 7, 52, 54, 56, 63, 85, 196

United Nations xi, 65, 72, 73, 75
United States Senate, Internal Security Subcommittee 46, 76, 93

Victoria College (University of Toronto) ix, 17, 19–20, 25, 51

Willoughby, General Charles 53, 58, 61, 62, 64, 197
Wittfogel, Karl August xi, 63, 65